Praise for

In *Unfettered Spirit,* Dr. Robert D. Cornwall roots through the fertile soil of his traditions and unearths the gifts that it has to offer. He then sets the table for Progressive Christians, and gives us the nourishment that we need to move into a New Great Awakening. Throughout the pages of *Unfettered Spirit,* Dr. Cornwall hosts this banquet with the knowledge of a well-read academic and the wisdom of a seasoned pastor.

Rev. Carol Howard Merritt
Author of *Tribal Church* and *Reframing Hope*

The church of the early twenty-first century is in one of the most uncertain periods in our history. What will the church be like in ten years? In five years? What soul-deep questions will the Christian community face? To be faithful, what risks will we have to face? Most importantly, where will we get the power to navigate the uncharted waters of the future? Dr. Robert Cornwall, distinguished minister of one of Detroit's most distinguished congregations, Central Woodward Christian Church (Disciples of Christ), a church historian by trade, and a biblical expositor by inclination, points a way forward; reclaiming the gifts of the Holy Spirit. Drawing from the deep well of scripture, from penetrating knowledge of our culture and of congregations, and most of all, from the power of the Spirit itself, Dr. Cornwall explains these gifts and relates them in practical ways to the church today. This book focuses on how the Spirit not only fills individuals but builds up the church as community for study, worship, caring for one another, and for mission outside the walls. As far as I know, this is the best discussion of the gifts of the Spirit in the current church. The congregation that embraces these gifts will navigate into the next years with a sense of adventure, discovery, and power.

Ronald J. Allen, Ph.D.
Professor of Preaching and Gospels and Letters
Christian Theological Seminary, Indianapolis
Author of *Reading the New Testament for the First Time*

Bob Cornwall here shows that the gifts of the Spirit are not owned by the pentecostal-charismatic wing of the church. Rather, the time is now for mainline churches to reappropriate the full spectrum of the spiritual gifts for their contemporary tasks. The result may include the sought for revitalization of the historic Protestant tradition as it seeks to bear appropriate witness to the living Christ in a pluralistic world.

Amos Yong, Ph.D.
Dean, Divinity School, Regent University
Author of *Spirit of Love*

Bob Cornwall has provided the body of Christ with a view of the Holy Spirit's work that is rooted in the deep streams of church history, founded on the scripture and engaged in the raw edges of current experience and theological reflection. I recommend the book for those of us in the Pentecostal world because we often fail to remember that Pentecost has never left the church – the inextinguishable flame of God's working is evident throughout church history and here now. I recommend the book for the church at large because it is a good reminder that the God we serve cannot be domesticated and that in an encounter with this undomesticated God there is the potential to flourish.

Ray Wheeler, DMin.
Adjunct Professor of Leadership,
Bethesda University, California and Executive Coach.

Reading a book by Bob Cornwall is like sitting down for a conversation with your smartest and yet most gracious friend. This book, packed with notes and quotes from the brightest and best in the church, serves notice that the spirit of God is alive and well and ready to lead the church to a new and bright day.

Dr. R. Glen Miles, Senior Minister
Country Club Christian Church (Disciples of Christ)
Kansas City, MO.

UNFETTERED SPIRIT:

SPIRITUAL GIFTS FOR THE NEW GREAT AWAKENING

Robert D. Cornwall

Energion Publications
Gonzalez, FL
2013

Copyright © 2013, Robert D. Cornwall

Scripture quotations are taken are taken from the New Revised Standard Version Bible, Copyright © 1989 by the Division of Christian Education of the National Council of the Churches of Christ in the U. S. A. Used by permission. All rights reserved.

Cover Image: © Rolffimages | Dreamstime.com
Used by permission.

Cover Design: Henry Neufeld

ISBN10: 1-938434-59-5
ISBN13: 978-1-938434-59-4

Library of Congress Control Number: 2013941597

Energion Publications
P. O. Box 841
Gonzalez, FL 32560

energionpubs.com
pubs@energion.com
850-525-3916

Table of Contents

Foreword v
Preface xi
Introduction 1
Refreshing Winds and Purifying Fires: 15
Gifted by Grace: 35
Discovering Our Spiritual Potentialities 53
The Spirit and the Christian Life: 75
What are the Gifts of Love? 93
Gifts of Leadership 99
Gifts of Word 111
Gifts of Service 131
Gifts You'd Like to Avoid, but Shouldn't! 141
Becoming the Spirit-Empowered Body of Christ 157
Living and Working Together as Church 175
Get Your Hands Dirty: 195
Reflections on Spiritual Gifts and the Ordained Ministry 209
Bibliography 221

Foreword

An African American spiritual proclaims "You've got to move when the Spirit says move." God's Spirit is free as the wind and unexpected in her revelations. As Acts of the Apostles proclaims, God's energetic and enlivening presence shows up in the strangest places: in fire and wind propelling a small group of women and men into the streets, in the bold request for baptism by an Ethiopian eunuch, in the transformation of a persecutor to a proclaimer, in a dream that opens the door to welcoming unclean Gentiles into the church as equals, in songs and prayers from prison, and in congregational leadership embracing women as well as men. The Spirit of God, described in Acts of the Apostles, is unhindered. I believe that this same Spirit is alive and free today within the church and the world.

The end of Christendom and the rise of postmodernism and pluralism have led to spiritual vertigo among many Christians, both lay and clergy. The old ways no longer work. Even megachurches find it difficult to reach persons in their 20's and 30's. Christianity's reputation among young adults parallels the biases against Jesus' followers in the first century. Thirty percent of persons under thirty describe themselves as "spiritual but not religious" or consider themselves as "none" and do so for what they believe to be good reasons. They see the church as sexist, reactionary, homophobic, anti-science, anti-intellectual, and intolerant. Perhaps, worse than this, they see the church as irrelevant and unimportant in their quest for meaning. The church in their eyes is a relic from a bygone era and has little to do with their professional, personal, and family lives. Spirituality can be found elsewhere with far less baggage and fewer demands.

Many clergy and laypersons are paralyzed by grief and hopelessness as they see the church being pushed to the margins of cultural and personal life. Some protest vehemently at the reality that the USA is no longer a Christian nation: their recent initiatives against contraception, an Islamic center near ground zero in Manhattan, and their attacks on pluralism in the public and educational sectors are the last gasp of a dying faith. Mainstream and progressive Christians are faring no better than their conservative counterparts as they look at membership losses, institutional downsizing, and aging congregants. It is clear that we cannot evade or deny the realities of pluralism, postmodernism, and post-Christianity; we must open ourselves to creative transformation. In embracing the religious and cultural realities of our time along with the presence of God's unfettered and surprising Spirit, the margins may become the frontiers of a new spiritual movement that will energize, enliven, and empower mainstream and progressive Christians and bring new life to struggling congregations. Could God's Spirit be calling us to the next great awakening, as Diana Butler Bass suggests? Do we need to hold a "rummage sale," as Phyllis Tickle asserts, to get rid of unnecessary and outmoded doctrines and practices?

At the heart of this potential great awakening is the recovery of the experience and embodiment of the gifts of the Spirit within the church. Bob Cornwall sees the future of the church as involving awakening to God's Spirit. Cornwall images a spirit-empowered church that is sensitive to God's gifts in personal and community life. A spirit-empowered church expects great things and this expectation leads to expecting great things from ourselves and our communities. The church has too often "played small" and expected too little from itself and God when Jesus challenges us to do greater things. If we ask and knock, we will experience life-changing and mission-inspiring surprises. Cornwall's project involves an adventure of the Spirit which gives life to the description of the body of Christ as an interdependent and gifted community of faith.

The words of I Corinthians 12 challenge us to make no small plans either personally or corporately. The "mind of Christ" moves through the body of Christ, holistically at work in tandem with the Spirit, calling forth gifts, providing guidance, and nurturing possibilities. The church is called to be a laboratory for discovering and embodying our vocations within the body of Christ. Each member matters and makes a difference in the well-being of the whole. No one is without gifts or inspiration to contribute to the whole. In discovering our gifts, we experience personal fulfillment and promote the vitality of Christ's body. Each gift reaches beyond itself to nurture the community and broader world as well as the individual.

Congregational vitality bursts forth when congregants choose to see themselves as members of Christ's body and then live God's adventures in their lives. The gifts of the Spirit awaken us to wonder and challenge us to go beyond our current comfort zones. Whether or not a congregation grows numerically, a Spirit-empowered community will be lively and faithful. It will not envy larger churches, with their praise bands, youth groups, cradle-to-grave programs, mall-like atmospheres, sophisticated websites, and ATM machines. It will rejoice in God's presence right where it is and will, by its faithfulness, fulfill its vocation to bring life and light to the world. No one knows how many plants come from a small mustard seed or how many are fed from just a few loaves and fish. Nor does anyone know how many persons are transformed through the efforts of a humble congregation.

I believe that good theology involves the interplay of *vision, promise, and practice.* Spirit-empowered congregations and spirit-enlivened persons believe that God is active in our lives, the Spirit in moving in all things, and that the details of our lives matter to God and are the materials with which the Spirit works to bring healing and transformation to us and the world. Spirit-empowered congregations and Christians affirm that we can embody God's Spirit as our deepest reality. While there is no norm for spirit-empowered living, each of us is touched by God for our fulfillment and service to the world. Spirit-empowered faith takes the interplay of theology and practice seriously. The Spirit of God intercedes and speaks within our lives in sighs too deep for words, seeking good in all things, and giving us energy to fulfill our vocations. We awaken to this Spirit through adventurous practices, many of which have inspired Bob Cornwall's reflections, such as: intercessory and petitionary prayer, thanksgiving, discernment and examination of conscience, healing touch, imaginative thinking, and service to the world. Spirit-empowered congregations are missional and emerging – they see all of life as a mission in which we are blessed to be a blessing. They open to otherness through diverse forms of worship and community. Making no small plans, they expect great things from God and themselves. Holistic in nature, they make no distinction between action and contemplation, but see both as necessary for claiming our vocation as God's partners in bringing beauty and healing to the world.

Bob Cornwall provides a vision for today's Christians, centered around living out our gifts in creative and life-transforming ways. We are gifted, even when we are unaware of it. As a community of gifts, the church can bring out the best in its members and invite persons to unexpected and undreamed of adventures as God's companions in healing the earth. I am grateful for Bob Cornwall's willingness to share his spirit-empowering vision. It is needed more now than ever as a creative and hospitable response to the needs of religious seekers and persons of all faiths.

Claiming our role today as participants in the body of Christ requires honesty and commitment. As Bob Cornwall asserts, we need to ask ourselves as individuals and communities the following questions: "Do you truly believe that God is present in the world? And, do you believe that God is working through us to break down the walls that divide us from God, from each other, and from the world? And if you do, do you believe that you have been gifted and empowered to participate in this ministry that takes down the walls of egoism, suspicion, greed, self-interest, and hatred?"

If you answer "yes" to these questions, you will be joining a great communion of saints, including Abraham and Sarah, Elijah and Elisha, Jeremiah and Isaiah, Amos and Micah, Mary and Joseph, Paul and Peter, and Mary of Magdala and Lydia. You will find yourself in the company of Dorothy Day, Muriel Lester, Howard Thurman, Martin Luther King, Dietrich Bonhoeffer, Dag Hammarksjold, Oscar Romero, Mother Teresa, and Desmond Tutu. You will discover that within your own sense of inadequacy lie seeds of personal transformation and social change, whether on the micro or macro levels.

Bob Cornwall's insights will not automatically add members to your congregation nor will they guarantee spiritual growth without effort. We are to work out of salvation with fear and trembling – or awe and excitement – knowing that God's grace and giftedness invites, empowers, and energizes us to live out the gospel in our time.

Bruce Epperly
Advent 2012

Preface

Many years ago, as a teenager, I left the Episcopal Church of my birth for a Pentecostal church. Like many others my age, the church of my birth didn't seem to be speaking to my spiritual questions. Although it wasn't the signs and wonders, which often mark the Pentecostal experience, that initially caught my attention, over the course of time I imbibed its spirituality, and it helped define my understanding of the Christian faith. As time passed, during the latter stages of my college years, I began to drift away from this spiritual home, feeling that something else was needed to broaden my experience of the Christian faith. Yet, even as the Episcopal church of my youth left its mark on me, so did my sojourn among the Pentecostals. Still, even though my theology and practice would change in the years that followed, my spiritual life continued to be influenced by this important part of my journey. I have not lost the sense that the Spirit of God, whom I embraced during this period of my life, continued to be present with me, even if my understandings of the nature and purpose of God evolved. I am, ever shall be, it would seem, a Charismatic Christian.

The book you're about to read is the product of almost thirty years of reflection and writing. Some things take time to develop, and this book is one of those things. It's not that I didn't try to publish it; it's just that the book wasn't yet ready to share with the broader public. So, I continued to develop and expand my ideas and thoughts about the Spirit of God and the Gifts that God chooses to pour out on the church. And now, it seems, is the time to share this vision with the church at large.

Why now? Perhaps it is because the church finds itself at a moment of transition, a moment of awakening. Even as questions continue to be raised about the institutional viability of the church, people continue to pursue spiritual things. Diana Butler Bass has raised the question of what Christianity might be like after religion, and suggests that whatever the church will look like going forward, it will be marked less by institutions and more by spiritual awakenings. Some call it the Great Emergence or the Age of the Spirit or the Fourth Great Awakening. Whatever the name is that we give this period of history, it's clear that things are changing, and the unfettered Spirit of God seems to be at work opening new doors and creating new opportunities for ministry in this world. I therefore, offer this book up as a contribution to this New Great Awakening that is stirring within and outside the church. While I understand why some would choose to be "spiritual, but not religious, I am convinced that life-changing spirituality that touches the world in positive ways will be embodied in community.[1]

I recognize that many books have been written on the topic of Spiritual Gifts, and I make use of many of them in this book, but I do believe that with this book I have made a vital contribution to the conversation. While these many books represent a wide range of beliefs and positions regarding the Spirit and the Church, what I bring to the discussion is my own journey, with all of its own twists and turns. What I offer is a perspective that begins with my current place as a Disciples of Christ pastor, who has tasted the Pentecostal fruit and who continues to return to this tree for sustenance. My own sense of church and ministry is rooted in my evolving experience and understanding of the work of the Spirit and the Spirit's

---

[1] Diana Butler Bass' *Christianity after Religion: The End of Church and the Birth of a New Spiritual Awakening*, (San Francisco: Harper One, 2012), chapters 8-9. On the question of whether one might be spiritual but not religious, see Lillian Daniel's book *When "Spiritual but Not Religious" Is Not Enough: Seeing God in Surprising Places, Even the Church*, (New York: Jericho Books, 2013), chapter 1.

gifts. If in the course of reading the book you discern some interesting conversation partners, know that these represent different stages of my own engagement with the question of giftedness and the church. What I've discovered along the way is that we can learn from many conversation partners, and that these conversations create open new vistas that are often neglected when we stay too close to our original tradition.

Hopefully it becomes clear that part of my rationale in writing this book is to make sense of my own experience. Of course, such a motivation is insufficient for publishing a book and asking others to read along. Therefore, I'm hoping that you, the reader, will ask yourself what it means to be part of a Spirit-empowered church that is touching the world with the love of God.

As we look forward into the future and seek to make sense of this new spiritual awakening, we'll need to ask questions about the viability and importance of institutions. We'll need to wrestle with what it means to be spiritual and religious, which I believe is the future for the church. Spirituality without a religious home, without traditions and community, won't endure. But institutions without spirituality will wither and die. If I understand correctly, the message that Diana Butler Bass, and others like her, are sharing with the church is that we must seek to find this proper balance.

Yes, I believe that the Spirit of God is alive and at work empowering communities of faith to live fruitful lives of faith in this world – but we must be willing to let the Spirit move. We mustn't quench the Spirit, even though we must be discerning as to where the Spirit is truly at work in our midst. We must be willing to admit that too often the institution, especially the clerical hierarchies, suppress the movement of the Spirit. My prayer, therefore, is that this book can stir the hearts of the people of God to recognize that we mustn't try to fetter the Spirit, but instead allow the Spirit freedom to break down the barriers that keep the church from experiencing true spiritual awakening.

Although my vision of the church might not be as flat as that developed by Tony Jones, I'm in agreement with Tony and Jürgen Moltmann that God is calling us, equipping us, whether ordained or not, to do the work of the ministry. In an afterword to this book I write a reflection on the role of the ordained ministry in a Spirit-empowered church, but whatever our understanding of ordination, surely ministry is something we all share in. It's not the sole domain of the ordained, for God has gifted and called each of us to engage with God's Spirit in building the realm of God. In my Disciples tradition, we believe that baptism serves as the first point of ordination, so that all baptized members who have been authorized by the church can baptize, celebrate the Lord's Supper, Teach, and Pray. Disciple theologian Stephen Sprinkle writes:

> Following the divine imperative given to the apostle Peter, that what God has cleansed, we are not to call common, Disciples have honored the work of the Holy Spirit in the life of the baptized believer, and have opened ourselves to the priesthood of all believers in a thorough-going way. Our understanding of baptism has led us to this high opinion of the laity, yet in such a way as not to denigrate the clergy.[2]

This relatively flat understanding of ministry, with its high valuation of the priesthood of all believers, while also recognizing the valid ministry of clergy, which my Disciple tradition affirms, fits well with a gift-based understanding of ministry. But we must recognize that the Spirit must remain unfettered if we're to truly experience the benefits of this new awakening.

A book like this, especially one that has been under construction for as long as this one has been, has many contributors. Some names and faces I've forgotten, but they've contributed with their questions and engagements with me along the way. Some names,

---

[2] Stephen Sprinkle, "The Disciples Vision of Christian Baptism" in *Baptism and Belonging: A Resource for Christian Worship.* Keith Watkins, ed., (St. Louis: Chalice Press, 1991), 20.

however, need to be lifted up, so I'll start with two of my youth ministers, Ray Wheeler and Delvin Ford, who tried to help me make sense of my own struggles with Pentecostal experiences. They might not agree with all of my positions, but they played an important role early on in my development. The ideas that form this book were planted and watered during my seminary years at Fuller Theological Seminary, and two of my professors helped provide needed resources that would help me make sense of my evolving views. While a M.Div. student at Fuller, I took a class called *Spiritual Gifts* that was taught by Russ Spittler and Mel Robeck, both of whom are members of the Assembly of God church. This class was especially helpful because Russ and Mel pushed me to read widely across the religious spectrum, allowing me to forge an understanding of spirituality and Christian practice that made sense of my own experiences. In many ways this book has its origins in that class. From then on I continued my readings, and made teaching on spiritual gifts an important part of my own ministry. I taught Bible studies and seminars, introducing people to the topic and sharing with them gift inventories so that they could discern their own calling. While a professor of theology at Manhattan Christian College, I had the opportunity to offer a course on Spiritual Gifts – I tried to do with them what Russ and Mel had done for me. After leaving MCC, I have continued to teach on spiritual gifts at each of the churches I've served as pastor. I've even tried my own hand at framing a gift inventory.

As this manuscript began to take shape, I've shared it with many different people, and their comments have helped me develop my ideas. I've received words of encouragement and advice from Mary Helen Parsons, Linda Shelton, Steve Kindle, Keith Watkins, Beth Gaede, Jon Berquist, Amos Yong, and many others besides them. As every author must note – they're not responsible for the contents of the book! Only I can take responsibility for the ideas and content of this book.

Besides those named I want to also thank Bruce Epperly for writing the foreword to the book, and to my publisher Henry Neufeld who chose to offer me a contract on the book. In offering the contract, I'm able to bring to a close this part of my journey with the Spirit of God. But this journey isn't yet complete. I expect that this will only be the beginning of a new chapter.

In offering this book to the public, my hope is that it will prove to be a blessing to those who walk in the Spirit with me. My prayer is that it will help move the church in all its variety to embrace the gift of the Spirit, along with the gifts that the Spirit brings into our midst. As you read, I pray that you the reader will claim your own calling and recognize that God has empowered you to do ministry in the name of Jesus and in the power of the unfettered Spirit. And as we do this, perhaps the world can look at us and say of us – "God is in this place!"

Introduction

As a child, I was taught a rhyme that went like this:

This is the church,
This is the steeple.
Look inside.
And see all the people.

The message is simple – the church is the building in which people gather to worship. It has a steeple and pews. It might even have stained glass windows. The rhyme made a lot of sense in an age when a majority of Americans were members of institutional churches, where membership in the institution had its privileges. This was especially true in the 1950s and early 1960s when a nation of joiners embraced not only the church but fraternal and social organizations. Back in the day, one was likely to be a member not only of a church, but also of some other organization like the Elks or Lions (or its auxiliary if you were a woman), Rotary or PEO, the Masons, and of course, if you were a parent, the PTA. The Scouts were big (both for boys and girls – and yes, Campfire was popular as well).

In many ways the church wasn't all that different from the other groups in town, except that the churches were more specifically religious. If you built it people came, and a grand building boom ensued as the parents of baby boomers took their children to church for a bit of Christianizing. But the question that needs to be asked of our congregations today is one Paul asked of the Corinthians two millennia ago, will the stranger entering the doors of our churches say of us: "God is in this Place?"

This question – whether God is truly present in our congregations – needs to be taken seriously as we consider the state of the church in these first decades of the Twenty-first Century. It's clear that institutional forms of religion have experienced decline, but does this mean that God is no longer present? Was God more present in congregations back when they were thriving in the post-World War II era?

It's true, the institutional church did flourish in the years following World War II, but then this was true of all manner of organizations that blossomed as the Baby Boom era burst onto the scene. It wasn't just the churches. Think about those fraternal organizations that boomed at the same time. My father joined the local Elks Club during the late 1960s, right after they built a brand new building equipped with the best swimming pool in town. That's where I learned to swim along with most of my friends. In recent years the club's dwindling membership filled in the pool with cement, and then when they no longer had the funds to maintain it, they sold the building and took up residence in smaller quarters. Does that sound like what's happening in many of our churches?

As for the church, in some places it may still have some influence and importance (especially if it's a mega-church), but this influence has waned considerably in recent years. Newer new generations have emerged on the scene who are much less likely to be joiners than their parents or grandparents. In part this is due to the fact that with the growth of two-earner families, time has become precious. Rather than join a group, besides the one on Facebook, many are now "bowling alone"[3] or perhaps with just a few close

---

3 For a full discussion of trends and changes over the past century see *American Grace: How Religion Divides and Unites Us* by Robert D. Putnam and David E. Campbell (New York: Simon and Schuster, 2010). Robert D. Putnam, *Bowling Alone: The Collapse and Revival of American Community,* (New York: Simon and Schuster, 2000).

Unfettered Spirit

friends. There's simply no time for organizational life – no room for committee assignments.

Although the old is passing away, is it possible that a new day is dawning? Harvey Cox speaks of an age of the Spirit emerging in our midst. In this new age of the Spirit the focus will be on "spiritual experience, discipleship, and hope," rather than on hierarchy, dogma, and institutions.[4] It might seem odd to some that Cox, who predicted a half century ago that secularism would seize the day, would now speak so positively of the in-breaking of an age of the Spirit. But perhaps he was not completely wrong in his assessment. It's true that religion and spirituality continue to play a significant role in human existence, but over the last half century the way that this spiritual dimension is expressed has changed rather dramatically. The forms and roles that religion takes have evolved in tandem with a growing secularism in the broader culture. Most religious institutions are fragile – including many Christian denominations, both conservative and liberal. One could also say that many fundamentalist groups, whether Christian, Jewish, Muslim, Buddhist, or Hindu, exist as resisters to the broadening reach of secularism. More liberal or progressive faith communities have found it more difficult to withstand the onslaught of secularism, probably because they've been more open to change in doctrine and in social practice (though not necessarily as adept in embracing change in worship style).[5]

To go back to the rhyme with which I opened the conversation, it's possible that when we open the doors, there will be a lot fewer wiggly fingers present than before. But this needn't lead us to give up hope. Still, if the church is to become more than a museum of past religious practices it will need to rekindle the missional spirit

---

4   Harvey Cox, *The Future of Faith,* (San Francisco: Harper One, 2009), 8. On this season of change also see Diana Butler Bass' *Christianity after Religion: The End of Church and the Birth of a New Spiritual Awakening,* (San Francisco: Harper One, 2012).

5   See Doug Pagitt, *Church in the Inventive Age,* (Minneapolis: Sparkhouse Press, 2010), for a "spirited" analysis of this reality.

that marked the earliest Christians. Much has been written about the missional church and the term itself has become rather elastic. That we're talking about mission taking place in our communities and not just overseas is a good sign that the Spirit is calling the church to move forward into the future. Yet, it's likely that we still don't fully understand what this will mean for our churches. We're still discerning what it means to be church in a globalized and religiously pluralist world. How do we proclaim Jesus as Lord even as we seek to listen to and learn from and walk with those whose faith professions are different from our own? For many of us, the call to mission doesn't simply involve telling people they need Jesus if they want salvation. Indeed, we are in the midst of rethinking what salvation truly is. Still, the conversation about being missional communities is a hopeful sign that the church in all its variety is heading in the right direction.

Yes, there's something happening in our faith communities. Harvey Cox, Diana Butler Bass, Philip Clayton, Carol Howard Merritt, Eric Elnes, Doug Pagitt, Brian McLaren, Tony Jones, Bruce Epperly, and other progressive Christian voices have offered notice that there are green shoots breaking through the earth giving notice that the Spirit of God is on the move. Communities of faith, many of which have existed for decades, are once again bearing strong witness to a new work of the Spirit.[6]

These communities of faith are full of the Spirit, but they're not necessarily your typical "spirit-filled" congregations. They're

---

6   See Diana Butler Bass's *The Church for the Rest of Us,* (San Francisco: Harper One, 2006), for examples of these kinds of churches. See also Philip Clayton's *Transforming Christian Theology for Church and Society,* (Minneapolis: Fortress Press, 2010), Carol Howard Merritt, *Reframing Hope: Vital Ministry in a New Generation,* (Herndon, VA: Alban Institute, 2010), Eric Elnes, *Asphalt Jesus,* (San Francisco: Jossey Bass, 2007), Tony Jones, *The Church is Flat* (Minneapolis, JoPa, 2011), Doug Pagitt, *The Church in the Inventive Age,* (Minneapolis: Sparkhouse, 2011), and Bruce G. Epperly, *Holy Adventure: 41 Days of Audacious Living,* (Nashville: Upper Room Books, 2008).

open to the movement of the Spirit of God, but they're not likely to see themselves as Charismatic or Pentecostal. Many see themselves being progressive in their theology and have strong social justice commitments. Although there are a number of communities that stand at the vanguard of this new work of the Spirit, many other like-minded communities are still struggling with their sense of identity. While open to the Spirit, they're still discerning what this openness might mean for them. I write this book from the perspective of being the pastor of one of these long-established congregations that is deeply rooted in an institutional model and yet is struggling to find a new missional identity. As such, I write this book with similar communities of faith in mind.

A Spirit-Filled, Emergent, Missional and Progressive Community of Faith

The movement of the Spirit that is stirring moderate and progressive congregations, whether they have historically identified themselves with evangelical or mainline Protestantism, often see themselves as being emergent or missional.[7] These terms – emergent and missional – can be seen as expressions of a renewed sense of the church as a community called by God to engage the world today in such a way as to bring transformation not only to the church but to the world. These are movements that seek to burst through old boundaries that have stifled world-changing ministry. As faith communities begin to examine and reflect upon their core identities and practices, they have begun to discern how and where they should be engaged.

This process of discernment – acts of introspection – will need to keep two parties in mind – God, the author of this missional calling, and the stranger, the person who lives outside the walls of the faith community. In the age of Christendom it was assumed

---

7   Alan Roxburgh speaks of the need for congregations to develop their core identity, before they can discern their calling in the world. Alan Roxburgh, *Missional Map-Making: Skills for leading in Times of Transition.* (San Francisco: Jossey Bass, 2010), 127ff.

that everyone in Western Society was a Christian – or at least recognized that the culture was Christian. Church and state mixed, with the state either teaching or backing the teaching of religion to the masses. That day is long past. Large numbers of people, especially among the younger generations know little about the God whom church folk claim to worship. What does the person whom demographers have come to call the "nones" see or hear when they walk into a typical mainline Protestant church? Will they feel welcome and safe? Or, will they find a culture and environment that is not only foreign and strange but foreboding? Beyond the person who has little exposure to the church's theology and practices, we might consider other persons who venture into the community. There are any number of boundary issues that need to be considered – gender, age, ethnicity, language, socio-economic, and cultural differences that impact one's experience of God and the church.

When the stranger enters the community of faith, does what they hear and see suggest that the denizens of the church are, in the words of Paul, "out of your mind?" Or, do they hear and experience a message that discloses the secrets of their hearts, so that in response to their encounter in this place they fall before God in worship? Or to put it a bit differently, is it possible, that the stranger might enter into the church and declare: God is in this place (1 Corinthians 14:20-25). For many progressive/mainline churches this might seem like an odd expectation, but why is that? Why can't we expect God's Spirit to move in such a way that lives are changed dramatically due to their encounter with God?

This is the question that haunts the church in an age of wars and rumors of wars, an age of hate speech, drive-by shootings, growing intolerance, terrorism, bombings, and kidnappings. How do we bear witness to God's grace and love and presence in this context? The questions become even more daunting because religious people seem to be stirring up much of the heat, while more moderate and progressive voices appear to be lost in the shuffle. Indeed, the news that is heard from pulpit and pew isn't always good. Whether it's "fire and brimstone" or bewailing lost influence, it often seems as if the church has lost sight of its mission. And yet the church possesses good news. This is news that if it's shared will resonate with the hearts of people who face such a wearying barrage of negativity.[8]

There are people out there, some who will enter and some who will never enter – at least not without a gentle invitation – into traditional houses of worship, who are looking for words of hope and peace. They want to worship a God who will open up the secrets of their hearts so that they might find in God a source of healing grace. And so the question remains, if the stranger walks into the church what will she or he find? What will it take for them to say: God is in this place?

The world around us is groaning as if with labor pains. It's waiting for its redemption; it's waiting for a new start (Rom. 8:22ff; 2 Cor. 5:17ff.). Paul says that the Spirit of God is in our midst interpreting our groans and cries to God in sighs too deep for words. Paul says that God hears and acts in our lives, changing us, transforming us through the renewing of our minds (Rom. 12:1ff). God hears and God acts by pouring out on the church a Spirit who brings gifts and callings. Transformed by our encounters with this Spirit of God who hears our cries, we can become partners with God in world changing ministries.

You have heard it said before, change happens one step at a time. This adage is true. Change of vision begins as God discloses to us the secrets of our hearts so that we can bow before our God in worship. When we hear God's voice calling out to us, saying: Who will go? Who will be my voice? We know that our hearts have grown warm and the covenant of God is within us, when we hear a voice from within say: "Here I am, send me." When we hear the call and we say in response "send me," then we will know that

---

[8] Martha Grace Reese's series on evangelism and the mainline churches – *Unbinding the Gospel* (Chalice Press, 2007), *Unbinding Your Heart,* (Chalice Press, 2008), and *Unbinding Your Soul,* (Chalice Press, 2009), uncovers the mainline aversion to evangelism and provides resources for recovering one's voice.

God is in this place (Is. 6:8). World changing ministry begins with our personal life-changing encounters with the God who creates the heavens and the earth. From there we can see God moving in families, in churches, and in communities that lie beyond the walls of the church.

According to Genesis, God made a covenant with Abraham that carried with this promise: the world will experience blessings through Abraham's offspring (Genesis 12:1ff). It's a promise that is held dear by the Jewish people, who are Abraham's offspring. It's also a promise held dear by Christians, whom, as Paul suggests, have been grafted into the people of God and are thereby now children of Abraham and heirs of the blessing (Gal. 3:29). As children of Abraham we hear a call to be a blessing to the nations; we hear the call to engage in world changing ministry, a ministry that works for peace, justice, and healing (salvation) of a fallen, fragmented, and often chaotic world. Not only do we hear this call, we also receive the promise that the Spirit of God has gifted us with the tools necessary to accomplish this ministry in the world (1 Cor. 12:7).

I believe that the kind of church that the stranger is looking for offers both a sense of meaning for life and an opportunity to engage in work that makes a difference in the world. This is, I believe, the message that Jesus has entrusted to his church. It's a message that offers hope of reconciliation with God and with humanity, and ultimately with creation itself. The wars and rebellions of today are really nothing other than signs of our alienation from God, from neighbor, and from creation.

> *So if anyone is in Christ, there is a new creation: everything old has passed away; see everything has become new! All this is from God, who reconciled us to himself through Christ, and has given us the ministry of reconciliation; that is, in Christ God was reconciling the world to himself, not counting their trespasses against them, and entrusting the message of reconciliation to us* (2 Cor. 5:17-19).

This is our calling: Be messengers of God's act of reconciliation in Jesus Christ. The question is, how? And the answer lies within us,

Unfettered Spirit 9

in the gifts and callings that God has placed on our lives. Full of the Spirit, we embark on a ministry of transformation. This call to be ministers of reconciliation goes not to us as individuals, but to us as the church, the body of Christ that is visibly present in the world.

Opening Up the Circle of the Spirit – Becoming an Outward Looking Church

If the church is the body of Christ that has been called and empowered to engage in world-transforming mission outside the walls of the church building, what does this body look like? In short these communities take many forms and can be small or large, but they all have this in common – they have opened themselves up to the leading of God's Spirit. Whether house church or mega-church, these Spirit-empowered communities are outward looking and are committed to bringing into play the world-healing presence of God's Spirit. The goal isn't rescuing the perishing so they can enjoy the afterlife, but instead they seek to be harbingers of God's reign on earth as in heaven. In doing this, the church fulfills God's promise to make Abraham's offspring a blessing to the world. The church does this, as they follow the lead of the Spirit, in breaking down the walls that divide us from one another (Gal. 3:28). As we exhibit God's love for humanity, we expand God's reign over the creation. When God reigns over all, peace reigns as well.

It's clear to many of us that the church has to be more than simply an institution that exists for its own sake. It won't survive simply as a social club or even as a service club. The future is bright if we can recognize that religion as we've known it in its institutional forms is now dead. That's not to say that structure will disappear, but no longer will the people of God focus their attention on sustaining the institution for the sake of the institution. In this new vision for the church, the people of God will begin to again see themselves as spiritually-gifted to engage in ministry that touches the entire world of God's creation.

The organic nature of the body metaphor highlights both the diversity and the interconnectedness of the spiritually-gifted

Christian community. Because every member of Christ's body is uniquely equipped for service, we will need each other if we're to truly live out our call to be a missional community. There is no benefit to anyone in being a lone-ranger. I can do only so much by myself, but together there is power.

We who see ourselves as part of the body of Christ need to ask the question: Do you truly believe that God is present in the world? And, do you believe that God is working through us to break down the walls that divide us from God, from each other, and from the world? And if you do, do you believe that you have been gifted and empowered to participate in this ministry that takes down the walls of egoism, suspicion, greed, self-interest, and hatred? I write this book believing that more is required of us than simply revitalizing the church so that it can limp along for another generation, offering chaplaincy service for the current members. Buildings and committees are tools for service, but they're not ends in themselves.

I write this book with mainline Protestants in mind, though I hope others will find it a helpful read. This faith tradition has long believed that the church is called to do more than simply save souls. Although too often we have taken up what H. Richard Niebuhr called the "Christ of Culture," at our best we have seen our calling as that of being transformers of culture. We have seen our calling as embracing not only heaven, but also earth. At our best we have advocated for equality and justice as signs of God's reign on earth. We believe that the world created is at its heart good and when broken it can be mended and healed. We also believe that when God is at work in the world bringing redemption and reconciliation, God makes use of God's people

Although Mainliners influenced in part by the Social Gospel, made justice a priority, we tended to ignore evangelism. Perhaps we got complacent believing that the culture was largely Christian and thus we needn't share our faith stories with our neighbors. For some it seemed even undignified to share that which is private with others. More recently, there has been a resurgence of interest in evangelism. Perhaps it has come about out of concern for dwindling numbers, but while we understand that the good news can be shared without words, sometimes words are necessary – especially in an age where there is much spiritual confusion. And so, we have begun to tell our story – though hopefully not in a way that is coercive or judgmental – so that we might point toward the God who is at work in our world.

These twin concerns for living the faith and sharing the faith reflect the growing sense within these churches that we must reclaim our missional calling to engage in God's effort at bringing into existence the realm or kingdom of God on earth as it is in heaven. If we're to take up this calling, there is need of spiritual empowerment and spiritual-giftedness. In this book, I seek to offer my vision of what this kind of spiritually empowered and gifted church might look like as it embraces its missional calling.

Although decades ago discussion of spiritual giftedness might have been limited to Pentecostal communities, the idea that God gifts us for ministry has penetrated mainline Protestantism. Congregations often make use of gift inventories to organize themselves. We've used it to encourage greater involvement by members in the ministry of the church. We've even hoped that this exercise could help stem the tide of decline and encourage church growth. I've engaged in this myself over the years. With this book I'd like to build on this legacy and expand the discussion by placing it in a broader conversation about what it means to be progressive, missional, and Charismatic. What does it mean for the church to be spiritually endowed to engage in meaningful mission? Could discovering our own individual and congregational giftedness help us discern a sense of purpose as well as freeing us to be God's agents of reconciliation, healing, and love for the world?

In developing my own theology of spiritual giftedness, I have started with Scripture and the biblical call to service of God and neighbor. Our own sense of calling is reflected in those of persons such as Isaiah, who heard God call out: "Whom shall I send, and who will go for us?" With Isaiah we are invited to say: "Here am I; send me" (Is. 6:8). This voice that calls us to live in relationship with God and engage in loving service to the world is embedded in the stories, images, and metaphors found in the pages of the two testaments. This witness is amplified by the answers of all who have answered that call to service in the affirmative, that great cloud of witnesses, who by their dedication and service have shown us a way of faithful living. We even hear a voice of support from those who embrace other faiths.

Buddhist writer Thich Nhat Hahn has written that "for Christians, the way to make the Holy Spirit truly present in the church is to practice thoroughly what Jesus lived and taught. It's not only true that Christians need Jesus, but Jesus needs Christians also for His energy to continue in this world."[9] For Jesus to touch, heal, renew, and redeem this world that we inhabit, he will need us to be his hands and his feet, and if we're to engage in this work we will require the gifts and empowerment of God's Spirit.

The purpose of this book is to encourage God's people, especially people who are part of Mainline Protestant churches, people with moderate to progressive understandings of theology, to embrace the message that God is present and active in their midst and that God is providing gifts that will transform lives, churches, and the world itself. In the course of the journey we will take together, we will consider more fully the nature of God's church, its calling to be in the world, and the gifts of the Spirit that enable us to fulfill our call to ministry. If the phrase "call to ministry," seems narrow and limiting, it's important to note that while some among the people of God have been set aside by ordination for specific forms of ministry that center on leadership and teaching, *all* Christians have been called to share in the ministry of the Spirit, a ministry that pushes us beyond the walls and into the world, for that is where the Spirit is at work. Indeed, we've all been given a "manifestation

---

9   Thich Nhat Hanh, *Living Buddha, Living Christ,* (New York: Riverhead Books, 1995), 73. For a pneumatological/Pentecostal discussion of interreligious discussion focusing on hospitality, see Amos Yong, *Hospitality and the Other: Pentecost, Christian Practices and the Neighbor,* (Maryknoll, NY: Orbis Books, 2008).

of the Spirit for the common good" (1 Cor. 12:7). And when Paul speaks of the common good, it's likely that his vision is broader than simply the faith community itself.

Wouldn't it be wonderful if the stranger who enters our churches could see God's presence in such tangible ways that their lives would be turned upside down? This can happen when we open the gates of our hearts and let the Spirit begin to move, bringing to us God's power and gifts so that our lives will be transformed and we can become agents of God's reconciling love. In the following pages we will see how God can accomplish this through our churches.

The book itself is composed of three sections, the first set of chapters explore the theology behind spiritual gifts, including the way in which we understand the person of the Holy Spirit, the methods and pathways of discovery, and the way in which we can nurture a spirituality that undergirds the use of gifts. Part two provides a set of definitions for a wide variety of spiritual gifts that may be present in the persons who inhabit these churches, including gifts of leadership, word, and service. We will even discuss what some call power gifts, expressions of the Spirit's presence that may raise issues about definition and even propriety among moderate and progressive Christians – gifts such as healing, exorcism, and miracles. Finally, in part three we'll look at how a gift-based understanding of ministry can be implemented in the church. I've added an afterword that looks at the question of ordination. The book includes study questions at the end of each chapter. A gifts-discovery inventory that matches up with the definitions in this book can be found at the publisher's website. Congregations using this book can download the inventory for their own use.

Thought Questions

1. Consider the World in which we live, what message does the church have to offer it?

2. What would a world-changing, world-transforming faith look like?

3. What role might the church play in such a world-transforming action?

I

Refreshing Winds and Purifying Fires:

The Spirit Descends Upon the Church

On a hot steamy afternoon there is nothing better than the feel of a cool refreshing breeze descending upon you. With this burst of cool air you throw off the lethargy and sleepiness and find yourself renewed and ready to go. Sometimes we find ourselves feeling as if we're trapped in a place full of stale and stagnant air, which leads to the feeling that life is seeping from our bodies. What is true of us as persons can be true of the church as well. As a result we may find ourselves simply not caring anymore about life or relationships. But is this where we want to be, especially when it comes to our life of faith? Or are we ready for something new to blow into our lives?

It's possible that I'm an idealist, but my sense is that most of us do care about life and faith. We want to know God intimately and share in authentic fellowship with others. We want to feel compassion and mercy. We want to see the world transformed, and we want to make a difference in the world. We know that there's more to life than staleness or malaise that many Christians have been experiencing. We're ready to jettison "religion" for "spirituality." We know that church is more than simply another social club, but sometimes it feels like one. When we feel this sense of malaise, it is good to experience that life-giving breeze that comes as the Spirit of God blows upon us, inspiring, empowering, and gifting us to embark on a new journey of faith. As Paul puts it: "The old things have gone away, and look, new things have arrived!" (2 Cor. 5:17).

It does seem as if we're living in an age of transition. The old is falling away and something new seems to be rising. Some call this a new spiritual awakening that is marked by a collapsing of self-perpetuating religious institutions that are inwardly focused, and instead moves toward an outwardly focused, missional, emergent, experiential, spiritually rich reality. As Diana Butler Bass suggests, the signs of this new awakening include "egalitarianism, communalism, environmentalism, economic life, and mutual responsibility" all of which are "being born from the emerging spirituality, opening the possibilities for new forms of compassion toward others and toward the planet."[10]

Yes, there are signs all around us that the refreshing winds of the Spirit are moving into our midst, so that the people of God might be refreshed, renewed, cleansed, forgiven, and empowered. Having been refreshed and renewed, we can join together and bear witness in word and deed that God is truly in this place.

There are numerous signs that suggest that people both inside and outside the church want a deep and abiding relationship with God. All the surveys suggest that even a large majority of those deemed "nones," that is those who have chosen not to affiliate with any religious tradition or community, still want to be in fellowship with God. It's the kind of desire that St. Augustine spoke of when he suggested so many centuries ago that our spirits will not rest until they find rest in God. Although this desire for union with God can be self-centered, many of those seeking this connection with the Spirit of God understand that any link to God should lead to transformed relationships with one's neighbors and with the creation itself. The keystone story of the Christian pathway to spiritual transformation is found in Acts 2. The Pentecost story begins with a promise and a commission. According to this story, before

---

10 Diana Butler Bass, *Christianity after Religion: The End of Church and the Birth of a New Spiritual Awakening*, (San Francisco: Harper One, 2012), 259.

ascending into the heavens, Jesus told his followers to wait upon the Spirit before beginning their mission to carry the good news of the kingdom to the ends of the earth (Acts 1:8). This small band of disciples waited patiently until the day of Pentecost, when the Spirit fell upon them like "a mighty wind." At that moment, as the Spirit of God fell upon this gathering, it quickly became apparent that this room couldn't contain the Spirit of God. Soon, the whole city – a city full of pilgrims – begins to hear the disciples, all of whom are empowered by the Spirit of God, proclaim the message of Jesus to the gathering crowd (Acts 2). When the Spirit came upon them, the disciples were ready to give their witness to the resurrection of Jesus. Whatever fear and anxiety may have been resting on them gives way to the Spirit's empowering presence. Now they knew what their purpose was, what they were called to do, and so with the Spirit blowing at their sails, they embark on a new course, to share the good news to the ends of the earth.[11]

If you take a journey through the Book of Acts, you'll see the Spirit empower and guide this new movement of ordinary people as they take up extraordinary callings. Because of this movement of the Spirit a community of faith comes into existence, which will be called Christians, and they will leave an indelible mark on the world. The Spirit drew these first disciples together, empowering and gifting them, so that they could bring to their community a word of healing. As Peter said to the man sitting in the city gate: "I have no silver or gold, but what I have I give you; in the name of Jesus Christ of Nazareth, stand up and walk" (Acts 3:6). This has been the message of the church, when the church has truly understood its calling: God won't leave your life unchanged.

---

11   John offers a rather different, quieter version of Pentecost. In John, Jesus gathers the disciples together and breathes the Spirit into them. Though it is not as dramatic, it is just as effective. In both versions Jesus empowers the people of God for service (Jn. 20:19-23). For an accessible but rather full engagement with the role of the Spirit in the story of Acts, see Amos Yong, *Who is the Holy Spirit? A walk with the Apostles.* (Brewster, MA: Paraclete Press, 2011).

When that earliest community of faith gathered for worship and prayer, they comforted each other and gave generously to those in need. At our best, we continue this tradition. We serve meals to the hungry and provide homes for the homeless. We lift up the downcast and bring healing to the hurting. Such a church, to quote Fred Craddock, is "going out and serving other people who are not even grateful, hurting when anybody else hurts, emptying their pockets for other people's children, building a Habitat house when their own house is in bad need of repair and the paint is peeling, going to the woman's house and mowing her lawn when their own grass is twelve inches high."[12] But, not only do we engage in immediate acts of mercy, again, at our best, we organize and band together, to call upon those in authority to act with justice. In this we follow in the footsteps of the prophets. We do this, as a community, because the Spirit is there to build the community and empower our voices.

The message of Pentecost is simple: When the Spirit begins to move in our midst, expect things to change. When the Spirit is moving in our hearts we begin to focus on the needs and concerns of our neighbors. This leads us to practice the ancient art of hospitality and advocacy for justice and peace. It is, as Amos Yong puts it:

> Pentecost thus inaugurates a restored Israel and God's kingdom by establishing new social structures and relations. Note that the gift of the Spirit is not withheld from any of the 120 men and women who gathered in the upper room (Acts 1:14-15), the divided tongues of fire rested on each one and enabled each to either speak or be heard in foreign languages.

In this new vision of God's people there would be equality among women and men, and if taken seriously, it would call into question social structures such as slavery. He writes further: "In effect, the restoration of the kingdom through the power of the Spirit actually overturned the status quo."[13]

---

12 Fred B. Craddock, *The Cherry Log Sermons*, (Louisville: Westminster/John Knox Press, 2001), 69.
13 Amos Yong, *Who is the Holy Spirit?* 14-15.

Unfettered Spirit

With the coming of the Spirit, the call to change the world begins to resound in our midst. The point of Pentecost is not the spectacle of tongues of fire, but rather with these tongues of fire something new has emerged that will bring a new covenant reality and the created order under the rule of God. This work begins with this gathering of people in the Upper Room, but it doesn't stay in the room. We may want to control the Spirit, but it's clear that the doors and the windows of our buildings can't contain or constrain the Spirit. Although there's risk involved in opening the doors of our churches to the refreshing presence of the Spirit, but if we do this, then we will begin experiencing the full meaning of the two great commandments – loving God and loving our neighbor.

Staying Alive:
The Church Living in the Spirit

The two foundational principles of the Christian faith are the commandments to love God and love neighbor. These are principles that Jesus embodied fully, and when empowered by the Spirit of Love, we can join him in embodying these principles, even if we do so imperfectly. Unless there is love, everything done in the name of Christ comes to naught (1 Cor. 13:1-3).

A living and vibrant church will be marked by a love that's expressed through acts of hospitality, justice, compassion, and mercy. This life of the Spirit is rooted in vibrant worship of the God who created and now seeks to reconcile the world (*kosmos*). Such a community looks beyond its own walls and sees fields ripe for harvest, fields in which the Spirit is already present and at work. We hear the question, "where can I go, that the Spirit is not already there?" In the words of the Psalmist, we pray:

Where can I go from your spirit?
Or where can I flee from your presence?
If I ascend to heaven, you are there;
If I make my bed in Sheol, you are there (Ps. 139:7-8).

Knowing that the Spirit's presence isn't limited to church buildings, it would seem that the work of the church isn't limited to what is deemed by our culture as being religious. It encompasses all of life's experiences, from politics to family life to popular culture. Such a reality was termed "religionless" Christianity by Dietrich Bonhoeffer.

It would be nice if we could say that we've reached the point where such a reality was fully present, but that's far from the truth. There's too much of the "world" in the church, and not enough of the church in the world. But, if we're willing to give the Spirit room to move, then the church, even with its institutional markings, can be transformed into a community that relinquishes itself of its cliques and inward focus, and its suspicion of all that is new. What is envisioned here has come to be called the missional church, a church that not only engages in mission, but mission is its very identity.[14]

We start from the premise of Pentecost, that the Spirit of God is already present in the church and in the world. Although some might take from Pentecost the idea that when the Spirit moves it's with loudness and spectacle, such an interpretation would miss the point. We don't experience the presence of the Spirit as either loudness or coerciveness. The Spirit may come as a mighty wind, but the Spirit also comes as a gentle breeze, and in this movement of the Spirit, gifts of service are shared with the church so that it can touch the world. In addition, as we discover spiritual gifts we begin to recognize that every person in this world has something of value to offer to the world. With the Spirit present, all things become new, including our relationships with our God and with our neighbor. No longer will we look at life from a human point of view (2 Cor. 5:16).

Later in this book, we'll talk about how we can discover spiritual gifts as well as working to tune them and focus them so that

---

[14] See, among other resources, Gary V. Nelson, *Borderland Churches: A Congregation's Introduction to Missional Living,* (St. Louis: Chalice Press, 2008).

Unfettered Spirit

we can engage in ministry both inside and outside the church. For this to occur there must be a sense of interplay between the Spirit and the community.

For Christians, our relationship with Jesus has both vertical and horizontal dimensions. If we're to love God with our entire being this will play out in our relationships with our neighbors.

When asked about the identity of the neighbor whom we're called to love, Jesus told a parable about a Samaritan who showed compassion for the man in a ditch, when the religious authorities passed him by. It's clear that the definition of neighbor is much broader than we've often imagined. It includes family, co-workers, school-mates, church members, and the person lying in the gutter or in the prison. Genesis 1 declares that we're all created in the image of God – men and women, young and old, rich and poor, gay and straight. Each of us bears the imprint of the Spirit's presence, whether we live inside or outside the Christian community.[15]

What then is the nature of this Spirit that animates and empowers the church and enables both vertical (divine-human) and horizontal (human-human) relationships? What is this life-giving force that's present in our churches and in our lives?

God is, we confess, spirit. God is without material form, and yet God is more than an ephemeral wisp of smoke – as if to say, God is there and yet not there. Mindful of the limits of human

---

15 As I consider the presence of the Spirit in my neighbor, I am mindful that my neighbor may not "acknowledge" Jesus as lord. My Jewish, Muslim, Hindu friends are people of faith who desire to live as servants of God. What then should my relationship with them be like? My consideration of this question is fueled by my own involvement in interfaith dialog coupled with a strong confessional faith in Jesus Christ as Lord and Savior, personally and universally. On this question see Amos Yong, *Hospitality & the Other: Pentecost, Christians Practices, and the Neighbor,* (Maryknoll, NY: Orbis Books, 2008), Eboo Patel, *Sacred Ground: Pluralism, Prejudice, and the Promise of America,* (Boston: Beacon Press, 2012), and Brian McLaren, *Why Did Jesus, Moses, the Buddha, and Mohammed Cross the Road? Christian Identity in a Multi-Faith World,* (New York: Jericho Books, 2012).

images and metaphors, we confess that God is more than an impersonal force that can be manipulated for human benefit. That is, God is something more than the "Force" of the popular *Star Wars* sagas. However we understand personhood, the biblical portrayal of the Holy Spirit is that of an intimate presence of God in human life. This Spirit is a divine presence that is both personal and free from human manipulation; as the immanent presence of God, the Spirit remains a transcendent "determining subject" who is free to act.[16] With regard to the Spirit, we can't merely say the right words or perform the proper rituals and expect the Spirit to act.[17] When we experience the Spirit's presence and activity, we do so with openness to the unexpected. But, when the Holy Spirit acts in our lives, we're awakened to new possibilities for life and we're energized to carry them out.[18]

In trying to understand the person, character, and work of the Holy Spirit of God, we must turn to the person of Jesus. In the gospel of John, we hear that the advocate will bear witness to Jesus. Therefore, to know the Spirit is to know Jesus. We know what the purpose of the Spirit is by looking to Jesus' life, ministry, and teachings. A good shepherd will not run from danger (Jn. 10:11ff). A loving father welcomes home the prodigal with open arms (Lk. 15:11-31), the loving person forgives without count. Enemies are

---

16 On the contrast between the biblical portrayal of the Spirit and that found in Star Wars see Bryan Stone, *Faith and Film: Theological Themes at the Cinema,* (St. Louis: Chalice Press, 2000), 134-35. See also Jürgen Moltmann, *The Spirit of Life: A Universal Affirmation,* Margaret Kohl, trans., (Minneapolis: Fortress Press, 1991), 286.

17 Such an understanding of God is present in some forms of Pentecostalism, in which a prosperity based gospel, suggests if you have the right amount of faith and the audacity to demand God to act on your behalf, you can have what you want. TV evangelists pray for hurricanes to hit elsewhere and for millions to be received so they can stay on the air raising money.

18 Jürgen Moltmann, *The Source of Life: The Holy Spirit and the Theology of Life,* Margaret Kohl, trans., (Minneapolis: Fortress Press, 1997), 10-11.

embraced, persecutors resisted gently but earnestly. You'll know the true Spirit of God, and be able to test those who claim to speak for God, because the Spirit, as Fred Craddock reminds us, "does not speak apart from or contrary to the historical Jesus (John 16:12-15). Rather, the Spirit keeps the voice of Jesus a living voice in the church."[19]

What Does the Bible Say?

Biblical Images of the Spirit

In answering the following question – who is the Holy Spirit of God? – we would be wise to start by looking at how the Spirit is present in the biblical story. The Spirit is described using a variety of words that have important nuances. Words like breath, wind, fire, comforter, advocate, power, presence, all give us a sense of the person, the ministry, the presence of the Spirit of God. Let us, then, take a look at some of these words.

Breath, Wind

The Hebrew word *ruach* and the Greek word *pneuma* are often translated in scripture as Spirit, but these words have a broader set of meanings that can help us better understand the nature of this Spirit that is blowing gently through our lives. These two words can be translated as breath and wind, both breath and wind connote freshness and power, life and energy.

Consider that the Spirit sweeps like the winds "over the face the waters" at creation (Gen. 1:2), and the heavens are created by the word of the Lord and "their host by the breath *(ruach)* of his mouth" (Ps. 33:6). In this Psalm both Word and Spirit come together in the acts of creation. Then, in creating the first human, God breathes life into the man (Gen. 2:7). Ezekiel envisions the

---

[19] Fred Craddock in Fred B. Craddock, et. al., *Preaching Through the Christian Year, B,* (Valley Forge, PA: Trinity Press International, 1993), 284-85.

breath of God resurrecting the exiled and dispirited people of Israel (Ezk. 37:1ff). In Ezekiel, Israel is pictured as a valley of dry bones, which come to life as the breath of God enlivens them. When Jesus tells Nicodemus that he must be born of the Spirit, we learn that the Spirit, like the wind, blows where it wishes (Jn. 3:5-8). When the risen Christ sends the disciples out into the world to bear witness to him, he breathes the Spirit into them (Jn. 20:22). At Pentecost, the Spirit falls on the infant church like a "violent" or "mighty" wind, empowering the gathered church for service (Acts 2:2).

Each biblical image pictures God offering the breath of life to humanity. Whether that life is conceived in physical or spiritual terms it still comes from the one God, who blows where God wills (Jn. 3:8). The breath of God is the empowering Spirit that brings the church to life and stirs within it joy and hope. Enlivened by the breath of God, the church is more than a religious institution; it's the very living body of Christ.

Fire

Fire offers light, provides energy, and it purifies. We welcome fire, but we also fear it. In the words of John the Baptist, the one who is coming will baptize not just with water, but also with the Holy Spirit and with fire (Mt. 3:11; Lk. 3:16-17). At Pentecost a flame rests on each person gathered in the Upper Room, with the flame serving as a tangible sign of the Spirit's presence (Acts 2:3). John's promise, Luke tells us, is fulfilled.

It's in this context that we hear Paul's instructions to the Thessalonians: don't quench the Spirit – in other words, don't pour water on the Spirit's flame. Don't suppress or extinguish the passion and fervor of the spiritual life (1 Thess. 5:19). Or, as a mentor writes to a protégé in ministry, rekindle and fan into flame the gift first given to him through the laying on of hands (2 Tim. 1:6-7).

The image of fire as a symbol of God's presence predates Pentecost. It has a rich pedigree. God often appears to the people of God in the form of fire. God famously appears to Moses from within a burning bush on Mt. Sinai (Ex. 3:2). Then, God leads the Hebrews across the Sinai desert as a pillar of fire (Ex. 13:21-22). When the sojourners got to Horeb they, like Moses before them, heard God speak from within the midst of the fire (Deut. 4:14). Then there is Elisha who sees God's protective presence shielding him from his enemies as a ring of fire (2 Kings 6:17).

The Spirit of God, who comes to us in the form of fire, is, as Scripture so richly suggests, the light on our path that leads us forward. Like a blazing fire in the night, the Spirit leads us on our journey toward the place where God is at work. The Spirit is also the fire that purifies our lives of sin and our need to keep control of things that are of no consequence. Like gold, the impurities of life are burned off through trial and difficult experiences, driving us toward placing our trust in the one who brings new life. In the words of Zechariah, a sinful Judah is purged of evil through a refiner's fire: "I will put this third into the fire, refine them as one refines silver, and test them as gold is tested. They will call on my name, and I will answer them" (Zech. 13:9; cf. Is. 66:15-16). The Spirit lights within you and me the passion for God and the things of God. When we focus on the things of God, when we let the Spirit loose, our hearts catch fire with a burden for the world in which we live.

Presence

God is everywhere. You can't get away from God. This is what the Psalmist says of God: "Where can I go from your Spirit? Or where can I flee from your presence?" (Ps. 139:7). Jonah tried to get away from God by boarding a ship sailing for Tarshish. He thought God was limited by geography or national boundaries, but he found out that this wasn't true. God isn't afraid of water and the lines on the map won't keep God out either. You can run, but you can't hide from God, because God is present everywhere.

The Christmas song rings out: "You better watch out, you better not cry, you better not pout," because Santa knows if you're "naughty or nice." That's not the point of recognizing God's presence. Yes, God knows better than Santa when you're naughty or nice, but the point is not that you should watch your "p's and q's" lest God "gets you." Instead, the point is that in Emmanuel the transcendent God is present for us. Through the Spirit, God initiates a loving relationship with us. It's here that we receive the promise: "I will never leave you nor forsake you" (Deut. 31:6, 8).

God, in Christian theology, becomes present to humanity in the person of Jesus. In the words of John, "the Word became flesh and lived among us, and we have seen his glory, the glory as of a father's only son, full of grace and truth" (Jn. 1:14). In Jesus, God has walked in our shoes, tasting life as we live it, tasting death as we do. Even temptation did not pass God by, but Jesus remained faithful though having tasted life as we live it. Yes, in Jesus, God faced temptation as do we, but did not sin (Heb. 4:14-15). In the words of Paul, God humbled God's self, in an act of self-emptying revelation. Not even death itself was withheld (Phil. 2:6-8). What transpired in the life of Jesus, God becoming manifest to humanity, is extended to us by the Spirit, who makes the God known in Jesus present to all humanity.[20]

Our assumption of God's universal presence through the Spirit is humanized by the Christian belief that God became present to us in a person: "The Word became flesh and lived among us" (Jn. 1:14). The question remains: How is God present to me as a child of God? Scripture gives us at least two important ways of understanding God's "particularized" presence with us. One means of

---

20 There are a number of ways of understanding God's relationship with creation. "Panentheism" is one possible way of understanding God's immanent presence with creation. Panentheism, in contrast, to pantheism, affirms the presence of all things being within God, while positing a necessary differentiation between God and creation. See Marcus Borg, *The Heart of Christianity,* (San Francisco: Harper San Francisco, 2003), 65-70. But one can also understand God's ever present presence along more traditional lines, though a stronger demarcation between God and creation is made. The point is that God is not so "wholly other" that God cannot interact with creation.

Unfettered Spirit

the Spirit's presence is corporate – in the church – but this does not mean the Spirit is not present to us as individuals. Help can be found to understand both the corporate and individual dimensions of God's presence in the image of the Temple.

Ancient Judaism believed that God's presence dwelt in the Tabernacle/Temple. The Ark of the Covenant was understood to be carrying God's presence, God's *kabod* or glory. This *kabod* or glory is what made the Temple holy. In Rabbinic Judaism the concept of the *Shekinah* emerged to describe God's specific, self-willed presence in the world (*immanence*).[21] Taking this understanding of the particularized presence of God, the *kabod* or the *Shekinah* to heart, we can better understand the New Testament concept of the church being the Temple of the Holy Spirit (1 Cor. 3:16-17; 2 Cor. 6:16; Eph. 2:21-22). They also help us understand the image of the human body being a "temple of the Holy Spirit. Paul wrote to the Corinthian church, saying: "do you know that your body is the temple of the Holy Spirit within you, which you have from God, and that you are not your own? For you were bought with a price; therefore glorify God in your body" (1 Cor. 6:19-20). Although this particular passage speaks to the issue of sexual morality, the idea that the body is a temple of the Spirit suggests that God's Spirit is present in the world wherever God's people are present. Therefore, even as the Ark of the Covenant provides blessings to those who faithfully came into contact with it (1 Sam. 5:1- 7:2) – and a word of judgment on those who seek to deny the Spirit's presence – when the Spirit-indwelt people of God are present, blessings are possible. This means that the Spirit's ministry takes place not just within the church walls, but wherever the "temple" (the body) is present.

---

21   Moltmann, *Spirit of Life*, 48. David S. Ariel, *What Do Jews Believe? The Spiritual Foundations of Judaism*, (New York: Schocken Books, 1995), 22-23. Rachel Timoner, *Breath of Life: God as Spirit in Judaism*, (Brewster, MA: Paraclete Press, 2011), 51-54. Walter Brueggemann, *Ichabod Toward Home: The Journey of God's Glory*, (Grand Rapids: Wm. B. Eerdmans Publishing Co., 2002).

Helper/Advocate

John's gospel offers a unique description of the Holy Spirit that makes clear the connection between Jesus and the Spirit. In chapters 13-17 of John, as Jesus gives his last instructions to the disciples, Jesus describes the Spirit as the Paraclete (*parakaletos*), the one who comes alongside us, as helper, comforter, counselor, strengthener, and advocate. John's gospel offers the ascension as the point at which Jesus passes the baton to the Holy Spirit who indwells the disciples, who continue the work of Jesus. The Spirit comes to serve as a tutor, reminding the disciples of what Jesus taught them during his life.[22] With the coming of the Paraclete the Spirit of Jesus is universalized, enabling the people of God to bear witness to the one in whom God became incarnate.[23] Thus, even as Jesus bore witness to the Father (Jn. 8:14), so the Spirit bears witness to the Son (Jn. 15:26-27). The Paraclete, the Spirit of Christ, not only bears witness to Christ but is the Spirit of Truth (Jn. 14:17). For those who seek the truth, the Spirit will lead them to it (Jn. 16:13).[24]

These various nuances of the word *parakaletos* offer further definition of the Spirit's presence in human life. As helper, the Spirit empowers members of the body of Christ to serve and care for their neighbor. As comforter the Spirit comes alongside us, bringing hope to the hopeless and comfort to the grieving and suffering in our midst. In this idea of the Spirit serving as advocate, we see the Spirit giving witness to Jesus, putting forward his case to humanity. The image of counselor speaks of one who offers guidance and direction. It is just one Greek word, and yet it offers so many possibilities for us to engage one another in Jesus' healing presence.

---

22 The image of tutor is found in John Castelein's article, "The Doctrine of the Holy Spirit," in *Essentials of Christian Faith*, Steve Burris, ed., (Joplin, MO: College Press, 1992), 83.
23 Welker, *God the Spirit*, 223-24.
24 Welker, *God the Spirit*, 225.

Power

The explosiveness of dynamite should help us grasp the biblical understanding of the power of God's Spirit. The Greek word for power is *dunamis*, from which we get the word dynamite. As the "Power of God." the Spirit does the unexpected, going wherever the Spirit wills (Jn.3:8). This is not a form of power that we can control. Think of the hurricane or tornado – both storms have great power that cannot be controlled. Such is the nature of God's power, not that it is destructive, but that we can't tame God's power.

Barbara Brown Taylor picks up the sense of the power of the Spirit's presence in her reflections on the Pentecost story.

> This is the Spirit, who blows and burns, howling down the chimney and turning all the lawn furniture upside down. Ask Job about the whirlwind, or Ezekiel about the chariot of fire. Ask anyone who was in that room on Pentecost what it was like to be caught up in the Spirit, and wither it is something they would like to happen *every* Sunday afternoon.[25]

Could we be comfortable with a Pentecost like experience every Sunday? With Taylor, I'm not sure any of us is quite ready for such a demonstration of power. But, Pentecost underlines the biblical picture of the Spirit being that energy of God that cannot be domesticated, possessed, or even harnessed. Yet, the Spirit freely enters the community bringing to it energizing power. We might not be able to harness the power of the Spirit, but the Spirit remains present, infusing our lives with life changing energy. When coupled with the gifts and abilities God provides the people of God, world-changing ministry is truly possible. Thus the church can be a force that brings to the world God's transforming love through both word and deed.

In affirming the power of God's presence in human experience, we must recognize the troubling aspects of power. Lord Acton's statement concerning the corruptibleness of power, especially in

---

25 Barbara Brown Taylor, *Bread of Angels,* (Cambridge, MA: Cowley Publications, 1997), 67.

its absolutist forms, should warn us against taking the power of the Spirit for granted, as if it is there to do our bidding. Ever mindful of this caution about the danger of power, it is power — consider modern electricity — that makes things run, enabling the completion of untold numbers of tasks. Power is both dangerous and beneficial. Receiving the power of the Spirit of God requires discernment and careful handling. So, be sure that you and your congregation are "well-grounded."

The Spirit of God is the divine expression of power. It is power that creates and transforms. It is power that brings to life that which is dead and dry. Even as the Spirit, in Ezekiel's vision, resurrects the dry bones of Israel, the Spirit comes upon the church at Pentecost like a mighty wind and transforms a small dispirited band of disciples into motivated witnesses to Jesus Christ. Empowered by the Spirit, the church set out to fulfill Jesus' commission to preach the gospel to the ends of the earth (Acts 1:8).

Although Pentecost uniquely marks the birth of a new movement of the Spirit, it's also the model of future experiences of the Spirit. As a read through the Book of Acts demonstrates, this isn't the only time the Spirit inaugurates something new by filling a community or a person with power so that the community or person might bear witness to God's presence in the world. We see this not only in Acts, but church history offers many other stories of God's birthing of new movements of the Spirit. Think for a moment of the Franciscans, Luther and the Reformation, the two Great Awakenings, the ecumenical movement, the Social Gospel movement, the women's movement, Vatican II, Pentecostalism, and the various theologies of liberation. There is, as we've noted, much talk about whether we're witnessing the beginning of a new spiritual awakening. What we can say about each of these awakenings is that they appear to be expressions of the Spirit's presence in the world and serve as an invitation to embrace God's new work.

Returning to Pentecost, we see the birthing of a new community of faith that's empowered by the Spirit, and coming in the wake of this moment are the people and the communities that have

Unfettered Spirit

been empowered and equipped by the Spirit to bear witness in word and deed to the person and ministry of Jesus Christ. Stanley Grenz helpfully suggests that in Pentecost the "coming of the Spirit on the group signified the creation of the Spirit-endowed, Spirit-empowered, Spirit-led community."[26] What began that day has continued to spread beyond the Upper Room to the far corners of the earth. We are the heirs of the Pentecost event, at least if we're willing to allow the Spirit to draw us into service in the world.

UNITY IN THE ONE SPIRIT OF GOD

The Spirit empowers, but the Spirit also unifies. It's believed by many that Pentecost reversed Babel's confusion of languages. While Genesis describes, metaphorically, the separation, the fears, the confusions experienced by an alienated humanity (Gen. 11:1-9), Pentecost, with the gift of languages that makes the gospel understood, offers a sign of reunion.

Speech in other tongues, that is in languages or sounds that are unknown or foreign to the speaker, occurs four times in Acts and in each case it comes as the church reaches across humanly-constructed boundaries to fellowship. The first occasion could be seen as less the crossing of a barrier and more the opening of a door to a new experience of the Spirit, but the others are more focused on crossing boundaries. In the first instance, the voices speak of Jesus to the Jewish Diaspora; the second instance is more implicit than the others. Tongues are not mentioned, but something happens to confirm the outpouring of the Spirit on the Samaritan believers, bearing witness to the extension of God's reign to include the outsider. Though Luke does not offer a description of the event, traditionally it has been assumed that a gift of languages occurred (8:16ff). Tongues mark the crossing of another boundary, that which separates Jew and Gentile. Cornelius and his household receive a gift of tongues as confirmation of God's invitation to

---

26 Stanley Grenz, *Theology for the Community of God*, (Nashville: Broadman and Holman, 1994), 482.

Gentiles to join in the kingdom of God (Acts 10:46ff). The final passage is somewhat different, in that the recipients are Jewish disciples of John the Baptist who know of Jesus but not of the Holy Spirit (Acts 19:1). Again tongues seem to represent a sign of inclusion. This pattern is intriguing, but it does not provide an explicit or normative precedent for the church.

Each of these images used to describe and understand the Spirit, from breath/wind to power, from comforter/advocate to divine presence, speak to God's immanent presence both in creation and in human experience. They also underline God's freedom to act. Traditional Christian theism emphasizes God's transcendence, sometimes to the point of losing all contact between creator and creation. Although we need to remember that God is not a human being, that God does transcend human experience, both the doctrine of the incarnation and the doctrine of the Holy Spirit remind us that God also resides in and with creation. Perhaps we can even see God encompassing creation within God's being.

Jesus declared himself to be a bearer of the Spirit. He claimed the mantle of the one on whom the Spirit of God had fallen.

> *The Spirit of the Lord is upon me, because he has anointed me to bring good news to the poor. He has sent me to proclaim release to the captives and recovery of sight to the blind, to let the oppressed go free, to proclaim the year of the Lord's favor"* (Lk. 2:18-19).

Jesus' own sense of calling to Spirit-endowed ministry points us toward our own calling. This calling is to make known God's work of reconciliation. It's a call to join with God, who dwells within us by the Spirit, in a ministry that will inaugurate a new creation, a world that is not only better, but one that will reflect the love that is God. Endowed with the Spirit, we will shine God's light into the world's darkness.

The Spirit has come into our midst, serving as a refreshing breeze, a purifying fire, and an empowering wind of God. As the Spirit shines the light of love into our world of darkness, we can re-

Unfettered Spirit

discover the path that leads back to God, and as a result, experience reconciliation with our neighbor. The Spirit is moving in our world today, breaking down the barriers and extending to anyone who is open, the eternal benefits of God's reign. If we are open to the Spirit, we will discover wonderful gifts that enable us to minister to this world in which we live in partnership with our God. This is our calling as Spirit empowered ambassadors of reconciliation (2 Cor. 5). How we can claim this calling for ourselves is the subject of the rest of this book.

Thought Questions

1. Consider your experiences/lack of experiences of God's presence. What about them would you consider life changing?

2. Think on the images of the Spirit: Wind, fire, presence, power. In what ways do these images help you better understand your place in the church and in the world?

3. If the Spirit is truly a force that cannot be harnessed by human power, how might order and harmony be found in church?

2

Gifted by Grace:

Why We Are All Charismatics!

> Grace is something you can never get but can only be given. There's no way to earn it or deserve it or bring it about any more than you can deserve the taste of raspberries and cream or earn good looks or bring about your own birth.[27]
>
> Frederick Buechner

The word charismatic may have a somewhat dubious ring to it, at least in Mainline Protestant circles. Despite what some might think of the term, I'd like to claim it for progressive and moderate mainline communities of faith. I want to be able to say: I'm a charismatic and you are too! Of course, if you're going to accept this label, you'll want a proper definition of the word.

Since the Greek word *charis*, from which we derive the words charisma and charismatic, can be translated as grace, we could define a charismatic as being one who has tasted God's favor or grace. This favor or divine grace is expressed through wonderful gifts (*charisms*) that enable us to not only experience God's love but in turn to share that love with one's neighbors. It is for this reason that we call these charisms "gifts of grace." They're not something we've earned, but they come to us as a result of God's abundant love for the world. As a result of this outpouring of divine grace, which

---

27 Frederick Buechner, *Wishful Thinking: A Seeker's ABC*, rev. ed., (San Francisco: HarperSanFrancisco, 1992), 38.

comes to us as an expression of God's love, we manifest this love and this grace through gifted and empowered benevolent actions.

In the opening chapters of Genesis, God fashions humanity from the dust of the earth and breathes life into this creation (Gen. 2:7). The Hebrew word *ruach* can be translated both as breath and spirit, and so as we read this passage from Genesis 2, we hear a witness that God breathes the Spirit and thus life into humanity. The Spirit is, therefore, linked to the gift of life. If life is the result of God's breath, then can we not say that God's essence, that is God's Spirit, is present within each of us? Therefore, as a result, the seed of the Holy Spirit is within us, which means, as Buddhist writer Thich Nhat Hanh puts it, inside us we "have the capacity of healing, transforming, and loving. When we touch that seed, we are able to touch God the Father and God the Son." Having received the gifts, the *charismata* of the Spirit, we're prepared to share the life that God has invested in us with the rest of Creation. And this makes us all charismatics.[28]

Since spiritual gifts are signs of grace and not personal acquisitions, or even marks of personal holiness, there is no hierarchy of giftedness. With gifts being expressions of grace, we can, with Anne Lamott, say that even if we don't understand the mystery of grace, we can know "that it meets us where we are but does not leave us where it found us. It can be received gladly or grudgingly, in big gulps or in tiny tastes, like a deer at the salt."[29] Grace gives us freedom to explore, to try, and to fail, and then to try again. It is this forgiving and empowering love that heals the shame, which suggests that our lives don't have value. Grace, according to Lewis Smedes, "is the gift of being accepted before we become accept-

---

28 Thich Nhat Hanh, *Living Buddha, Living Christ*. (New York: Riverhead Books, 1995), 15. Jürgen Moltmann, *The Source of Life: The Holy Spirit and the Theology of Life*, Margaret Kohl, trans., (Minneapolis: Fortress Press, 1997), 19, 180. Moltmann suggests that we are charismatic even if we have yet to discover our giftedness. It is inherent in faith.
29 Annie Lamott, *Traveling Mercies: Some Thoughts on Faith*, (New York: Anchor Books, 2000), 143.

able."[30] That is, grace is a state of being for which we do not have sufficient words, but it's a state that allows God's people to step out boldly and live in ways that are redemptive and bring healing to relationships within the communities we inhabit. When our communities are full of people who live into these signs of grace, then surely the rest of the community will say – God is in this place.

What Is a Spiritual Gift?
Characteristics of the Spirit's Gifts of Grace

If spiritual gifts are signs of divine grace, then what forms does this grace take? If we look at the gift lists in Romans, 1 Corinthians, and Ephesians, it becomes clear that there is a wide diversity of gifts, and these lists are only suggestive and not definitive. We could say that the possibilities are limited only by the imagination. One could even say that as people embrace their giftedness, they become – as individuals – gifts of God to the world.

To say that a person is a divine gift, doesn't mean they're better than anyone else, it simply means that they have become expressions of divine love in the community. It also means that whatever the gifts of God, they're expressed in and through our personalities, temperaments, abilities and talents. The gifts that we bring into our communities may or may not involve what we would deem natural talents, that is, innate abilities. The ultimate test of a gifts value is its usefulness in contributing to the welfare of the faith community and the world itself. As a result, since the church is a community of persons gifted and called by the Spirit, the church that is gifted and empowered by the Spirit becomes an instrument of grace in what is clearly a broken world.

The church is the gathered people of God, called together in Christ and gifted by the Spirit. These gifts share certain characteristics, even if one of these characteristics is diversity of expression.

---

30   Lewis Smedes, *Shame and Grace*, (San Francisco: Harper San Francisco, 1993), 108.

Gifts Are God's to Give

If God is the source of "every generous act of giving, with every perfect gift" (Jas. 1:17), and God's acts of giving occur in the manner and timing of God choosing (I Cor. 12:11), then we, as recipients, are called to live in gratefulness and trust, knowing that God will not leave us bereft of what we need to join in this ministry of service to the world. Although the ways and manners of creation are a mystery, we can affirm a divine interest in our potentialities. Who we are as persons, including our abilities and our personalities, influences our choices and our success in life. As people of faith, we affirm the premise that in God's infinite wisdom, God is involved informing us as persons.

The gift lists we find in the New Testament suggest that God uses natural abilities and occasional additional endowments of the Spirit to touch the world with divine love. Whether they are part of our constitution as a person (the gift of teaching perhaps) or an occasional sign of the Spirit's empowerment (an act of healing), gifts of the Spirit do not belong to the individual as a possession to be taken for granted. Gifts come to us by the sovereign choice of the Creator who calls on us to use these gifts wisely and appropriately to create a common good for humanity. We do not choose the gifts; the giver chooses the appropriate gift for each recipient. Although these gifts are sovereignly given, we have the freedom to choose how, when, and where we use them. We can use them appropriately or inappropriately. Therefore, we each serve as "stewards of the manifold grace of God" (1 Pet. 4:10).

ABUNDANCE AND VARIETY: NAMING THE POSSIBILITIES OF THE SPIRIT'S GIFTS

There is no end to the number and variety of gifts available to the church. The church of Jesus Christ is not homogeneous. It isn't one size and color fits all. The unity of the Christian community isn't rooted in uniformity or conformity. This gifted community of faith mirrors the breadth of human experience and existence.

The church is composed of gifted people who differ in age, gender, race, life situations, and economic status. We come together not on the basis of our common interests and backgrounds; we come together in the Spirit who bridges our differences. In our baptisms the barriers that divide us are gone. "In Christ there is neither Jew nor Greek, slave or free, male and female" (Gal. 3:28).

Offering a variety of gifts, activities, and services, the Spirit moves through the community of faith like a refreshing breeze, enlivening and empowering the community's worship, fellowship, and service (Rom. 12:6; I Cor. 12:4-6, Eph. 4:11-12). As we discover these graciously bestowed gifts of the Spirit, we find ourselves celebrating the differences that exist within the church. We can also affirm that these differences are the product of the one Lord, one God, and one Spirit who is the bond of unity (1 Cor. 12:4-6).

The gift lists – found almost entirely within the Pauline letters (Ephesians may or may not be the work of Paul, but it is rooted in the Pauline tradition, even if not from his hand) – cover a wide spectrum of gifts. Although there is significant overlap between the gift lists, the differences are suggestive not only of diversity, but also of the tentative nature of the lists. (See chart on page 40.)

Comparison of Gift-Lists[31]

Since these lists are merely suggestive and representative, we don't have to limit ourselves to this small sample of possibilities. Scripture itself offers other possibilities such as craftsmanship, hospitality, intercessory prayer, celibacy, and musicianship.

What are your gifts? Look inside yourself. What do you see? What are the possibilities? I know people who are wonderful musicians and their music draws my soul to God. There are artists whose sculptures and paintings inspire and challenge. Others find

---

[31] There is an additional non-Pauline list that should be noted. 1 Peter 4:10-11 has a brief list of spiritual endowments that is limited to service and speech gifts, a list that is more a categorization of gifts than an actual list.

1 Cor. 12:8-10	1 Cor. 12:27-28	1 Cor. 12:29-30	Romans 12:6-8	Ephesians 4:11
Prophecy	Apostles Prophets	Apostles Prophets	Prophecy	Apostles Prophets Evangelists Pastors
Wisdom Knowledge	Teachers	Teachers	Teachers	Teachers
Faith Miracles	Workers of miracles	Workers of miracles		
Healings	Healings	Healers		
Discernment	Assistance Leadership		Leaders Ministry/service	
			Exhorters Givers Compassion	
Tongues Interpretation of tongues	Tongues	Tongues Interpretation of tongues		

themselves able to live a life of poverty and celibacy, taking on themselves burdens that I, as a husband and as a father, am unable to take on.

Creating Communities of Faithful Service

Diversity and unity seem so opposite and contradictory. The message of church growth pundits was homogeneity as the key to growth – birds of a feather flock together. Human experience does suggest that there is truth to this teaching, but is it a true expression of God's realm? Although it seems to cut against the grain of conventional wisdom, diversity and unity are deemed to be hallmarks of the Spirit endowed community of faith.

Although American ideology suggests that we are to find unity in our diversity, we find it difficult to truly embrace this message. For one thing, many have embraced an ideology of "rugged individualism." We tend to honor those who "pull themselves up by their bootstraps," so that square-jawed John Wayne represents the vision of the "can-do" American spirit. But is that the vision that Jesus has for his community? Unfortunately, many American Christians have embraced this Americanist vision, and so finding unity in the midst of our diverse gifts has been difficult. Although the entrepreneurial spirit, with its attendant encouragement to take risks, try new things, and blaze new trails, is important to the welfare of the community, there is a danger here in the tendency to go it alone. There is value in this spirit of adventure, but the church isn't simply a gathering of independent individualists. It's a *community* gathered and formed by the grace and love of God. It's a body, a system that is more than the sum of its parts. Although it is very diverse, it is one body of Christ.[32]

---

32 C. Kirk Hadaway, *Behold, I Do a New Thing*, (Cleveland: Pilgrim Press, 2001), 40-42. A counterpart to the rugged individualist is the entrepreneur, who is willing to take risks to build a business or institution, often from nothing. As a typology of church life, such leaders fit into Hadaway's "charismatic leader-follower model that leads not to an

There are challenges to creating communities of faithful service, but the Spirit's gifts help create these communities, so that unity can be experienced in the midst of diversity. As we discover and begin to understand these gifts of the Spirit, we'll start to realize our dependence on each other. This realization leads to the recognition that we have a duty to work for the common good (1 Cor. 12:7) and build up the body of Christ (1 Cor. 14:12). As a body whose members depend on each other, when one suffers, all suffer, when one rejoices, all rejoice (Rom. 12:15; 1 Cor. 12:7, 25-26). Therefore, when a family suffers the death or illness of a loved one or loses a job, the community comes alongside and provides a meal, housekeeping assistance, or just an ear to listen.

This support for one another is the essence of body building, which comes naturally to the Spirit-gifted community. It comes without guilt inducing coercion or expectation of something in return. Such selfless acts come out of a sense of love for the body, a love that is rooted in the grace that is the foundation of the Spirit's gifts. But, for this grace to become evident, our giftedness must be fed and nourished by our relationship with the living God, whom we know in the person of Jesus Christ. Therefore, our ability to hear and respond to this call to use gifts to build the body is fed spiritually as we attend to our prayers, our study, our worship, and our fellowship with one another.

The key to understanding the role the gifts play in the life of the church is to think in terms of the health of the human body. A healthy body is one that has harmony and balance, with every part working together as one. As with the human body, this bal-

---

"incarnational community of faith" but an institution dependent on the leadership of the entrepreneurial founder/leader who has effective control of the congregation. There is additional danger in this model; as such charismatic leaders often lack accountability, which portends greater possibility of moral failure, financial malfeasance, or destructive behavior, all of which have been witnessed in recent years. There is also the problem of what happens to the church once the charismatic leader is no longer able to effectively lead the church.

ance within the body of Christ lasts only temporarily. It must be continually attended to or it falls out of harmony.[33] Therefore, even as we must continually attend to proper diet and exercise to keep our own bodies in proper working order, the same is true of the body of Christ. Spiritually healthy churches are ones that emphasize worship, prayer, study, teaching opportunities, and fellowship. These are the foods and vitamins that nourish the body.

Proper diet, however, is not enough. Our bodies also need exercise or our muscles will atrophy. By using our gifts to teach, to build houses for the homeless, to call on the home bound, to lead grief support groups, or to lead worship, we build and strengthen the body of Christ. When we use our gifts we help create an environment where God's message of reconciliation can take root and lives will be changed.

Gifted and Trained for Ministry

If you are a Christian, you are a minister. Your ordination comes with your baptism. One characteristic of spiritual gifts is that they provide the skills needed to engage in ministry, whatever form that ministry takes. There are, it seems, people who are gifted and called to train others to use their gifts for ministry in the church and in the world. It is one of the functions that the ordained ministry takes on. In Ephesians 4, we read that God gives "pastors and teachers, to equip the saints for the work of ministry" (Eph. 4:12-13). The image of the player-coach is instructive in understanding the relationship of pastors to the rest of the community of faith. As a player-coach, the pastor-teacher provides leadership and instruction while sharing, with the team, in the game itself.

---

33 Peter L. Steinke, *Healthy Congregations: A System's Approach,* (New York: Alban Institute, 1996 16.

Gifts and Servanthood

Both Jesus and Paul envision the body of Christ in a non-hierarchical way. In this realm of God, no one lords it over the other. Therefore, all ministries are an expression of servanthood. It is the testimony of Mark that Jesus "came not to be served, but to serve" (Mk. 10:45). Henri Nouwen suggests that, like Jesus, those called to ministry "stand in this world with nothing to offer but his or her own vulnerable self." In this way Jesus himself revealed to humanity the nature of God's love.

The great message that we have to carry, as ministers of God's word and followers of Jesus, is that God loves us not because of what we do or accomplish, but because God has created and redeemed us in love and has chosen us to proclaim that love as the true source of all human life.[34]

In that context we can understand the call to be good stewards of God's gifts to us. They aren't possessions; they're divinely given resources for servant ministry. So, whether we speak, lead, or serve in helping or caring ministries, we do so in the power and grace of the Spirit of God, so that "God may be glorified in all things through Jesus Christ" (1 Pet. 4:10-11).

GIFTS: MANIFESTATIONS OF PRESENCE AND POWER

Spiritual gifts are an expression of God's love for the world. They are the tools with which a Spirit-empowered people of God build up missional communities of faith so that they can be the means by which God reconciles the creation to God's self.

Gifts and Talents: What is their relationship?

In envisioning what a spiritual gift might be, we need to explore the relationship between what we normally call a natural talent and what we would call a spiritual gift. Are the same or are

---

[34] Henri Nouwen, *In the Name of Jesus: Reflections on Christian Leadership*, (New York: Crossroad Publishing, Co., 1989), 17.

they different realities? A quick glance at the Pauline lists suggest that it's probably best not to offer an either/or answer to the question.

In my mind, it's probably best not to make a sharp distinction between gifts and talents, in part because a sharp distinction leads to separating abilities and passions into sacred and secular categories. It's best not to limit how and where the Spirit can work in the world. In the mystery of creation, we can recognize that what we call talents are in reality divine gifts of grace. We can use them for our own purposes or, in gratitude to the creator, use them in the work of God's kingdom. A gift's usefulness to the community of faith is rooted in our appreciation of the one who is the true source of all talents and abilities, the Creator.

The biblical discussions of creation witness to the mystery of human life. There is a strong sense that humanity is created to be in relationship with God. Consider the implications of the Psalmist's affirmation of God's attention to the details of our formation as individuals.

For it was you who formed my inward parts;
You knit me together in my mother's womb.
I praise you, for I am fearfully and wonderfully made
(Ps. 139:13-14).

We don't have to take this passage in a deterministic or literalist manner to appreciate its message that because we're part of God's creation we're also "fearfully and wonderfully made." Every human being bears the image of God, and therefore they have tremendous value to God. No matter our backgrounds, skills, IQ, social class, we all have something to offer to the world. Who we are and what we do makes a difference. No one else can do what I do like I do it, and no one can do what you do quite like you do it. It's not just a matter of talent; it's also a matter of personality and temperament. Who we are is somewhat of a mystery, but the call to use our talents and abilities to create a community of faith that will witness to the love of our God, that is not a mystery.

Manifestations of God's Power

When we think of demonstrations of God's power some of the most powerful examples include the stories of Moses at the Red Sea, Elijah on Mt. Carmel, Jesus on the Mount of Transfiguration, and Paul on the Damascus Road. These experiences of God's presence seem so dramatic and powerful that we may wonder why we don't have the same experiences. We may wonder what's wrong with us. Still, there seem to be are no normative experiences of God's presence. Each of us can experience God's presence in a way that is empowering to our lives. It may not be "dramatic," but it will be powerful.

Whether the Spirit comes upon us in the form of a still small voice, a shudder of joy, a sense of warmth or peace, or something much more dramatic, whatever the form, these are manifestations of divine power. Whatever our experiences, we're all encouraged to examine them with deep spiritual discernment. As we begin to recognize that we have gifts from God that empower us to serve with joy and gratitude, we will then taste of the current of the Spirit's power coursing through our lives.

You might say that the Christian life isn't for the timid. To borrow from the title of a book by my friend Bruce Epperly, it's a "holy adventure."[35] The Spirit is the source of great energy that can electrify our lives. One of the things I appreciate about Pentecostal spirituality is that at its best it exhibits a sense of exuberance and freedom of expression that would benefit every church. Decency and order may be needed for a properly functioning church, why else would Paul provide such direct instruction to the Corinthian church – but the Spirit is not a force that we can contain with our rules and regulations. The God we worship and serve is a dynamic presence. Perhaps this is why so many religious movements have sought to return to the days of the book of Acts. Back then it

---

35 Bruce G. Epperly, *Holy Adventure: 41 Days of Audacious Living*, (Nashville: Upper Room Books, 2008).

seemed as if you could truly see and feel the Spirit's presence, why can't we reclaim that experience of divine presence?

Perhaps, if we embrace these gifts of the Spirit and set the Spirit free to work in our midst, we will see something spectacular happen in our midst. It doesn't have to be a spectacle, but shouldn't we expect something dynamic and powerful to happen in our midst when the Spirit is at work?

Spiritual Benefit of the Individual

God gives gifts to the church for the common good, which means that they are at their essence – others-centered. That said, can we not expect to experience blessings as a result of these gifts present in our lives? For one thing, the gifts build community, and we're part of the community. The gifts are intended to bring us into spiritual maturity – another benefit (Eph. 4:12).

While Paul discourages us from seeking spiritual benefits in isolation from the whole community (1 Cor. 12:14-26), our ability to hear God's voice as well as that of our neighbor requires that we attend to our own spiritual health. Spiritual dryness is a malady that can afflict every person, no matter how committed to God's calling. If we continually give of ourselves, without paying attention to the voice within that cries out for nourishment, we'll eventually self destruct. Let's remember that the call to love our neighbor rests in the recognition that we will love ourselves.

The table of the Lord, the Eucharist service, offers a good example of the interchange between the personal and the corporate experience of Christ's presence in the community. We come to the table as individuals, laying our lives before the Lord in an offering of praise, and we find unity in the one loaf and one cup (1 Cor. 10:16-17).

As we make use of spiritual gifts we find that our hearts are turned to the other. In seeking to encourage the other, we find wholeness for ourselves. How many times have we come back from serving a meal at a homeless shelter, or visiting with a homebound member of the church and not found ourselves blessed? Therefore, by focusing on the common good, we don't forget the needs of the individual. Participation in the community provides the opportunity to grow into spiritual maturity. In the end, maturity is expressed through our oneness with the head of the church, Jesus Christ (Eph. 4:14-16).

Recognizing our Interdependence

In making use of our spiritual gifts, we put our focus on the needs of others and at the same time discover our own dependence on the other as a source of God's love and grace. Spiritual maturity that comes as a result of this realization sets us free from the grasp of self-centeredness, greed, and envy (1 Cor. 13). It also helps us understand that ultimately we need each other.

The sense of community commitment that results from our exercise of spiritual gifts helps alleviate the problem of burnout and spiritual dryness. When we feel, as many of us have on occasion, the full load of responsibility, we become cut off from the springs of living water, the presence of the Spirit, and we begin to experience a sense of spiritual abandonment (Jn. 7:37-39). By discovering our gifts and then focusing our ministry in those areas of giftedness we can resist the tendency to do everything. We can recognize that there are others in the community who are able and may be willing to pick up jobs we're not especially gifted for. All of this relieves the unnecessary stress we put on our lives and the lives of our family as well.[36]

---

[36] As a pastor, in spite of my commitment to a ministry rooted in spiritual gifts, I have found myself pressuring parishioners into taking on jobs they felt neither called to nor were gifted to take on. I have also found myself taking on responsibilities that are better suited for someone else. The exigencies of "parish realities" can undo some of what we intend to accomplish by releasing the Spirit to work in our midst. There will be times when we will need to undertake tasks that lie outside our giftedness, but recognition of this reality can help limit those necessities.

I have long appreciated an analogy made by Thomas Hawkins, who points to the story of David and Goliath as a good example of what happens when we try to take on a job using someone else's gifts. In that story Saul offers the young hero his own armor. David tries on the armor but realizes that the armor doesn't fit. Instead of dragging that massive suit of armor onto the field, David goes into battle armed only with a sling (1 Sam. 17:38-40). Hawkins writes:

> We sometimes fail to perceive what David instinctively knew. We long for someone else's armor and achievements. We greedily seek that person's talents, believing we can defeat our giants if we are using someone else's gifts. Yet, it never works. We cannot put on someone else's gifts. We can effectively use only our own gifts.[37]

Although spiritual gifts have an outward directive, we will find immense benefit and blessing as we let go of the need to everything and instead choose to contribute our giftedness to the community of faith.

FINDING THE LINK BETWEEN GIFTS AND MINISTRY

I met a woman in a nursing home while visiting a member of my congregation. This woman wheeled herself into the room and asked me: "Are you a minister?" Although a bit startled by her question, I answered – Well, yes, I am." Both of us understood what she meant – she was asking about my professional religious credentials. Even though I didn't have clerical clothing on, she seemed to recognize that I was a religious professional. Now, there is an interesting twist to the story, as this woman had once been a part of the very congregation I now served as pastor, and so on that day I became her pastor.

The term minister often has this professional connotation, but it's not the only definition of minister. It's important to remember that everyone who is gifted by and with the Spirit is a minister,

---

37 Thomas Hawkins, *Claiming God's Promises: A Guide to Discovering Your Spiritual Gifts,* (Nashville: Abingdon Press, 1992), 28-29.

ordination notwithstanding. This book is rooted in an assumption that each Christian is gifted for ministry by the Spirit and ordained to that ministry in baptism. Therefore, no matter your professional status, if you are a Christian, you are a minister.

In recognizing that every person of God is called to ministry, we can narrow the gap between clergy and laity. Yes, clergy do ministry but they're not the only ministers. It's inappropriate to assume that the work of the laity is any less a form of ministry. I don't wish to negate the place of the clergy. Pastors serve a very important function in the life of the church, but what they do in church and community isn't the totality of the church's ministry.

Another way of asking this question would be: What aspects of church life should be considered off limits to lay people?[38] We could answer – none of them. Remember that Jesus didn't have any credentials – he simply heard his call and responded. So, whether we teach Sunday school, visit the homebound, lead grief groups, serve meals to the homeless, march for civil rights, evangelize our neighborhoods, preach, what we are doing is ministry.

Whatever form ministry takes, it is by definition an act of service. The Greek word for ministry (*diakonos*) can be translated in a variety of ways, but its most important nuance is that of servant. Jesus offers us a very pertinent model of servant leadership when he bowed down before his disciples and washed their feet (Jn. 13).

There's a second defining image of ministry, that of priest. Traditionally a priest is a religious professional who acts as an intermediary between humanity and God. The message of the gospel is that in Christ we no longer need human intermediaries. Jesus, who is now our high priest, serves as our mediator and point of access to the throne of God. However, even as Jesus is our high priest, each of us has been made a priest of God who is called to intercede not

---

[38] It is appropriate that I confess to be a member of a faith community that does not limit the celebration of the sacraments to the clergy. In the Disciples tradition both clergy and lay elders celebrate the Lord's Supper. See Keith Watkins, ed., *Thankful Praise: A Resource for Christian Worship*, (St. Louis: CBP Press, 1987), 15-16.

only for ourselves and for our neighbors as well (Heb. 10). Because we're part of the royal priesthood, a form of priesthood eloquently defined in 1 Peter 2:5-9, clergy aren't of necessity priestly intermediaries. Each of us has been empowered to join in the priestly service of intercession. Therefore, as one of the founders of my own tradition once wrote, "whatever constitutes *the worship of* God is the common privilege of all the disciples *as such.*"[39] As disciples of Jesus, baptized by the Spirit, we are servants and priests for all people, and thereby we are freed to join in the full ministry of God.

There is one caveat that I should add. To say that all are servant ministers and priests does not mean that we all have the same roles and callings. There is the need for freedom because freedom is the catalyst for change and new opportunities to serve. There is also a place for order – chaos and anarchy are not necessarily helpful to the cause of Christ. The gift lists themselves suggest that some are called to ministries of leadership. The ship needs a pilot if it is to navigate difficult waters. As we discover our gifts and join in the community of faith in service, it will become evident that some among us have specific gifts and callings for leadership roles. There is a place for the religious professional as well, as long as both clergy and laity understand that such a calling does not relieve the laity of their ministerial callings.

In discovering our gifts there is the additional need to discern where and when to use these gifts in ministry. The community will, if it is listening to the Spirit, help us discern the answer. In the process of discerning our gifts and calling, we may feel free to try out new ministry roles, even roles that might seem to lie beyond what we consider our gifts. When I became pastor, one area of ministry that I didn't feel comfortable with was that of the pastoral care of

---

39 Royal Humbert, ed., *Compend of Alexander Campbell's Theology,* (St. Louis: Bethany Press, 1961), 175. On the question of priesthood in the church, one would be wise to consult the discussion in *Builders of Community: Rethinking Ecclesiastical Ministry,* by José Ignacio González Faus. Translated by Maria Isabel Reyna and Revised by Liam Kelly, (Miama: Convivium Press, 2012), 25-40.

the sick and dying, and yet in time I discovered that I had a knack for it. So, don't be afraid to try new things. In time you will know if you ought to try something else instead. Whatever we do as the people of God is really an expression of the reign of God; as we join in ministry we are expanding the realm of God in this world, claiming spiritual territory for redemption.[40]

THOUGHT QUESTIONS

1. Taking into consideration etymologies, what does it mean to be a charismatic? How does this definition relate to one's self-understanding?

2. In what ways is it possible for you to understand God to be present in your life and what does this mean to the way you live your life?

3. Looking at the gift lists, do you see any gifts there that might describe your life? Are there other gifts/abilities not present there that might better define your life?

4. Considering this discussion of gifts and the presence of the Spirit in one's life, how might this help define a sense of your own ministry?

5. If we see these gifts as the foundation of Christian ministry, how does the ministry of the laity fit with ordained ministry?

---

40 Moltmann, *Church in the Power of the Spirit*, 302-4.

3

Discovering Our Spiritual Potentialities

> I began to see that the Holy Spirit never intended that people who had gifts and abilities should bury them in the earth, but rather, he commanded and stirred up such people to the exercise of their gift and sent out to work those who were able and ready. And so, although I was the most unworthy of all the saints, I set upon this work.[41]
>
> John Bunyan

If God is the giver of every good and perfect gift, then it would be unwise to keep the gifts of God hidden. Having been gifted and called to ministries as diverse as the persons who have received these gifts, it's incumbent upon us to discern the nature and purpose of these gifts. The place to start, as a community of faith, is to affirm in our own contexts the word that described the experience of the Corinthian church. That word, according to Paul, declared that the community had been enriched in every way through gifts of "speech and knowledge of every kind." They didn't lack any "spiritual gift as [they waited] for the revealing of our Lord Jesus Christ" (1 Cor. 1:4-7). If the church grasps this message, then the next

---

[41] John Bunyan, excerpted in *Devotional Classics: Selected Readings for Individuals and Groups,* Richard J. Foster and James Bryan Smith, eds., (San Francisco: HarperSanFrancisco, 1993), 243.

step is for God's people to discern and discover the nature and use of their own gifts, so that they might join together as one body in missional service to God and God's creation.

Embracing our spiritual potentialities, our giftedness, is to affirm that we are created in God's likeness, with a mandate to love and serve God. The implications for churches, especially Mainline Protestant churches, of the promise that the people of God can discover spiritual gifts that will enable and empower them to engage in the transformative work that accompanies the coming of God's reign is incredibly significant.

The reticence that some feel about this understanding of ministry in the church is that it runs counter to the long held belief that ministry is something that ordained clergy do, while the laity benefits from this ministry. This understanding of ministry creates a built in sense of dependency on clergy. The point here isn't to offer a critique of structure, for structure has its place. The question is – have we created a sense of dependency that undermines our ability to live into the mission of God?

The potential benefits derived from embracing the idea that the whole people of God are gifted for ministry are too great to ignore. In discovering their gifts, the people of God will first of all begin to grow spiritually as they throw off the shackles of dependency. From there the people, having understood that the Spirit is alive within them, can join together as a community and begin to share in ministry that brings hope and healing to a fragmented and broken world.

I once heard Jim Wallis speak to an audience in Santa Barbara and I remember him stating clearly that "religion is personal, but not private."[42] Wallis was speaking about the political implications of faith – of religion's place in the public square – but his statement covers all of Christian life. My faith in God and my decision to follow Jesus is incredibly personal, but it also has significant public implications.

---

42 Jim Wallis, Walter Capps Center, Santa Barbara, CA, (March 27, 2004).

Gifted people engage the world where they find it, and ministry in churches where people embrace their gifts will touch not only the people within the church, they will touch the world outside. The faith of the gifted will touch political, social, and environmental, issues. There is no area of life that the church's ministry does not touch, for gifted by the Spirit we are one body, with one purpose, to share the love of God with all people.[43]

What are the possibilities for ministry and mission? What ministries might God be calling us to take up? Jürgen Moltmann speaks to the wondrous possibilities that lie before us as people of faith.

> The person who believes becomes a person full of possibilities. People like this do not restrict themselves to the social roles laid down for them, and do not allow themselves to be tied to these roles. They believe they are capable of more. And they do not tie other people down to their own preconceived ideas. They do not imprison others in what they are at present. They see them together with their future, and keep their potentialities open for them.[44]

As we trust God, ourselves, and our neighbors, our "charismatic potentialities are awakened" and we begin to join in a ministry that makes a difference.[45]

The theology of giftedness begins with the premise that all the gifts necessary for the people of God to serve in ministry are present in the community. In our journeys of faith, if we open ourselves to the possibilities of service, we uncover these gifts. This is what Moltmann means when he speaks of "awaken[ing] our charismatic potentialities." This journey or pathway is one that takes time, prayer, and trust. It is likely that the path of discovery, of awakening

---

43 In this regard I have become convinced of the value of joining forces through community organizing to advocate for justice in the community through organizations such as PICO National Network.
44 Jürgen Moltmann, *The Spirit of Life: A Universal Affirmation*, Margaret Kohl, trans., (Minneapolis: Fortress Press, 1992), 187.
45 Moltmann, *Spirit of Life*, 187.

our potentialities, is a life-long one. When visiting a natural wonder such as Crater Lake, Yosemite, or the Grand Canyon, you're likely to notice something new and awe-inspiring each time you visit. What you discover today about your giftedness may be far different from what you discovered a decade ago. It will also be different from what you will discover ten years hence. The possibilities for service are as open as we are open to God's leading.

A Pathway of Discovery

So, how do we discern our spiritual potential? What steps must we take?

We can start by simply opening up our lives to the movement of God's Spirit. By letting the Spirit set us free from our fears and our spiritual inhibitions we become open to something new happening in our lives. We become expectant and receptive. With this sense of openness we are ready to explore and try out new possibilities in ministry. The pathway of discovery requires that we have a spirit of adventure. Consider the story of Lewis and Clark. They knew what they were looking for – a pathway from the eastern half of the United States west to the Pacific Ocean. In the course of their cross-country adventure they found a way to the sea, even though it wasn't the one they had envisioned. It was neither as direct nor as easy as they had hoped, but the journey changed them and it changed the world as they knew it. The same is true for those willing to undertake the adventure that leads to gifts discovery. It will change your view of your own self and your view of the world.

Discovering one's spiritual gifts isn't an exact science. There is no one precise way of uncovering one's gifts. There are many different methods of assessing one's gift potential, and over the years I've tried most of these assessment tools. Many of them are helpful, but none of them are fool proof. Their usefulness is often determined by the philosophies and theologies that undergird them. I've developed one of my own that can be downloaded from the publisher's website that's based on the principles found in other assessments, but is keyed more closely to the definitions provided in this book. It should prove useful in the course of exploring one's spiritual potential and life purpose. Scripture itself doesn't provide a "way of discovery," but, there are intuitive ways of discerning our gifts that involve paying attention to life-experiences, feelings, and one's passions. By making use of assessment tools, guided questions and meditation we can discern directions, strengths, and limitations.

As we begin this process of discovery we must also remember that God often calls us to minister outside the boundaries of our giftedness. Gift discovery does not limit our arenas of service, but it does help us set priorities for how and where we serve. Although there is no one path that will lead to discovery of the gifts, the following steps can help set the tone for discovering our gifts.

Living a Life of Discipleship

If one is a Christian, then by definition one is a disciple of Jesus Christ. Disciples are followers and students of a master teacher, and in the gospels the disciples of Jesus are pictured leaving behind everything to follow a new master. They leave fishing boats, tax booths, families, political causes, and take up a new path, one that leads to a new way of living. Dietrich Bonhoeffer has famously defined the life of discipleship as a costly path. It is rooted in grace, but it is a costly grace.

> It is costly, because it calls to discipleship, it is grace because it calls us to follow *Jesus Christ*. It is costly because it costs people their lives, it is grace, because it thereby makes them live.... Above all, it is grace is costly, because it was costly to God, because it cost God the life of God's Son – "you were bought with a price" – and because nothing can be cheap to us which is costly to God.... Costly grace is the incarnation of God.[46]

---

46 Dietrich Bonhoeffer, *Discipleship*, Dietrich Bonhoeffer Works, Volume 4, Geoffrey B. Kelley and John Godsey, eds., Barbara Green and Reinhard Krauss, trans., (Minneapolis: Fortress Press, 2001), 45.

Walking by the Spirit (Gal. 5:16-18) calls forth a life of discipleship, a relationship that is honed as we live out our callings to serve God. Discipleship is a life lived in commitment and relationship to Jesus Christ. This Jesus we know and experience as he is incarnated in the church, his body present for us. As we abide in the Spirit, we make it possible for God to reveal to us a way of serving in our worship, our study, our fellowship.

A life-changing relationship with God requires us to be receptive to the movement of God's Spirit in our lives. This means finding ways of spending time in the presence of God, and that will differ from person to person. The practices and disciplines that open our hearts to God can include corporate acts such as worship and more personal acts including prayer, fasting, journaling, meditation, writing, and even serving others. Some of us are more contemplative than others, while some are more active. It's important that we not impose one method or ideal upon the body of Christ.

What we need to find are what some call "thin places;" those places where the membrane separating the human and the divine become nearly transparent. We may, as Paul says, see the things of God as if through a mirror. What we can see and experience is only partially revealed, but we do have a sense that God is present and we can build upon that sense of God's presence (1 Corinthians 13:12). That is, we can open our lives and hearts to the work of God. This opening of the heart, according to Marcus Borg, is "the purpose of spirituality, of both our collective and individual practices through which we become open to and nourished by the Mystery in whom we live and move and have our being."[47]

---

[47] Marcus J. Borg, *The Heart of Christianity*, (San Francisco: Harper SanFrancisco, 2003), 161. On the nature of spiritual disciplines or spiritual practices see Richard Foster, *Celebration of Discipline*, (San Francisco: Harper SanFrancisco, 1978); Dorothy C. Bass, ed., *Practicing Our Faith: A Way of Life for a Searching People*, (San Francisco: Jossey-Bass, 2010); and Dwight J. Zscheile, ed., *Cultivating Sent Communities: Missional*

Unfettered Spirit 59

In our search for intimacy with God, we seek out those "thin places" where God might open our hearts not only to the presence of God, but also to the presence of our neighbors in our world. In the course of our walk with God we should become more compassionate beings. "The Christian life," says Borg, "is about a new heart, an open heart, a heart of flesh, a heart of compassion. The Christian life is about the Spirit of God opening our hearts in thin places."[48]

Commitment to a Life of Ministry

A heart open to God is compassionate and committed to the welfare of the neighbor; it is a heart committed to justice and peace in the world. Such a heart leads to commitment to ministry. Isaiah heard the call: "Whom shall I end, and who will go for us?" He replied: "Here am I, send me!" (Is. 6:8). In John's story of Jesus' resurrection appearances, Jesus tests Peter's commitment to him, asking three times: "Peter, do you love me?" Each time Peter replies, "Yes Lord, I love you." To which Jesus answers, then "feed my sheep" (Jn. 21:15-17). Our relationship with Jesus makes it possible for us to love as Jesus loved.[49]

Feeding the sheep, taking care of those who need God's love, showing compassion and mercy, these are acts of love. They are points of grace. They are acts of ministry. Discovery of gifts is related to our commitment to the life of ministry. Such service could include a form of full time vocational ministry,[50] but it's not limited to such forms of ministry. Answering the call to ministry requires from us commitment of our lives – our time, our resourc-

---

Spiritual Formation, (Grand Rapids: Wm. B. Eerdmans Publishing, Co. 2012).
48   Borg, *Heart of Christianity*, p. 162-63. See also Jan Linn, *The Jesus Connection,* (St. Louis: Chalice Press, 1997), 19-21.
49   Linn, *The Jesus Connection*, 15.
50   The issue of ordination will be discussed in a separate chapter.

es, our abilities, and our attention – to the task of expanding the boundaries of God's realm.

Exploring the Varied Nature of Spiritual Gifts

Our availability for use in ministry requires knowledge of what we are equipped to do. If we don't know of the Spirit's gifts, then we face limitations. As we explore the various gifts listed and sometimes described in Scripture, we may catch a glimpse of the areas of ministry we may be called to.

Study of scripture, especially texts such as 1 Corinthians 12-14, Romans 12, and Ephesians 4, offers a starting point for our explorations. With this study of scripture, reading broadly in the literature on spiritual gifts, ministry, and spiritual life, looking at these from different theological perspectives, will provide further insight. Participation in seminars, classes, and Bible studies that deal with gifts also can aid in exploration. The more exposure we have to different interpretations and definitions the better we can understand what it means to be gifted for service to God and neighbor. We'll also begin to notice parallels in our own lives to the gifts and ministries described in these resources.

This step of exploration requires discernment because writers and speakers on spiritual gifts are not all of one mind. Some proponents take a very mechanical view of giftedness– you are what you are gifted to be, or that the gifts are limited by one's theology – while others take a more organic view – gifts flow in and out of our lives as the Spirit continually moves in our lives, empowering us for service. The latter view doesn't limit God to a boxed set of gifts, but is open to whatever God might bring into our lives. It is the premise of this book that we should be open to whatever gifts God might bring into our midst that enable us to be harbingers of God's transforming love.

Consider Your Churchly Activities

One of the most frustrating aspects of most treatments of spiritual gifts – especially when it comes to the use of gift inventories – is that they assume significant experience in the church. For the person who is new to the faith or the church, there is insufficient ministry experience to build upon. Until you spend time in ministry in a congregational context, it's difficult to know where your gifts might lie. Despite these difficulties, it's possible for even the most inexperienced person to begin the journey of exploration.

If you're new to church life, take time to explore and experiment. Look at your daily life, your relationships and jobs. Do you see any parallels between these activities and the gifts you read about in scripture? For the more experienced person of faith, the path of discovery involves not only reflection on your life experiences, but also your experiences in congregational life.

To begin this reflection it may be helpful to consider the roles and offices you have held. Why not make a list of these offices and roles? As you reflect on these roles and offices, ask yourself: Did I enjoy this role? Did I experience a sense of fulfillment? As important it is to know what you enjoy doing, it's also important to know what you don't enjoy doing. In both cases, further reflection requires that we ask why we have these feelings. Once we have considered our roles and responsibilities, it is helpful to begin looking at the possible gifts that would be helpful in carrying out these tasks.

Experiment with the Spiritual Gifts

If we're going to uncover our spiritual gifts, we'll have to get involved in ministry. If we think we might have a gift, it would be helpful to use it in a meaningful way. This is especially important for someone who is new to church-life. But, if we begin to experiment, in time we'll begin to discern patterns of effectiveness and discover areas of ministry that don't seem to work for us. Beginning this process simply requires the willingness to volunteer to serve. If you think you might have gifts to teach, then why not volunteer to teach when the opportunity arises? Or, if you find yourself drawn to ministries of compassion, then perhaps you could visit homebound members. Our experiences in these ministries will help us reflect on our areas of giftedness. It is important that in experimenting with gifts that we give ourselves adequate time to fully experience the activity – unless it is obvious from the start that further experimentation would be fruitless. You may be a gifted teacher, but it will take more than one or two times to truly discern whether this is a gift. Rare it is that someone is a smashing success the first time out!

Examine Your Experiences in Ministry

Having done some experimenting, we're ready to do some reflecting. This is an intuitive process that requires honest assessment of our experiences of life in community. We'll also want to listen to members of the community, for as the Proverb puts it – in a multitude of counselors, there's great success (Prov. 11:14). In our reflections we may ask, prayerfully, the question of enjoyment, success, and passion. We can also make use of a variety of tools such as gifts inventories (one is provided in the appendix of this book). I should add a caveat here – although we need to attend to the voices of our community, we also need to pay attention to our own sense of calling and giftedness. Too often members of a congregation – usually benignly – try to be too helpful in the process, suggesting to people gifts that they themselves think are important and thus place this burden on the other person.

Enjoyment

The story of Jonah is a counterpoint to the theology of gifted ministry. In our reading of this story, we may conclude that God is in the business of calling people to undertake ministries they'd rather avoid. Haven't you felt, sometimes, that God is always calling you to take on jobs you'd just as soon avoid or to jobs you lack any interest in? It's easy to develop a martyr's complex, but while a call to ministry can and often does push us beyond our comfort zones, can we not at least consider where we find joy in this action? Joy, of course, isn't the same as having fun. Therefore, our joy won't make every job easy or without cost. The joy comes from the sense of accomplishment and knowing that the reign of God has been extended.

It's common sense that we would enjoy the things we're good at; therefore, it would also make sense that if God has gifted us in some way, then we should find joy in living out that gift. Enjoyment by itself, however, isn't a sufficient guide to giftedness. I enjoyed playing baseball and basketball, but I can't say that I was a gifted athlete. No matter how hard I tried, I never could overcome my own physical limitations. With regard to spiritual gifts, a person will generally have a sense of accomplishment and positive feelings about their ministry. In exploring your giftedness it would be helpful to make a list of those things you especially enjoy and then begin to ask whether those activities might have ministry potential. Could these gifts allow me to be of use by God to touch the lives of others with God's love?

Passion

What is your passion? I've been asked that question many times. The Latin word *passio* can be construed as suffering – thus we speak of the "passion of Christ." It also means, being moved by something. It's interesting that in classical theism, which is built upon Greek philosophy, especially Stoicism, to be moved or to suffer was considered a sign of imperfection. Therefore, if God is perfect, then God can neither suffer nor be moved. God was defined as having the quality of *impassibility*, which means that God is to be envisioned as being passionless. Of course if God is without passion, then God is also without compassion, which means that our affirmation that God is Love is meaningless.

The question standing before us is this: What are you passionate about? I can say that I'm passionate about making the world a better place to live in and helping people find their places of service in the church. I'm passionate about building bridges between people who share different religious traditions. I'm passionate about helping others understand their own faith commitments. So, what are your passions?

Passion stands at the heart of our calling to serve. As you examine your life, what do you feel passionate about? Does the situation of the homeless in our community move you deeply? What about the education of children? The care of the sick? Comforting the grieving? Perhaps you feel the need to speak out against the ills of society. We see in Martin Luther King, Jr. a passion for justice and in Mother Theresa a passion for those living on the margins. Jesus had passion for those left out by the religious and political elites. In exploring your own giftedness, it would be useful to make a list of the causes and the issues, the people and the needs, that move you deeply.

1.   4.

2.   5.

3.   6.

As you consider this list, ask the question: Which of the Spirit's gifts will allow me to pursue this passion?

Effectiveness

By definition "to be gifted," means you're good at something. A gifted child is a child who excels in their studies. Therefore, it's not enough that a teacher is diligent and excited about teaching. A gifted teacher should be able to effectively communicate with their students. Leaders should lead effectively, while people endowed with compassion (we are all called to be compassionate, but some are gifted for specific ministries of compassion) for the hurting

Unfettered Spirit

should be able to comfort the people they touch. You may not be effective every time you minister, but it should be the normal pattern. Ask yourself as you serve: Do I see God at work in this ministry? If not, then maybe you should move on to another ministry.

Giftedness does not mean that you forgo practice, training, and learning. To use a sports analogy, LeBron James; Michael Phelps; Venus Williams may be natural and gifted athletes, in fact they have been among the most gifted in their respective fields, but they still devote hours to training and practice. The same is true of musicians – Miles Davis didn't just pick up his horn during a performance and start playing powerful music, he worked hard to perfect his gift. Giftedness is only the starting point; each of us must then take what we're given and hone those skills. The gifted preacher still must spend time studying scripture, reading journals and books, and practicing their sermons. You might, on occasion speak powerfully without preparation, but that's only because you've been training for that moment. A gift is like a rough diamond, it must be cut and polished before it's ready for display.

Resources for Reflection on One's Experiences: The Use of Gift Inventories

One of the most popular tools for discovering spiritual gifts is the gift inventory. There are many inventories on the market, some of which you can access on-line. As assessment tools they help people reflect on their experiences in church and in life. Most of them ask questions about enjoyment, effectiveness, and passion. They will help one sort through one's ministry opportunities and feelings about them.

Gift inventories can be important tools in helping give a sense of giftedness, but you should use them cautiously and with discretion. As helpful as they can be, they're not foolproof. Instead of determining your gifts, they help you narrow the possibilities. As you make use of different inventories – it's helpful to make use of several of these tools – you'll discover that each inventory is defined by the theology, concerns, and interests of the creator of the inventory (which is why the one I developed is geared to more moderate/progressive Christians). The nature of the questions used should be a clue as to where the writer is coming from. Therefore, you may get different results depending on which inventory you use. You'll want to factor these theologies into your reflections.[51]

COMMUNITY AFFIRMATIONS

Spiritual giftedness is a community issue. The gifts of the Spirit empower and guide us as we make ourselves available to the reign of God. Gifts are expressions of the body of Christ; therefore there should be a symbiotic relationship between gifted persons as we engage effectively in our various ministries. That is, the community helps give a context for ministry. A teacher cannot teach without students; one cannot care for the hurting if one is not in relationship with those who are hurting. Therefore, it shouldn't be surprising that the community would play a role in helping us discern our areas of giftedness

The community's role can be seen as it encourages and guides individuals in using their gifts to express God's gracious love to the world. It also confirms our effectiveness in ministry. It's helpful to be told that a sermon or a class has effectively touched a person's life. Financial givers need to know that their gifts are valued. Givers

---

51   One of the most popular inventories is the Wagner-Modified Houts Inventory, which is often sold separately, but can be found in the revised edition of Peter Wagner's book, *Spiritual Gifts Can Help Your Church Grow*. This inventory reflects Wagner's "church growth theology" but it includes gifts such as tongues and healing. Other inventories, including the Trenton and the Wesleyan inventories, do not include so-called "sign gifts" but they add gifts such as craftsmanship. The Willow Creek Church publishes the *Networking* materials, which include inventories that are geared to their evangelical theology. Patricia Brown's workbook, *Spirit Gifts,* (Nashville: Abingdon Press, 1996), written from a mainline Methodist perspective, also has an inventory.

of compassion need to know that their efforts brought healing of the soul.

We need to hear from those who can help us monitor our feelings, because we may think that we have a calling or may believe that we are being effective, when in reality we are not being effective in our work. The discerning community lets people know when this is true and when it's not. If the majority of the members of the community don't feel that you have a specific gift, then perhaps you should reevaluate your ministry. This work of the community is difficult, requiring great sensitivity and compassion. It requires people who are gifted with discernment, because there is great danger of stifling the Spirit or a budding ministry if the community acts too soon. On the other hand if the community waits too long it could lead to great disappointment and even disruption of the community. It is the community's responsibility, however, to hold the members of the body accountable for their gifts.

A theology of giftedness doesn't limit our areas of ministry, but it should guide our focus in ministry. For example, we've all been called to share the story of what it means to be a follower of Jesus and child of God, but not everyone will channel their energy into evangelistic ministries. We've all been called to compassionate ministry, but not everyone's focus will be directed to ministries that feed the hungry or call on the home bound.

Personality Type and Spiritual Gifts

Gregory of Nyssa, a fourth century church leader and theologian, calls to our attention the blessings of being created in the image of God.

> Know to what extent the creator has honoured you above all the rest of creation. The sky is not an image of God, nor is the moon, nor the sun, nor the beauty of the stars, nor anything of what can be seen in creation. You alone have been made the image of the reality that transcends all understand-

ing, the likeness of imperishable beauty, the imprint of true divinity, the recipient of beatitude, the seal of the true light.[52]

As Christians we look to Jesus as the one who most fully expressed God's image in human form. Yet, the creation story teaches that each human being, male and female, has been created in God's beneficent image (Gen. 1:26-27). We bear this image not only in our giftedness for service but in our very being, our personhood. Who we are as individuals provides the context for sharing in service to God. Personality makes the difference. Two people can have the very same gifts and yet their ministries will be as different as night and day.

Are you extroverted? Or, introverted? Intuitive or sense oriented? The body of Christ reflects this variety of personality. Therefore, it's important to pay attention to the role personality, our personality, plays in the way we use our gifts and do ministry. Extroverts and introverts will probably do ministry very differently. One way is not better than the other, just different. The extrovert might enjoy the big stage, while the introvert the small group or even the one on one relationship.

There are several theories of personality types. These theories and the tools they engender, can be very useful in helping us understand ourselves and our place in the world and in the church, especially when taken together with this attempt to discern our spiritual gifts. Self-awareness will help each of us discern where and how we should make use of our gifts, whether in smaller settings or larger. They will help us understand how we work with people.

Carl Jung is the originator of the idea of personality types, by which he meant that people have "an innate predisposition to develop certain personality characteristics."[53] Jung's theories are the basis of the much used Myers-Briggs Type Indicator. The MBTI

---

[52] Gregory of Nyssa in *The Westminster Collection of Christian Meditations*, Hannah Ward and Jennifer Wild, compilers, (Louisville: Westminster John Knox Press, 1998), 18-19.

[53] Gary Harbaugh, *God's Gifted People*, (Minneapolis, MN: Augsburg Press, 1988), 20.

Unfettered Spirit

helps a person discover one's predilection toward four different sets of polar opposites: 1) extroversion or introversion, 2) sensing or intuition, 3) thinking or feeling, 4) judgment or perception. The question is: how will I as an INTJ do ministry as compared to the person who is ESFP? In addition to Myers-Briggs, there are a number of other personality evaluation tools, including the Taylor Johnson Temperament Analysis and the Enneagram Type Indicator.[54] Such resources need to be used with care and with the proviso that they are aids to self-awareness only.

THE GIFT ARRAY OF THE INDIVIDUAL

We live in an age of specialization. A car mechanic who can repair a Ford might not be able to work on a BMW. Fewer doctors go into family practice these days. Instead, they focus on specialized medical fields. The academic world is also increasingly specialized. There are very few Leonardo da Vincis or Benjamin Franklins alive today, making the omnicompetent "Renaissance Man or Woman" a relic of the past. When it comes to spiritual gifts it's easy to get caught up in this obsession with specialization. A too literalistic reading of the gifts texts might lead to the conclusion that each person has one gift, but experience suggests otherwise.

We are complex individuals with different interests, abilities, passion. Therefore, when it comes to spiritual gifts we should expect that most of us will have more than one spiritual gift. Even if one gift is dominant, most will exhibit a cluster of gifts. This mix of gifts gives identity and purpose to each person of God. It's this cluster of gifts that defines one's spiritual personality and creates

---

54 A Jung typology test can be found online at http://www.human-etrics.com/cgi-win/JTypes3.asp. Information on the Enneagram type indicator may be found at the website of the Lake Tahoe Wellness Institute: http://www.tahoeinstitute.com/Enneagram.htm. Also see Don Richard Riso and Russ Hudson, *Discovering Your Personality Type,* rev. ed., (Boston: Houghton Mifflin, 2003). The use of personality typology in understanding one's giftedness and ministry opportunities is discussed in some detail in Harbaugh's *God's Gifted People.*

within each person not only unique personality and temperament, but unique opportunities for ministry.

The kind of ministry we choose and the way we fulfill it will be influenced by this complex set of gifts in concert with our personality types and opportunities that present themselves. Focusing on the ministry of pastors, Brian Baucknight notes that the kind of pastor one is reflects one's giftedness. One pastor may find the greatest joy and fulfillment in preaching, while another will find it in pastoral care. One pastor might be best suited for rural ministry while another is equipped for urban or suburban ministry.[55] Each person is unique, even as each ministry is unique. The important thing to remember is that the church is comprised of all of these very unique individuals, joined together in Jesus Christ as one body.

Most mature Christians can fulfill a variety of ministries. From my own experience using gift assessments, I would venture to guess that most pastors have sufficient experience in the church that their "performance" on a gifts inventory might give the impression of at least a degree of omnicompetence. But, no pastor, any more than any other Christian, can do everything equally well. The question that each of us faces as we deal with spiritual gifts concerns the way these gifts fit together. In essence, we're talking about the spiritual chemistry of a person.

Since there are no omnicompetent Christians, the church's ministry can't be left to just one individual. There are times when we'll be required to work outside our areas of giftedness, but even then our gifts will influence the manner in which we fulfill this ministry. A gifts-mix doesn't necessarily determine our areas of ministry, but instead speaks to the styles of our ministries.

CHILDREN AND GIFTS

When the disciples sought to push the children away, Jesus asked that they be brought to him. To such persons as these, be-

---

[55] Brian Kelley Bauknight, *Body Building: Creating a Ministry Team through Spiritual Gifts*, (Nashville: Abingdon Press, 1996), 90-92.

longed the kingdom of God (Mk 10:13-16; Mt. 19:13-15; Lk. 18:15-17). Children are often spoken of as the future of the church, but they're more than the future, they're gifted members of the body whose place in the body needs to be recognized.

Congregations have a responsibility to provide spiritual nurture and care to children, and to pass on to them the traditions of the faith. Churches, whatever the form and timing of their baptismal practices, face the issue of when a child truly becomes a member of the community in their own right and not simply as an extension of their family. Is it at Baptism or Confirmation (depending on tradition)? If so, then children in believer baptism communities find themselves in a different situation than those in infant-baptism communities.

The question of the place of children can be seen in how children are treated at the Lord's Table. In the Disciple tradition, which practices believer's baptism, many churches require baptism before admitting children to the table – this was the practice of the church I formerly served – but we faced the question of how to respond to Jesus' call to include the children in the covenant community. If it's at the table that we encounter the living presence of Jesus, can the church bar children from coming to it? Disciple pastor Colbert Cartwright has written that "children learn relationships of love long before they know how to articulate love's meaning. They can express love before they can formulate its implications." Therefore "faith grows out of the experience of worship," which requires from the church a provision of a "common way of including children in worship that will affect what we believe about the church and God"[56] It's possible, therefore, that communion can serve as an opportunity for children, whether baptized or not, to experience God's nurturing and reconciling grace.

Even as the family seeks to provide a child with a place to grow and mature as a physical and emotional being, the church can provide that same child a safe place to mature as a spiritual

---

56 Colbert Cartwright, *Candles of Grace*, (St. Louis: Chalice Press, 1992), 80-81.

being. As members of the body, as branches of the vine, children discover their purpose and their abilities. They discover the love of God in their relationships with other members of the church and they begin to discover their mission as children of God. Delia Halverson suggests that "each of us has a personal mission, and that mission is our commitment to love God and follow Christ in a manner appropriate to our age and situation."[57] Halverson's point here is important. Children are just as gifted as adults, but it takes time, education, and maturity to discern what these gifts and callings might be. Therefore, it's important that steps be taken to encourage and nurture potential gifts.

Churches face the difficult question of how to find age appropriate ways of introducing children to Christian faith and ministry. We can do the same thing schools and Scout troops do, we can provide opportunities to serve the community. Within these children there are potentialities that have yet to be realized. They can't be realized until they get explored and developed. Childhood and adolescence is a time of experimentation, of trying new things in a safe environment.

This isn't the time to use inventories and personality typologies, at least not early on. Inventories require some involvement in ministry before reflection can actually occur, and most children won't have enough experience to make use of these tools.

The process of introducing children to faith and ministry can begin in the home as they observe their parents live out their own faith and ministries. If children see that the faith of their parents makes a difference in their lives, that they are transformed by God's love, and that they can experience God's love within the family, then they will be more open to exploring this faith themselves. But even children who do not come from families of faith can be introduced to it as they come into contact with loving and gracious members of the body of Christ. These older men and women (older

---

[57] Delia Halverson, *How Do Our Children Grow? Introducing Children to God, Jesus, the Bible, Prayer, Church,* (St. Louis: Chalice Press, 1999), 126.

Unfettered Spirit 73

in comparison to the child) can model for these children a faith that changes lives. Modeling of the faith involves our conversations, our devotional life, our service to God and neighbor in and through the church. Such introductions can't happen too early in life. If we feel that children need to wait until they are old enough to make a decision, they'll decide that it's not important; otherwise their families would have sought to nurture their budding faith journeys.[58]

Faith development comes in stages, with younger children especially needing experiential activities. Delia Halverson suggests that young children will "act, react, observe and copy." Therefore, she says, "interaction with others and opportunities to explore and test are vital in this [experiential] style. This is why it's important that we begin early to help children experience God through other persons and in the world."[59] My own experience as an acolyte during my elementary years likely contributed to my own growth in faith and service in the church. Children find that as they serve a meal at a homeless shelter with a group of church members, play an instrument in an ensemble, or read scripture in worship, that God seems more present to them.

We need to pay attention to our children's personalities. If a child is highly sensitive to people in pain or is willing to be friends with the friendless, might that not say that this child has a potential gift of compassion or pastor? If a child is always bringing friends to church, might that not say something about giftedness? The child who is conscientious about helping people, might that person not be gifted in service? By making it possible for children to taste ministry, they will begin to find their place in church and the world, that God might use the little ones to bring into place the realm of God.[60]

---

58 Halverson, *How Do Our Children Grow?*, 4-5.
59 Halverson, *How Do our Children Grow?* 128.
60 Delia Halverson suggests an exercise that begins with reading Matthew 24:14-30 and then offers a modern parable of three children discovering talents and then using them. Helping children reflect on their own experiences of success can help them become comfortable with their

Final Thoughts about the Pathway of Discovery

There isn't any one right way to pursue the discovery of spiritual gifts. There are, however, tools that can help the process. They each have their strengths and weaknesses. The key to discovering our place in the body of Christ is our awareness of the Spirit's movement in our midst. This means that we have to practice what the Buddhist writer Thich Nhat Hanh calls mindfulness, which can be defined as knowing "what is going on within and all around us."[61] Mindful of the Spirit's presence we will become beacons of God's love in a world that seeks to be loved by God. The gifts, they will emerge, as we faithfully follow the one who calls out of darkness and into the light.

Thought Questions

1. What has your church-life experience been? What opportunities have you had to experience ministry in the church?

2. What are your passions in life and how do they get reflected in your church experience?

3. In what ways does the church encourage your discovery and use of spiritual gifts? Do you experience affirmation? How might the church more effectively encourage people to discover and use their gifts (without manipulating them to fill slots)?

4. It has been suggested that personality type influences one's experience of ministry and one's use of spiritual gifts. Discuss ways in which personality type influences one's use of spiritual gifts.

---

abilities to serve God in the church. Halverson, *How Do Our Children Grow?* 131-32.
61   Thich Nhat Hanh, *Living Buddha, Living Christ,* (New York: Riverhead Books, 1995), 14.

4

THE SPIRIT AND THE CHRISTIAN LIFE:

THE MEDIUM OF GIFTED SERVICE

> Spirit of the living Christ, come upon us in the glory of your risen power; Spirit of the Living Christ, come upon us in all the humility of your wondrous love; Spirit of the Living Christ, come upon us that new life may course within our veins, new love bind us together in one family, a new vision of the kingdom of God spur us on to serve you with fearless passion.[62]

To serve God with a "fearless passion" is a high calling that requires nothing less than a close and abiding relationship with the living God. Some people speak of the spiritual life as a "walk," and walking can be considered a form of exercise. It takes discipline, even will-power, to accomplish. I know this from personal experience, for as much as I know the importance of walking for my physical health; it's easy to let other things crowd that activity out of my life. But, when I take the time to walk, to hike, ride my bike (which has become a rare occurrence), my body and my spirit are the better for it.

---

62 *The Complete Book of Christian Prayer,* (New York: Continuum Publishing Co., 1995), 407.

Spiritual gifts are, as we've discovered, tools for ministry, but they don't exist in a spiritual vacuum. Their effectiveness for the work of ministry is related to our spiritual health and receptivity to the leading of God's Spirit. Therefore, before we take a look at definitions of spiritual gifts, it would be helpful to take a brief look at the Christian life in general. Spiritual gifts are markers of the Spirit's presence, but they're not markers of spiritual maturity. There are other important markers that we need to consider, the most important of which is love (in all its forms). In regard to love it is important that we begin with a definition, for too often we talk of love in vague generalities.

Thomas Oord gives what I believe is the most concise and helpful definition of love, especially as it relates to the issue of spiritual gifts:

> To love is to act intentionally, in sympathetic/empathic response to God and others, to promote overall well-being.[63]

Love isn't just a feeling or emotion; it's a commitment to act in a way that "promotes overall well-being." This is but a basic definition. Oord expands this definition in relationship to specific forms of love, including *agape, eros,* and *philia* – all of which have a role to play in the life of the Spirit. Gifts of the Spirit carry the same intention, and thus are most effective when bathed in this kind of love.

With this basic definition in mind it's appropriate to say that without love, nothing of value can be accomplished. Paul speaks of markers of the Spirit's presence, fruit of the Spirit including: love, faith, hope, joy, justice, patience, compassion and peace (1 Cor. 13, Gal. 5). This is what salvation is about. It's not simply a one time act of confession. It's a lifetime spent moving toward wholeness. Justified (made right with God) by grace, received by faith, we take the first steps toward maturity in our baptism. In the course of a life lived in the presence of the Spirit, we begin to give evidence of

---

[63] Thomas Jay Oord, *The Nature of Love: A Theology,* (St. Louis: Chalice Press, 2010), 17.

Unfettered Spirit 77

the Spirit's work in our lives. Our growth in faith is facilitated by acts of discipleship. It is the purpose of the prayer offered up by the author of the letter to the Ephesians:

> I pray that, according to the riches of his glory, he may grant that you may be strengthened in your inner being with power through his Spirit, and that Christ may dwell in your hearts through faith, as you are being rooted and grounded in love. I pray that you may have the power to comprehend, with all the saints, what is the breadth and length and height and depth, and to know the love of Christ that surpasses knowledge, so that you may be filled with all the fullness of God (Eph. 3:15-19).

That is the purpose of the disciplined life, reaching the point where we might be "filled with the fullness of God." The question is this: how do we discipline and shape the heart to give evidence of this fullness of God's presence?

Spiritual giftedness is facilitated by attending to spiritual disciplines, disciplines such as prayer, study, fasting, and worship, and by receiving baptism and sharing fellowship at the Lord's Table. These actions help us as a church become receptive to the movement of the Spirit in the world. As we are receptive to this work of the spirit we find that faith, hope, and love are also manifestations of the Spirit's presence in our midst. Markers of the Spirit's presence and work, they provide the foundation for Christian community and ministry, both inside the church and outside the walls of the church. Without them the gifts of Spirit lose value and effectiveness. Gifts may differ from person to person, but faith, hope, and especially love are to be present in all God's servants. Their absence in the life of the believer and the church is telling.

Shaping the Heart

If we're to make responsible use of God's wonderful gifts for service, our hearts need to be shaped. To be shaped, they'll need to be softened. Jeremiah speaks of the Law being written on the hearts of the people of God, for "no longer shall they teach one another, or say to each other, 'know the Lord;' for they shall all know me, from the least of them to the greatest, says the Lord; for I will forgive the their iniquity and remember their sin no more" (Jer. 31:33-34). Marcus Borg perceptively writes of the heart:

> The heart is an image for the self at a deep level, deeper than our perception, intellect, emotion, and volition. As the spiritual center of the total self, it affects all of these: our sight, thought, feelings, and will.[64]

In my own life, experience has taught me the need for the shaping of the heart, so that I might be open to God's leading. I've been in the church my entire life, but that doesn't mean that this church experience has always given evidence of God's presence in my life.

I understand that the inclination of the heart may be toward evil (Gen. 8:21), but I'm grateful that it is possible for us to "incline [our] hearts to the Lord, the God of Israel" (Josh. 24:23). A receptive heart, allows for the Spirit to move in our lives. As we become receptive to God's Spirit, the Spirit softens our hearts toward our neighbors. The question is: How do I put myself in a position to become receptive to the Spirit's movements?

There are numerous and significant works on developing the spiritual life, and the reader should attend to these important works. But because the shape of the heart is important to the understanding and usage of spiritual gifts, I will speak briefly to several foundational disciplines: prayer, study, attendance at the Lord's Table, worship, and disciplining of the body. In these disciplines of the Spirit, God is released to shape our hearts and our lives, making us receptive to the love and grace God desires to share with us and with the world, that the world might experience redemption and transformation.

---

64 Marcus Borg, *The Heart of Christianity,* (San Francisco: Harper San Francisco, 2003), 151.

Unfettered Spirit

Prayer

What is prayer? Prayer is conversation, intercession, praise, submission, contrition and confession. One especially poignant answer is provided in the introduction to the *Little Book of Hours.*

> In prayer we pay attention as the Holy Spirit breathes God's voice to us, and we breath back our signs and songs of love and praise. We call out to the heart of God and listen to the word of God as it has been given through the centuries – words of Scripture, canticles, teachings and devotional readings When we pray, we add our own voices to this ceaseless chorus, taking our part in the song that has been sung since creation began.[65]

Harry Emerson Fosdick writes that "the thought of prayer as communion with God makes praying a *habitual attitude,* and not simply an *occasional act.* It is continuous fellowship with God, not a spasmodic demand for his gifts."[66] Therefore, the process of shaping the heart toward God begins as we open our hearts to God's Spirit in prayer. Such prayer comes daily, hourly, even minute by minute, as we seek in word or in silence the presence of God.

The Christian practice of prayer is not prescribed for us, as it is for our Muslim neighbors. For the Muslim, prayer is required five times a day. Akbar Ahmed writes:

> The daily prayers help Muslims to remember God and prevent them from incorrect or wicked acts. By bowing their heads to the ground Muslims accept the omnipotence of God. It also encourages humility and the notion of equality. They must pray even if they are in the middle of a war or suffering

---

65 *The Little Book of Hours: Praying with the Community of Jesus,* (Brewster, MA: Paraclete Press, 2003), ix.
66 Harry Emerson Fosdick, *The Meaning of Prayer,* (Nashville: Abingdon Press, 1980), 30.

ill health. The prayer helps them transcend the mundane and the everyday.[67]

For most Christians prayer is a voluntary, even occasional act. The timing comes at our choice, but as with the Muslim, our prayers are reminders of God's presence and sovereignty.

The life of prayer is not an easy one. Time in prayer can easily get crowded out of the schedule. It's easy to get distracted, especially if, like me, you're not an especially contemplative person. Finding a place that is quiet also is often problematic. But, Jesus took time away from the crowds and disciples to pray. He made it a priority.

Although prayer at its simplest is conversation, it's not the usual form of conversation we engage in. Unless we listen carefully and intently it can easily become a one way conversation. Prayer, Dietrich Bonhoeffer says, is not a natural act. But whether "the heart is full or empty" there is a need to speak with God. However, he says "no man can do that by himself. For that he needs Jesus Christ."[68] Jesus taught the disciples a form of prayer, a form rooted in the Jewish habits of prayer. It pledges honor and allegiance to the name of God, it acknowledges that God reigns now and in the future, on earth and in heaven. In our prayers we affirm our dependence on God's bread and seek God's forgiving grace – only that our forgiveness is conditional on our willingness to forgive our neighbor – and we seek God's protection from evil (Mt. 6:9-13).

Attending to the Word

God took human words and breathed life into them, making them the Word of God (2 Tim. 3:16). In these words of scripture, if we're attentive to the Spirit's leading, we can hear a word from God. For those of a more literalist bent, this process may seem rather easy to accomplish. You just read and apply. For those of us

---

67 Akbar S. Ahmed, *Islam Today: A Short Introduction to the Muslim World*, (New York: I.B. Tauris & Co., 2002), 33.
68 Dietrich Bonhoeffer, *Psalms: The Prayer Book of the Bible*, (Augsburg, 1970), 9-10.

Unfettered Spirit

who take a more critical perspective, the process isn't quite so easy. Hearing a word from God takes discernment and requires that we give attention to critical scholarship, especially when a text speaks in a way that seems contrary to either what we know from science or history or it runs contrary to the way we understand God to work. Thus, we must be aware of the cultural and historical context in which this word was formed, preserved, and passed on to us.

When given a careful reading, one that attends to the voices of the scholar, we can find in this ancient words that can guide us in our relationships with God, with humanity, and with the creation itself. And the word that should come forth from this document is one that calls forth a faithful community of compassion, of mercy, and of service.

Scripture, according to James Dunn, is designed "to produce well-instructed and disciplined adults, proficient and well-equipped in the graces and skills required for a positive role in church and society ('good work of every kind') and wise as to what makes for the wholeness of salvation."[69] The words of scripture, when read with open and critical eyes, may guide us in the way of love of God and love of neighbor. Scripture brings to our minds and our hearts the truth that sets us free, a truth that lays bare our anger and our bitterness. It exposes our rebellion, our need to be in control, and reminds us that we are not God (Job 38). Paul said that the purpose of the Law is not to make us right with God, but to show us the distance that lies between us and God (Rom. 7:7-12). The gospels reveal to us the person of Jesus Christ, in whose life, death, and resurrection, we discover a way back to relationship with God and with each other. As the Psalmist says: "The Law of the Lord is perfect, reviving the soul; the decrees of the Lord are sure, making wise the simple; the precepts of the Lord are right, rejoicing the heart, the commandment of the Lord is clear, enlightening the eyes; . . . ." (Psalm 19:7-8).

---

69 James D. G. Dunn, "The First and Second Letters to Timothy and the Letter to Titus," in *The New Interpreter's Bible,* (Nashville: Abingdon Press, 2000), 11:852.

Sharing at the Table

For me the Table of the Lord is the central act of worship. Regular attendance at the Eucharist serves to remind us that Jesus is truly present with us as we take this journey of faith. Bread and wine stand forth as witnesses that the Logos of God became flesh and dwelt among us (Jn 1:14). "I am the bread of life" Jesus tells the crowd in John 6. In him we find the answer to our spiritual hunger and thirst. Come and eat, Jesus says to us, eat of the bread of heaven.

For Jesus, table fellowship offered a way of inclusion. He was accused of eating with sinners and tax collectors. What was meant as condemnation was worn by Jesus as a badge of honor. In doing so he declared them clean, fit for relationship with God. Jesus does the same for us. By inviting us to the Table, Jesus declares us, like the sinners of his day, to be clean. Because we've been welcomed by him to his Table, we can join in fellowship with him and his people.

At the table we also celebrate the presence of the one who was crucified and buried and then raised by God from the dead. It's this risen Christ who cleanses us from sin and raises us to new life. When we come to the table we bring our biases, bigotry, racism, suspicions, our hatred, and hear the call to let go of them and embrace our neighbor. Jürgen Moltmann writes that "the Lord's Supper takes place on the basis of an invitation which is open as the outstretched arms of Christ on the cross. Because he died for the reconciliation of 'the world,' the world is invited to reconciliation in the supper."[70]

The table of the Lord is a place of welcome, a place where distinction of race, gender, social class, age, and sexual orientation, are irrelevant. The fact that we haven't experienced this reality in its fullness doesn't mean we should give up table fellowship. It only means that we will have to rely on the grace of God if we're going

---

70 Jürgen Moltmann, *The Church in the Power of the Spirit,* (Harper and Row, 1977), 246.

Unfettered Spirit

to return time and again in pursuit of the unity that the Table symbolizes.

The celebration at the table is an act of hope. Paul writes that "as often as you eat this bread and drink the cup, you proclaim the Lord's death until he comes" (vs. 26). Even as the table looks back to the decisive events of the cross it also looks into the future and the completion of God's act of reconciliation. Therefore, we may "rejoice and exult and give him the glory, for the marriage of the Lord has come, and his bride has made herself ready; to her has been granted to be clothed with fine linen, bright and pure – for the fine line is the righteous deeds of the saints" (Rev. 17:7-8).

The Table looks forward to a wedding feast to which the world is invited. No matter our backgrounds or theological differences, the Table offers us the opportunity to experience a moment of God's grace that is powerful enough to break down any barrier we put up. As Paul wrote: "Because there is one bread, we who are many are made one body, for we all partake of the one bread" (1 Cor. 10:17). Therefore, whether we are black or white, young or old, male or female, rich or poor, Catholic or Protestant or Orthodox, we are one in Christ when we share in the bread and cup. Although barriers remain that keep us from enjoying full table fellowship, this vision of the Lamb's wedding feast stands as a sign that the barriers will not prevail.

Singing in the Spirit

The Psalms invite us to sing new songs of praise and thanksgiving. In Ephesians we read a call to "sing psalms, hymns, and spiritual songs among yourselves, singing and making melody to the Lord in your hearts" (Eph. 5:18-20). Music is a foundational spiritual discipline. Although we live in an age of prerecorded music and professionalization, for the church and the people of God, singing in the Spirit sustains the life of the Spirit. Martin Luther wrote centuries ago:

"Next to the Word of God, music deserves the highest praise. She is a mistress and governess of those human emotions – to pass over the animals – which as masters govern men or more often overwhelm them. . . . For whether you wish to comfort the sad, to terrify the happy, to encourage the despairing, to humble the proud, to calm the passionate, or to appease those full of hate – and who could remember all these masters of the human heart, namely, the emotions, inclinations, and affections that impel men to evil or good? – What more effective means than music could you find?"[71]

Music comes in variations of style and form. It is contemporary and ancient, traditional and avant-garde. It draws our hearts heavenward and it binds us one to another.

Good church music is music that can be sung well by non-professionals. Worship is not a spectator sport, and therefore we should not leave the singing to the choir or the praise band. Song, our song, sets up everything else from the prayers to the preaching. Music should unite us, though in our musical tribalism it often divides. Worship offers a place for an expression of giftedness, of sharing the songs and the instrumental abilities that are inherent in our persons.

Music is foundational to corporate worship. It springs from our souls and trips memories within us. Maybe that is why singing the *Hallelujah Chorus* gives me chills. It is, therefore, an expression of spiritual life to be attended to with care, by pastors, by musicians, by church members. Therefore, sing the new song as the psalmist commands![72]

---

71 *Luther's Works*, Liturgy and Hymns, (Philadelphia: Fortress Press, 1965), 53:323.
72 For an extremely helpful discussion of the music and worship see Carol Doran and Thomas H. Troeger, *Trouble at the Table: Gathering the Tribes for Worship*, (Nashville: Abingdon Press, 1993), 47-92.

Disciplining the Body

John the Baptist received criticism for his ascetic lifestyle – no eating or drinking, the wearing of a coarse shirt – while Jesus was condemned for his perceived gluttony. In responding to these double-minded critics Jesus affirmed the possibility of fasting but not its necessity. For him, the kingdom of God required celebration, but a time would come when fasting would be appropriate.

Asceticism in whatever forms it takes is a denial of the body. It has a long history, not only in Christianity but in most religious traditions. Fasting from food, sexual relations, speech, can prove beneficial to our spiritual lives. Such restraint can focus our attention and remind us that ultimately we depend on the bread of heaven not human bread to sustain our lives.

The Virtuous Life

Legalism is an ever present temptation in religious communities. Lists of dos and don'ts can overwhelm people, and ultimately define who is on the inside and who is on the outside. Jesus' own actions led some to believe he was a sinner because he spent considerable time cavorting with people who weren't welcome in polite circles. The Christian community is open to all, but it isn't an "antinomian" community. I bring this Greek word into our conversation because some Christians have believed that since we live according to the principle of grace, there is no law and therefore we're free to do as we please (as long as we don't hurt anyone else). Paul seems to have dealt with such persons, and though he taught the primacy of grace, he also called believers to a virtuous life.

According to Paul's instructions to the Galatian churches, disciples of Jesus "walk by the Spirit" and don't give in to the desires of the flesh (Gal. 5:16). He contrasts flesh and Spirit and suggests that the works of the flesh involve immoral or licentious acts, idolatry and dissension, as well as drunkenness (Gal. 5:19-21). Instead, their lives should express the fruit of the Spirit: love, joy, peace, patience, kindness, generosity, faithfulness, gentleness, and self-control (Gal.

5:22-23). Although James is often contrasted with Paul, would Paul really disagree with James's conclusion that "faith without works is dead?" Paul may have emphasized grace, but James' message of works doesn't contradict Paul's message, it simply reminds us that grace, as Dietrich Bonhoeffer reminded us, is costly.

A Spirit-filled and empowered life will be virtuous, for the fullest expression of the Spirit's presence is love. Indeed, since love is the fulfilling of the Law (Rom. 13:8-10), and love is the expression of the baptism with the Spirit who is love, then the life of virtue is an expression of this love. Amos Yong writes:

> The Spirit's baptism of love means that followers of Jesus the Messiah are no longer bound to the letter of the law but that any edification of or peaceful overture to (Rom. 14:19; 15:2) the neighbor – strong or weak, friend or enemy, altruist or evildoer, as delineated I the earlier passage on love in Romans 12 – would be a fulfillment of the law.[73]

Our conversation about the relationship of the Spirit of Love to the idea of the virtuous life fits well with Benjamin Farley's definition of virtue as being "an activity of the whole person in conformity with love of God and love of neighbor."[74]

The call to the virtuous life isn't taken up by individuals in isolation. As Gordon Fee notes, the call to walk by the Spirit is directed not so much toward the individual, as toward the community. The fruit of the Spirit "are ethics for believers who are learning to live together as God's people in a fallen world."[75] The church, therefore, is "a community of virtues." Instead of having a Christian social ethic that announces the "peaceable kingdom" to the world, the Christian community is the Christian social ethic that models

---

73 Amos Yong, *Spirit of Love: A Trinitarian Theology of Grace*. (Waco, TX: Baylor University Press, 2012), 127-128.
74 Benjamin Farley, *In Praise of Virtue: An Exploration of the Biblical Virtues in a Christian Context*, (Grand Rapids: Wm. B. Eerdmans Publishing, Co., 1995), 160.
75 Gordon Fee, *Paul, the Spirit, and the People of God*, (Peabody, MA: Hendrickson, 1996), 115-16.

Unfettered Spirit

for the world the peaceable kingdom. As followers of the crucified Savior, Stanley Hauerwas writes, "they must be capable of being peaceable among themselves and with the world, so that the world sees what it means to hope for God's kingdom. Such people do not believe that everyone is free to do whatever they will, but that we are each called upon to develop our particular gifts to serve the community of faith."[76] Service to the community of Christ – the primary purpose of giftedness – leads ultimately to service of the world in which the community exists.

To get a sense of what the virtuous life looks like, we might turn to Jesus' "beatitudes." These are descriptions of life in God's realm, but we don't have to wait for some cataclysmic future event to enjoy living under God's reign. As we pray the Lord's Prayer, we pray that God's reign would be known on earth as in heaven.[77] In living according to these signs of blessing, we extend that reign in the world of God's creation and redemption. Jesus said, "my kingdom is not of this world" (Jn. 18:36), but that does not mean that the kingdom is not in this world. Its origins are with God and not with humanity. In the words of Jürgen Moltmann:

God's kingdom is as earthly as Jesus himself was, and anyone who looks at Jesus' end will say: through the cross of Christ the kingdom of God is ineradicably implanted in this earth. With the resurrection of the crucified Christ the rebirth of the whole tormented creation begins. So remain true to the earth! For the earth is worth it.[78]

There are blessings to be found in the midst of the poverty and grief of human experience. Those who are meek, and who hunger for righteousness (or simply hunger for food), those who are merciful and pure in heart, those who seek to make peace and those

---

76 Stanley Hauerwas, *The Peaceable Kingdom: A Primer in Christian Ethics*, (Notre Dame: University of Notre Dame Press, 1983), 102-3.
77 Robert D. Cornwall, *Ultimate Allegiance: The Subversive Nature of the Lord's Prayer*, (Gonzalez, FL: Energion Publications, 2010), 15-23.
78 Jürgen Moltmann, *Jesus Christ for Today's World*, Margaret Kohl, trans., (Philadelphia: Fortress Press, 1994), 20.

who are persecuted, they will know the blessings of God's realm. In being the blessed community, the people of God are salt and light to the world (Mt. 5:1-16).[79] The spiritual life is not centered on self – not just my personal relationship with God – it's centered in the community that lives in obedience to the one who is Lord, Jesus the Christ. But, if anyone should falter, we have a great high priest who can sympathize with our weakness, and yet provide the means of grace in our time of need (Heb. 4:14-16).

Fruit of the Spirit

I've already mentioned the fruit of the Spirit, and we return to them now. Jesus says of humanity, "you will know them by their fruits. Are grapes gathered from thorns, or figs from thistles?" (Mt. 7:16). The Christian community, if it's to be salt and light, will be a community that gives evidence of its relationship with God through the fruit it bears. Paul's list of the nine "fruits of the Spirit" stands as a marker of the church's spiritual health. On this basis, Phil Kenneson believes that the church is in fact seriously ill. In spite of apparent numerical growth, at least within the Evangelical community, the church today is "simply cultivating at the center of its life the seeds that the dominant culture has sown in its midst."[80] The nine "fruits" that serve as markers of spiritual health are "love, joy, peace, patience, kindness, generosity, faithfulness, gentleness, and self-control" (Gal. 5:22-23). Each of these markers of spiritual health undergird human relationships, they enable a person to put the needs and concerns of the other in a position of priority. While the fruit is a permanent expression of the Spirit's presence, spiritual gifts are temporary expressions designed for ministry within the body and in the world at large (1 Cor. 13:8).

---

79   Farley, *In Praise of Virtue*, 103-12.
80   Phil Kenneson, *Life on the Vine: Cultivating the Fruit of the Spirit in Christian Community*, (Downers Grove, IL: InterVarsity Press, 1999), 10-12.

If the fruit of the Spirit define Christian character, then love is the foundation of Christian life and experience (Eph. 4:17-19, Gal. 5:22-23). It defines the Christian faith precisely because God is love (1 Jn. 4:7-8). Ontologically, we could define love, in the words of Paul Tillich, not as emotion but as "the drive towards the unity of the separated."[81] Love (*agape*) seeks the best for the other, even when the intention of the other is evil. Again, I turn to Thomas Oord for help in providing a definition – this time, of *agape*.

I define *agape as acting intentionally, in response to God and others, to promote overall well-being in response to that which produces ill-being.*[82]

Oord calls *agape* as "*in spite of* love." Thus, it becomes the foundation of the ministry of reconciliation to which we have been called. This principle finds its connection to human life in the person of Jesus, in whom God reconciles all things to himself and makes all things new (2 Cor. 5:16-21, Eph. 2:11-22).

Abiding in God who is the ground of human existence is to abide in love (1 Jn. 3:7-16). Love, John Koenig writes, is "a necessary bridge between gift and task," in that it "directs the powerful charismata toward the welfare of others."[83] Love is the foundation of spiritual service, because love alone endures. Spiritual gifts – not tongues, prophesy, even martyrdom – no matter how beneficial they might seem, without love, have no value to the church or the world if they are not exercised in the context of love (1 Cor. 13).

---

81 Paul Tillich, *Love, Power and Justice*, (London: Oxford University Press, 1960), 24-25. Tillich is a philosophical foundationalist, which might put his position at odds with the nonfoundationalism of the post-modern movement; however, his position resonates with the biblical understanding of love's centrality to human existence. Without it life is not possible. See also Michael Welker, *God the Spirit*, John F. Hoffmeyer, trans. (Minneapolis: Fortress Press, 1994), 248-52.

82 Oord, *The Nature of Love*, 56.

83 John Koenig, *Charismata: God's Gifts for God's People*, (Philadelphia: Westminster Press, 1978), 151.

Much grief has come to the church because of immature understandings of the nature and purpose of spiritual gifts. Churches have tried to set people free to use their gifts only to see them used in an unloving, even destructive, manner. Pride, a critical spirit, even misplaced enthusiasm can undo even the most selfless acts. These problems could be avoided if love of neighbor was the primary motivating force in these acts of service. The discovery and use of these gifts is wonderful, but without love they divide rather than unite the body of Christ.

Paul's inclusion of an expanded treatment of the place of love in the exercise of spiritual gifts (1 Cor. 13) is compelling evidence that from the beginning of church history immaturity and selfishness could lead to abuse of spiritual power. A "charismatic" church can easily become home to coercive and destructive activities. In Corinth the unity of the body was threatened by those who would elevate the gift of tongues to preeminence in the community. The contemporary church faces a similar problem. In seeking to give attention to the role of the Spirit in the church, some enthusiastic partisans of the Spirit's work have given tongues a preeminence not warranted by scripture or Christian experience. The determining factor in the value of any spiritual gift is its usefulness in contributing to the welfare of the community, whether Christian or not. It is for this reason that Paul contended that the gifts that should have preeminence are those gifts that build or edify the body. Therefore, a tongue without interpretation doesn't achieve this purpose and should be used in private. Amos Yong bemoans the tendency among Pentecostals to emphasize power rather than love. However, he writes:

> The evidence of the Spirit is not just glossolalic utterance but the fruits of the Spirit, especially love, and their concrete manifestation in benevolent actions. Pentecostal missions involve the expectation that divine supernatural power will appear, although for some this is palpably felt not only in miraculous healings but in the feeding of the hungry, the clothing of those practically naked, caring for the orphaned, and the

ministering to the abandoned, oppressed, or marginalized of the world.[84]

Paul had to offer a word of correction to the Corinthian church because of its unhealthy attitudes toward spiritual gifts had led to dissension and even division. This divisiveness made the church unattractive to those outside the Christian community seeking a place that offered a healing and supportive home, where lives might be changed through an encounter with the living God, the God known in the person of Jesus.

Spiritual gifts don't have the same eternal value as divine love. Our use of these gifts is not the ultimate barometer of spiritual health. Love will persevere and it's as expressions of love that gifts endure. We may see the things of God dimly at this time, as if through a distorted mirror, but there will come a time of completeness when we will see God face to face (1 Cor. 13:12-13). As we use these gifts God gives us in an attitude of love and undergird the ministries that emerge from these gifts by giving attention to spiritual disciplines, the world will be able to look at our assemblies and say: "Surely, God is in this place" (1 Cor. 14:25).

---

84 Yong, *Spirit of Love*, 54. More will be said about tongues later in this book.

PART TWO

DEFINING THE GIFTS OF LOVE

5

WHAT ARE THE GIFTS OF LOVE?

> And I had a kind of vision of all of us coming together, bearing our different wounds, offering differing gifts. The preachers, prophets, healers, and discerners of spirits. Those who can describe the faith and those who can only live it. Those who speak in tongues and those who interpret. Those who write, and those who sing. Those who have knowledge and those who are wise only in the sight of God. Each of us poor and in need of love, yet rich in spirit. Each of us speaking in the language we know, and being understood. Pentecost, indeed.[85]
>
> Kathleen Norris

Looking back two millenniums to the first century experiences of God described in Scripture, we quickly realize that we live in a very different world. Even if we see ourselves as being postmodern, we're children of the Enlightenment, a movement that has challenged us to think scientifically and skeptically about our world. This skepticism that rightfully marks our worldview may make it difficult for us to see things in what we might call "spiritual terms." Even though horoscopes and spirituality are popular, our materialistic world view often makes us immune from incorporating angels, demons, gods, and devils into the way we think about the world. We look for mechanistic explanations whenever possible

---

85   Kathleen Norris, *Amazing Grace: A Vocabulary of Faith*, (New York: Riverhead Books, 1998), 349.

and find the notion of mystery problematic. Or, at least that was true until recently.

In recent years the overly materialistic/mechanistic Newtonian world view that has marked the Western world over the past three centuries has begun to erode. We've begun to realize that while science can offer answers to many of our questions, it doesn't answer all of them. There are some in our faith communities who've retreated to a pre-enlightenment worldview and seek to replace modern science with the kind of god-of-the-gaps world view, but such a move seems counter-productive and doomed to failure. As Dietrich Bonhoeffer reminds us, when we use God as a stop-gap explanation for the seemingly unexplainable, new scientific discoveries often fill the gaps and push God further away from us. Writing from prison he wrote that "we should find God in what we know, not in what we don't know; God wants to be grasped by us not in unsolved questions but in those that have been solved."[86]

In proposing that we embrace a theology of giftedness, I don't mean to suggest we seek to inhabit this pre-enlightenment world of an oft-intervening God. As I read the post-modern critique of Modernism, I see it broadening our field of vision so we can discern what is truly a God-inhabited world. We live in the world we know, so that even if we don't directly see the hand of God that doesn't mean God is necessarily absent.

Sometimes conversations about spiritual gifts start with rather supernaturalist assumptions. They assume an overly interventionist God. As my own theology of giftedness has evolved I have tried to take into account the realities of the world as we know it and the world yet to be discovered. I'm aware that positing an interventionist God is problematic, but can we not at least consider the prospect that there is more to our reality than what we discern with the five senses? As a child of the Enlightenment, I'm wary of

---

[86] Dietrich Bonhoeffer, *Letters and Papers from Prison. Dietrich Bonhoeffer Works, Vol. 8. Translated by Isabel Best, et. al* (Minneapolis: Fortress Press, 2009), 405-406.

Unfettered Spirit

much that passes as spirituality today, and yet a totally demystified world seems rather sterile.

Attempting to offer definitions of spiritual experiences that have their origins in a pre-critical, pre-enlightened age offers particular difficulties. If we're to welcome into our midst the Spirit of Pentecost and understand the message of Pentecost today it's important to consider what definitions of spiritual gifts should look like in this post-modern age. As I look at these gifts, I'm mindful of Walter Wink's discussion of the powers and principalities, a discussion that suggests that behind the material there is a spiritual dimension, a spirituality that can be discerned and affirmed where possible and redeemed where necessary. In other words, it is necessary that we use spiritual lenses two millenniums old to examine our place in the world. Wink is helpful here when he writes:

> Christianity's lack of credibility is not a consequence of the inadequacy of its intrinsic message, but of the fact that its intrinsic message cannot – simply, categorically, cannot – be communicated meaningfully within a materialistic cosmology."[87]

Although Wink doesn't deal with spiritual gifts in his books, there is, I believe a parallel between what he does in his books and what I'm trying to do here. That is, I'm suggesting that there's a way of engaging our world that allows for the spiritual – post-materialist – dimension to have its say. It's in this sense that the search for spiritual gifts is a charismatic enterprise.

We begin the journey of discovery by affirming that the Spirit of God is at work in our world, unmasking the powers and empowering us to engage the powers that be.[88] By offering definitions of

---

[87] Walter Wink, *Unmasking the Powers: The Invisible Forces that Determine Human Existence*, (Minneapolis: Fortress Press, 1986), 6.

[88] Wink's three volume work on the powers speaks of naming, unmasking, and engaging the powers. By defining and appropriating the gifts of the Spirit the church is able to accomplish these tasks. See also Winks, *The Powers that Be: Theology for a New Millennium*, (New York: Galilee Books, 1998).

gifts listed in scripture, tentative though these definitions may be, we can begin to find our place in God's mission of redemption. By naming these gifts and offering them to the world, we unleash the Spirit to blow through the world, bringing refreshment and new life to a world that is groaning for God's transforming presence.

Spiritual giftedness is about walking in the power of God. When we walk in the power of God's Spirit, our words and actions demonstrate that God's grace is available to the world. They bring glory to the creator by acknowledging God's empowering presence. There is, as we've seen, a wide array of possible expressions of the Spirit's work in the world. In many ways, they're as diverse as the people of God. Therefore, if it's nearly impossible to limit the number of gifts, it's even more difficult to define them with any definitiveness. My definitions, therefore, aren't definitive. Instead, I see them as a tool to make sense of patterns of experience and opportunity.

As we begin to venture into these definitions, it may be helpful to consider the question that began the book: What will the stranger see when she or he wanders into our congregations? What will they hear and experience? Will they sense that the Spirit of God is moving in our midst? Will they discern in our words and actions a desire to offer comfort to the hurting as well as challenges to the complacent? Will they find Spirit filled and led people offering prayers for healing, advocating justice for the marginalized and offering help to those in need – sharing homes with the homeless, tutoring children, preparing food for the hungry, mowing lawns for the elderly? Whether inside or outside the walls of the church, do our words and activities suggest to the stranger that God's transforming and gracious love is at work in our midst? Spiritual gifts offer hope that "in Christ all things become new" (2 Cor. 5:17).

Regarding the gifts and their definitions, there are five primary gift lists, all Pauline in nature, which suggest a total of nineteen gifts. The differences in the lists suggest that we should not seem them as being exhaustive, but merely suggestive. Experience and the imagination can be helpful in considering other possibilities.[89] While there is the danger of oversimplification in offering categories, it makes sense here to break the gifts into four categories: word, leadership, service and power.

In the following four chapters we'll attempt to provide useful definitions for these gifts of the Spirit. Such definitions are not easy to come by. There is, understandably, a tendency to impose contemporary meanings on these words. It's likely that any attempt at providing modern definitions will inject a degree of anachronism as well. With the following definitions, I have attempted to root them within critical exegetical practice. As you read through these definitions ask yourself the following questions:

1) Do I recognize myself in this definition?

2) Do I recognize someone else who might have this gift?

3) What would this gift require of me in terms of training, time, effort, commitment?

4) How might this gift make a difference to my life, the life of the church, the life of my community?

---

[89] In examining the various gifts I will be making use of a number of works including: Colin Brown, ed., *The New International Dictionary of New Testament Theology,* 3 vols., (Grand Rapids, MI: Zondervan, 1975); C.E.B. Cranfield, *Romans,* International Critical Commentary, (Edinburgh: T. & T. Clark, 1979), vol. 2.; James D. G. Dunn, *Jesus and the Spirit,* (Philadelphia: Westminster Press, 1975); Gordon D. Fee, *The First Epistle to the Corinthians,* The New International Commentary on the New Testament, (Grand Rapids: Wm. B. Eerdmans, 1987); Gordon Fee, *God's Empowering Presence,* (Peabody, MA: Hendrickson, 1994); George T. Montague, *The Holy Spirit: Growth of a Biblical Tradition,* (New York: Paulist Press, 1976); Alan Richardson, ed., *A Theological Wordbook of the Bible,* (New York: Collier Books, 1950). Other works will be noted as they are used.

6

Gifts of Leadership

>Leadership, like other work of the people of faith, depends upon the vigorous and responsible use of the talents God has given to each of us. It depends upon the work of the Spirit weaving those talents into a rich tapestry. It is the marvelous and mysterious working of God through our lives and work that we call grace. Leadership is a gift from God, confirmed by the church, for the service of others and the upbuilding of the body of Christ.
>
>Lovett Weems[90]

Congregations need leaders if they're to fulfill their missional calling. Leaders are called to equip, guide, and build up the community of faith so that the community or congregation may live out its own calling to love God and the world. Although Scripture doesn't prescribe a specific form of church structure or leadership, it presumes that leadership will be present. In the beginning, Jesus may have set aside the twelve as primary leaders, but it's clear that a variety of forms emerged in the early years of the church. New ministries and new forms of leadership emerged as they were needed. It's also clear from reading the Pauline texts, along with Ephesians and the Pastorals, that gifts of leadership were present and recognized by the early Christians. Therefore, whatever we say about gifts of leadership should take into account the freedom of

---

90 Lovett H. Weems, Jr. *Church Leadership: Vision, Team, Culture and Integrity*, (Nashville: Abingdon Press, 1993), 17.

the church to organize itself in ways that are appropriate to the times and the contexts.

Leadership gifts help mobilize the church to fulfill its ministry of joining with God's Spirit in transforming the world in a way that reflects God's vision of shalom. In a gift-based model of the church, ministry is a shared vocation. It presumes that there is equality among members, and that the church needn't be hierarchical. I say needn't be, because I don't want to cast aspersions on more hierarchical systems. If they reflect the vision of God and they free the people of God to make use of their gifts of ministry, then so be it. I am, however, of the belief that hierarchy tends to get in the way of Spirit-driven ministry. On the other hand, even if we affirm the idea that the "church is flat," to borrow from Tony Jones, this affirmation needn't preclude strong and effective leadership. Monarchical it's not, but in what ways is it democratic?[91]

Both monarchy and democracy can lead to tyranny in the church – either tyranny of the one or the tyranny of the majority. A church that's beholden to one leader or a cabal of leaders will fail to fulfill its calling, but a community that shuns the voice of the minority will also fail to fulfill its calling.

In thinking about the way church leadership can function effectively in a missional context, I've become convinced that one of the best ways of doing this is to look to the model of congregation-based community organizing. The community organizing model is built on the premise that powerful organizations are built on the foundation of a broad community of empowered and trained leaders. In this model there is an organizer, who helps train and keep the community of leaders moving toward their value-laden goals. Kendall Clark Baker, who has long experience in this form of community life, has envisioned his own calling as that of "organizing pastor." That is, the pastor doesn't just organize things,

---

91 See José Ignacio González Faus, *Builders of Community: Rethinking Ecclesiastical Ministry*, (Miami, FL: Convivium Press, 2012), 60ff. Tony Jones, *The Church Is Flat: The Relational Ecclesiology of the Emerging Church Movement*, (Minneapolis: JoPa Productions, 2011).

organizing is the defining point of ministry. It helps integrate the roles of prophet, priest, and king (preaching/teaching, worship leadership, and administration/organizing).[92]

Although there isn't one defined form of leadership in congregations, there are qualities and qualifications that help define what leaders should be like. Thus, in the Pastoral Letters, which were likely written in Paul's name sometime after his death to encourage young leaders to be resilient in their ministries, the letters name several qualifications for holding a leadership position. Leaders should have high moral virtue and learning, should be hospitable and able to teach, have respect at home and in the community (1 Tim. 3:1-7; 4:6-16). Although these letters suggest a more institutionalized form of community than we find in Paul's undisputed letters, they can help us better understand the role of the leader in a gift-based church. We read the charge that the mentor pastor gives to Timothy: "proclaim the message; be persistent whether the time is favorable or unfavorable, convince, rebuke, and encourage, with the utmost patience in teaching" (2 Tim. 4:2).

To be a good leader, one must have a sense of vision, wisdom, common sense, compassion, and skills that enable one to motivate, guide, and when necessary even prod people toward the desired direction. Leadership, it would seem, is founded upon a foundation of moral integrity and ethical values.

Jesus contrasted the world's understanding of leadership with God's vision of leadership. In this vision of leadership, we're to be servants rather than lords. So, in an age when more and more pastors are called upon to serve as congregational CEO's, this is an important consideration. From personal experience in pastoral ministry, I know that it's impossible to absolve one's self of administrative responsibilities. The very fact that one receives financial remuneration from the congregation, suggests that certain rather mundane tasks will fall on that person, if for no other reason than

---

92   Kendall Clark Baker, *When Faith Invades the Public Square: Mixing Politics and Religion through Community Organizing to Enhance Our Democracy,* (Cleveland, OH: Circle Books, 2011), 177-178.

such a person likely has the time (due to not having another form of employment) to fulfill this need. Yes, there are important administrative tasks to which pastors must attend themselves. The point isn't that pastors/ministers don't serve in this capacity, but we must be careful about how we comport ourselves. While there is much to learn from the business world about leadership, this must be tempered by values that are defined by our faith. So, given the variety of leadership responsibilities that are present in the church, what kind of leader would Jesus want for the church?

In contrast to visions of leadership that focus on control (lording it over others), Jesus' vision of leadership leads to freeing and empowering others to take up their own calling to ministry in church and world.

With an eye to gifts, calling, and mission, congregations can discern how to organize themselves – whether it's episcopal, presbyterian, or congregational. If the church is open, the Spirit can move in and with any of these structural forms – though if a gifts-based understanding of the church is implemented, even hierarchical churches will begin moving toward a less hierarchical form. Structure isn't really the issue. Instead, the issue is making sure that leaders are – spiritually sensitive and able to empower others to fulfill their own divine calling. Among the gifts that would come under this category are various forms of leadership, apostles/missionaries, the gift of pastor, and the gift of discernment. The style of leadership called for in the church is one of service, compassion, and grace, but it's also something needed within the church, from pastors, elders, and chairs of committees.

LEADERSHIP / ADMINISTRATION / GOVERNMENT (KUBERNESIS / PROHISTAMENOS)

As we've already noted, leadership takes many forms. In a congregation you may find pastors/ministers, women and men who've presumably heard a call from God to a defined form of ministry and as a result they've been educated/trained/equipped for ordained, vocational ministries. You may also find elders (or equivalent), moderators, chairs of ministry groups (also known as committees and task forces), and more. Some time ago Kennon Callahan declared that the day of the professional minister was over, having died along with a churched culture, but this form of ministry continues to persist, though others have joined Callahan in his assessment. While this alleged death of the clergy may have been overly exaggerated, what Callahan offers in its place fits with the realities facing the church today. Callahan proposes the principle of the missionary pastor, the leader who is able to maneuver in a changing, pluralistic world. Such a vision fits well with the recognition that the church needs to be missional if it is to live out its purpose in the world today. Even if most established congregations may not have fully made this transition, the point is well taken.[93]

I'm not in the position to provide a complete description of what effective leadership looks like, but in providing a rather brief definition of effective leadership, we can point to two specific gifts that we should expect to be present in local congregations.

Paul uses two different Greek words to describe what is essentially one form of ministry: *kubernesis* (1 Cor. 12:28) and *prohistamenos* (Rom. 12:8). The root of the word *kubernesis* describes the work of a pilot or helmsman who steers the ship, and. Plato uses the word to describe the statesman who guides the ship of state. Its Hebrew equivalent, *tahbûlôt*, speaks of wise direction or counsel (Prov. 1:5; 11:14; 24:6). The importance of proper and wise administration is seen in the admonition found in Proverbs: "Where there is no guidance, a nation falls, but in an abundance of

---

93 Kennon L. Callahan, *Effective Church Leadership: Building on the Twelve Keys*, (San Francisco: Harper & Row, Publishers, 1990), 3-4. In considering the gift of leadership, books by Callahan, Weems, Kirk Hardaway, and Peter Steinke are a good place to start. On being missional, see Gary V. Nelson, *Borderland Churches: a Congregation's Introduction to Missional Living*, (St. Louis: Chalice Press, 2008). Kendall Clark Baker's idea of "organizing pastor" fits well with this understanding – Baker, *When Faith Invades the Public Square*.

counselors there is safety" (Prov. 11:14). Although these two terms are often listed as separate gifts (administration and leadership), both terms describe people called of God to guide the church in its affairs so that the people of God remain true to their calling and purpose. Paul calls on those gifted and called to lead and guide the congregation to do so with diligence (Rom. 12:8).

With both terms, *kubernesis* and *prohistamenos*, Paul affirms the necessity of strong leaders. The leaders for the church are people who have the vision and personal qualities to pilot the church as it navigates the waters of a sometimes hostile, sometimes skeptical, and often confused but hurting world. Such leaders work to bring people together, to encourage them to discover their own gifts and callings, and help them mobilize for ministry in the world. True Christian leaders do not try to lord it over others, but at the same time they attend to their task with diligence and strength of conviction.

Leadership gifts can be seen in the life of Elisabeth, a young woman who joined the small church where I once served. She helped organize and guide the congregation's young adult group so that it could grow and serve the congregation and community. Not only did she help them plan social events, but she encouraged the group to begin service projects. Over time, new people began to join the group, and she also began to take on other roles in the church. Eventually, she was hired in a part time capacity to work with the children. Her ability to encourage, envision, equip, and empower members of the group truly gave evidence of the Spirit's presence.

Apostle/Missionary (apostolos)

In traditional Christian thinking there were twelve apostles, plus one (Paul). They were given a unique and unrepeatable founding role. Their number symbolized the twelve tribes of Israel and their calling was to bear eyewitness testimony to the resurrected Christ (Acts 1:21-26; 1 Cor. 9:1). If the definition of an apostle is

Unfettered Spirit

limited to being an eyewitness of the resurrection, then this gift is truly extinct. There is, however, another way of understanding this gift. We can best understand the apostolic gift if we look to Paul's own missionary calling, and extrapolate from it the foundations of a ministry focused on pioneering church planting. Living as we do in an increasingly unchurched world, even in predominantly Christian nations, this missionary gift is especially needed. There's a need for women and men who are gifted and called to plant new communities of faith that can both flourish and make a real difference in their communities.

In the age of Christendom, we imagined the work of a missionary to take place in a far off land, such as Asia or Africa. We think of people like Paul, St. Columba, William Carey, and Mary Slessor, men and women who crossed cultural boundaries to bear witness to the good news of Jesus. But there are boundary crossing ministries that are possible in our own back yard as well. Consider the possibility of creating an intentional community in an urban setting, where a group of Christians live together in community investing themselves in the wider community. The New Monastic Movement is a good example of this.[94]

If we understand this gift to be that of missionally creating new communities of faith, for new and often untouched peoples – and young adults living in the United States are as much an untouched people as any group living in another country – this is a gift that is very much present for today.

Pastor (poimenas)

When you read Ephesians 4:11-12 you come across pastors and teachers who are called upon to "equip the saints for the work of the ministry." Is this a reference to a spiritual gift or an office?

---

94   On the nature and purpose of intentional community, including the new monasticism, see the book by David Janzen – *The Intentional Christian Community Handbook: For Idealists, Hypocrites, and Wannabe Disciples of Jesus*, (Brewster, MA: Paraclete Press, 2012).

Could it be both? Could you be gifted at pastoral care and not be ordained to the leadership office of pastor?

As an office, the church has understood the role of the pastor as that of "minister of word (preaching) and sacrament (celebrant of the Eucharist and baptism)." Thomas Oden, in his definitive book on classical pastoral theology, defines the role of the pastor in these very terms.

> "The pastor," concisely defined, is a member of the body of Christ who is called by God and the church and set apart by ordination representatively to proclaim the Word, to administer the sacraments, and to guide and nurture the Christian community toward full response to God's self-disclosure.[95]

This has been the definitive definition of the pastorate since Pope Gregory I. Such a ministry has its place in the context of the gift-based church, but it doesn't seem to exhaust the meaning of what it means to be gifted as a pastor.

When you look at the nature of pastoral care – ministries of encouragement, counseling, intercessory prayer – you realize that there is more to it than just an administrative church office. Pastors (whether clergy or lay) offer solace to the grieving, guidance to the struggling, support to the uncertain. One's effectiveness in such ministry, of course, is related to one's level of training and education. Those with the pastoral gift could engage in ministries of visitation, counseling, and the giving of comfort. They might lead grief groups or serve in hospitals as chaplain's assistants. Those gifted in this area might serve as elders or as part of a pastoral visitation team. Stephen Ministries is a wonderful program of training and support for non ordained Christians to take part in a full range of church ministries. Selection/invitation to join in such teams is related to recognition – whether internal or external – of giftedness to share in ministry with the elderly, the sick and injured,

---

95 Thomas Oden, *Pastoral Theology: Essentials of Ministry*, (San Francisco: Harper & Row, Publishers, 1983), 50.

Unfettered Spirit

the grieving, and the struggling.[96] The possibilities are many, and worth pursuing.

Discernment (diakrisis)

Healthy communities of faith need people with gifts of discernment. But, what is this gift of discernment? According to Walter Wink "discernment doesn't entail esoteric knowledge, but instead it is the gift of seeing reality as it really is."[97] Yes, faith communities need people who can see reality as it really is, so that they can recognize the difference between what is good and what is evil, what is relevant and what is irrelevant, what leads to wholeness and healing and what doesn't. As Wink also notes, such a gift of the Spirit enables one to see the spiritual dimension that lies behind the material.

Although the idea of spiritual warfare is off-putting to many Christians, especially those like me who find themselves left of center, there's something to be said for this imagery. Without discernment or the ability to see the spiritual behind the material, it's likely that we'll end up fighting spiritual battles with human weapons, even though the battle requires spiritual weapons. In the words of the author of Ephesians: "put on the whole armor of God" (Eph. 6:11), for the battle is with spiritual forces. Scripture is the Spirit's sword, the offensive weapon of choice (Eph. 6:10-17).

In a community that is open to the leading of the Spirit, there is great need for the gift of discernment to be present. This is doubly necessary in a community comprised largely of converts (1 Cor. 10:20) who might be easily led astray by charismatically inclined leaders. History is replete with examples of false prophets and false messiahs, with Jim Jones and David Koresh being good examples. It is, therefore, important that the church have the ability to distinguish between what is true and honorable and what isn't. Paul

---

96 There are a number of good foundational training sessions and structures for lay pastor, including the Stephen Ministry program.

97 Walter Wink, *Engaging the Powers: Discernment and Resistance in a World of Domination*, (Minneapolis: Fortress Press, 1992), 89.

called on the church to consider carefully the words of the prophets, to determine the source of these words (I Cor. 14:29). But it's not only the "prophetic" that requires discernment. Every day the church faces important issues that challenge its identity and purpose: politics, culture, human self-centeredness. Who will help the church remain true to its purpose and calling? Who will help them discern whether they're hearing an authentic word from God or a word that emerges from within our own self-centeredness, or even a word that has a more dark and sinister source? Other questions that might be raised by those who are spiritually sensitive include: Does this word comport well with what is known of God? What is the fruit of the one who brings the message?

The church must have the tools to test (*dokimazō*) the spirits (1 John 4:1-6). Those gifted for the ministry of discernment must rely on God's spirit and work in the context of the community. Criteria for this ministry of discernment may include "common sense, shared community values, or a set of doctrinal standards."[98] Throughout history the church has looked to creeds, the 'Rule of faith" (*Regula fidei)*, and to Scripture for guidance in discerning the voice of the Spirit. At the center of the process of discernment is one's fidelity to Jesus as Lord. Paul declared that no one speaking by the Spirit would deny the Lordship of Christ (1 Cor. 12:3). Those gifted and called to this ministry will be of great assistance to the church, but their ministry must be undertaken in love. Indeed, it requires a distinct humility to hear and consider various perspectives. This isn't a ministry to be engaged in lightly, for the Spirit moves as the wind and so great attention must be given to the ways of the Spirit of God.

---

[98] Cecil M. Robeck, "Discerning the Spirit in the Life of the Church," in *The Church in the Movement of the Spirit,* William R. Barr and Rena M. Yocom, eds., (Grand Rapids: Wm. B. Eerdmans Publishing Co., 1994), 34-35, 39-40.

Thought Questions

1. What is the definition of leadership from a Christian perspective?

2. How would a Spirit-centered or Spirit-empowered leadership look like?

3. What does the ministry of apostle look like and how might the church give support to this missional form of ministry?

4. We think of pastor as an office, in what way might it be a spiritual gift? If it is a spiritual-gift how might one use this gift in service inside and outside church?

5. The final leadership gift is that of discernment. What is this gift and how might it be used in the life of the church? What are some examples you've seen in the life of the church?

7

Gifts of Word

> My Little children in the Lord God Almighty, this is my joy that you all be ordered and guided by the mighty power of God. Know that Voice that speaks, the sound of the words, and the power of them. For words without power destroy the simplicity, bring up into a form and out of obedience of the Truth. Therefore, walk in the power of the Truth that the name of the Lord God may be glorified among you, his renown may be seen in you and among you, and all the world maybe astonished, and the Lord admired in the ordering of his people who are guided by his wisdom.
>
> George Fox[99]

Words have the power and potency to both create and destroy. John's gospel opens with the declaration: "In the beginning was the Word, and the Word was with God, and the Word was God." Everything, John seems to say, has its beginning in this Word of God, a Word that took flesh and made a life among us, and in doing so this enfleshed Word revealed the nature and the purpose of God to humanity (Jn. 1:1ff). Yes, the word has great potency. It's as Frederick Buechner notes:

> Words are power, essentially the power of creation. By my words I both discover and create who I am. By my words

---

[99] George Fox in *Devotional Classics,* Richard J. Foster and James Bryan Smith, eds., (San Francisco: HarperSanFrancisco, 1993), 219.

I elicit a word from you. Through our converse we create each other.[100]

There is both the possibility of creation and destruction in the words we speak. The tongue, as James so aptly reminds us, is like a fire that sets ablaze the forest (James 3:5-6). Therefore the tongue must be controlled so that it can do good rather than ill.

Gifts of word involve all manner of speech and communication. Through them God creates new life and new possibilities for humanity. When used with discernment and care, words can offer praise to God and grace to those who share life with us. In this category of gifts I include prophecy, wisdom, knowledge, teaching, exhortation, evangelism, intercessory prayer, tongues, and interpretation of tongues, music, and witness/martyrdom. Each gift provides an opportunity for God's voice to be made known in the world. They can be part of our lives for a season or a lifetime, but each gift is an expression of the Spirit who blows where the Spirit wishes.

Since gifts normally emerge out of the church, the church plays a central role in enabling this word of God to go forth into the world. Discernment is necessary, because not everyone claiming to speak for God has a word from God. There is a constant warning against false prophets who speak on their own behalf or on behalf of powers other than God. Their words may sometimes sound pious and enticing, but they can be quite destructive to the common good. For this reason, Paul told the Corinthian church to let the prophets speak, but then have the congregation weigh what was said (1 Cor. 14:29). The first letter of John offers similar advice, calling on the churches to "test the spirits to see whether they are from God; for many false prophets have gone out into the world" (1 Jn. 4:1). The criterion for knowing if a word is from God is threefold: Confession of Jesus as Lord (1 Cor. 12:3; 1 Jn. 4:2), love (1 Cor. 13:1-3); and benefit to the body (1 Cor. 14:3-5). You

---

100 Frederick Buechner, *Wishful Thinking*, rev. ed., (San Francisco: Harper-Collins, 1993), 121.

Unfettered Spirit

could say that this process of evaluation involves a combination of common sense and inspired insight.[101]

Prophet (prophētēs)

In the popular imagination, modern prophets are half-crazed schizophrenic pronouncers of doom. They inhabit street corners wearing sandwich boards, uttering nonsense about UFO's, earthquakes, and nuclear attacks. Like the psychic, such prophets usually speak of the future in fatalistic terms. Caught up into spiritual ecstasy, they lose control, but such is not to be the case with the prophets who speak a word from God to the Christian community. According to Paul's instructions to the prophets at Corinth, the spirit of the prophet is under the control of the prophet. This is because God is not a God of disorder but of peace (1 Cor. 14:32-33).

If we're to understand the prophetic gift it's helpful to get a sense of what a prophet is and does. The place to see what a prophet is and does is to look to the Hebrew Bible, where we find the words and descriptions of prophets such as Amos, Elijah, Jeremiah and Isaiah. Walter Brueggemann offers this helpful description of prophetic ministry.

> [P]rophetic proclamation is an attempt to imagine the world as though YHWH – the creator of the world, the deliverer of Israel, the Father of our Lord Jesus Christ whom we Christians come to name as Father, Son, and Spirit – were a real character and an effective agent in the world. [102]

Brueggemann notes that contrary to both conservative and liberal perspectives, biblical prophets neither predict events nor are they social activists. Instead, the prophet helps stir the imagination so that we can see where and how God is at work in the world.

---

101 James D. G. Dunn, *The Christ and the Spirit,* Vol. 2, "Pneumatology," (Grand Rapids: Wm. B. Eerdmans Publishing Co., 1998), 278-81.
102 Walter Brueggemann, *The Practice of Prophetic Imagination: Preaching an Emancipating Word,* (Minneapolis: Fortress Press, 2012), 2.

Now, it's true, that the prophetic word tends to be counter-cultural and prophets often "cross swords" with the powers that be. Prophets tend to open up our vision to the world as it is and the direction we're heading. In other words, prophets tend to have a long view, rather than a short one. What is clear is that the idea that the prophet speaks unerringly about the future relies on a fatalistic view of the world, one that isn't shared by scripture.

If we look at the prophets at work, we do see them challenging social and political problems in society. We see this in Amos's statements of judgment on a people that engaged systemic abuses of the poor and marginalized. Thus, he charged his own people with selling "the righteous for silver, and the needy for a pair of sandals" (Amos 2:6). He warns of the nation's impending destruction, but with his warning comes a word of hope: "seek the Lord and live" (Amos 5:5-6).

I think we can see the spirit of these biblical prophets in the work of people such as Desmond Tutu, Martin Luther King, Jr., and Oscar Romero. These are figures, two of whom were assassinated, who were led by the Spirit to speak out, and as a result they force us to recognize the presence of social and political evils in our midst and call on us to take action. All of us are called to speak out against injustice, though not all are equipped and commissioned for a leading role.

There is the second form of prophetic activity, that of the visionary, which can be seen in passages of Isaiah and Ezekiel. In the words of these prophets, one finds statements of hope and promise of a new beginning. A day is coming, they say, when the people will walk with their God and peace will reign. This will be a day when the wolf and the lion will lie down together without fear.

In churches today we often talk about the need for vision, but usually what we mean is that we need to draw up a mission statement and a plan of action that will lead to church growth. It's a vision that is focused on our own existence – growth in numbers and the expansion of the budget. Visioning that is truly prophetic pushes us as individuals and as congregations to look at the world

Unfettered Spirit

in a new way. It's as Brueggemann suggests, practicing the prophetic imagination. Although even the call to be missional can be self-serving. In principle the idea of being missional envisions moving the congregation beyond the borders of its usual experience to engage the world outside the walls of the church in ways that transform the community around it. This takes visionary leadership – people who can describe and define what the world outside the walls of the church looks like and how they might engage it in effective ways.

A visionary word can define a pathway whereby the community of faith can own its calling to feed the hungry, enable the jobless to find jobs, and the homeless find homes. A visionary word can help guide the community in becoming partners with God in this process. Although the idea of being a "community organizer" has received bad press, a visionary is one who is able to organize the community to do the work of God in the world.[103]

When Martin Luther King cried out those famous words "I have a dream," he was offering a vision for a nation influenced by a spiritual heritage. King called on the nation to look beyond the surface to find a common humanity upon which to build a future. As a result of this visioning of a new community of neighbors, the politicians enacted important civil rights legislation. It also pushed Christians to look inside their churches and see if they were more a part of the problem than a solution. I wish I could say that this process has been a roaring success, but perhaps we need to take the long view and recognize that God's vision of a redeemed and transformed culture takes time and courage to implement.

There's a third way of understanding the prophetic gift. Interestingly enough, it's probably the one we're most familiar with, even if we don't equate it with the work of a prophet. If the prophetic gift is seen as the offering of a word from God by an "inspirited" person,

---

103 On the work of congregation-based community organizing, see Kendall Clark Baker's *When Faith Storms the Public Square: Mixing Religion and Politics Through Community Organizing to Enhance Our Democracy,* (Cleveland: Circle Books, 2011).

then the definition should incorporate the work of the preacher. As an inspired person, such a prophet brings to the community a word of love, consolation, challenge, or instruction. Such prophets inhabit the pulpits of our churches when they seek to build the faith of God's people through careful and sound teaching. We find these qualities in the teachings of Jesus and Paul, as well as in the words of history's great preachers, from John Chrysostom to Martin Luther, from Fred Craddock to Barbara Brown Taylor. True preaching speaks from the heart of God to us. As Barbara Brown Taylor writes, "Every sermon begins and ends with God." This is true because "the word of God is what a preacher wrestles within the pulpit and because it is a living word, every sermon is God's creation as well as the creation of the preacher and the congregation."[104]

Although the prophetic gift can take a variety of forms, ultimately the prophet speaks to "other people for their up building and encouragement and consolation" (1 Cor. 14:3). Such prophets help us view ourselves, our congregations, and the world around us through the eyes of God. The result of their words will be the world stopping in and recognizing that God is in this place (1 Cor. 14:25).

WORDS OF KNOWLEDGE (LOGOS GNOSEOS)

Some gifts appear to the modern reader as strange and enigmatic. Utterances of knowledge and wisdom fit this category. It's not possible to offer an exact definition for these *charisms,* and yet they stand before us waiting to be defined and used. We know from Paul's first letter to the Corinthian church that knowledge (*gnosis*) and wisdom (*sophia*) were much sought after gifts. Possession of such gifts seemed to enhance the stature of the person in the con-

---

[104] Barbara Brown Taylor, *The Preaching Life,* (Cambridge, MA: Cowley Publications, 1993), 77.

Unfettered Spirit

gregation. In spite of the problems inherent in this set of gifts, Paul sought to reclaim them for use by the church.[105]

In its original context, a word of knowledge would seem to be a word spoken about cosmic realities. That is, it's a word concerned with the spiritual dimensions that lie behind the powers and systems that reign in this world. We see this in Paul's discussion of what lies behind the material idols in Corinth (1 Cor. 8:4).[106] Such a word when offered to the church aids in discernment of the truths of faith, truths that without inspired insight remain a mystery. Such insight and words of knowledge should lead us to prayer, worship and to acts of redemption of those forces symbolized by these idols, powers, and systems.[107] Such knowledge that is Spirit-inspired builds up the lives of those it touches. The intent and purpose of this gift is defined in Colossians, which speaks of being "filled with the knowledge of God's will in all spiritual wisdom and understanding, so that you may lead lives worthy of the Lord, fully pleasing to him, as you bear fruit in every good work and as you grow in the knowledge of God" (Col. 1:9-10). This gift provides insight into the spiritual dimensions of the world so that the church might move knowledgeably forward with its ministry of unmasking and engaging the spiritualities that oppose the vision of God for the world.[108]

WORDS OF WISDOM (LOGOS SOPHIA)

There is wisdom and then there's wisdom! We should pray that God would give us a spirit of wisdom; "Therefore, I prayed, and understanding was given me; I called on God, and the spirit of wisdom came to me" (Wisd. of Sol. 7:7). But, what is meant

---

105 James D. G. Dunn, *Jesus and the Spirit*, (Philadelphia: Westminster Press, 1975), 217-18.
106 Dunn, *Jesus,* 218.
107 Montague, *Holy Spirit*, 152.
108 Walter Wink does not address the issue of the spiritual gift under consideration, but his discussion of the powers would seem to parallel this activity of the Spirit. See especially his *The Unmasking the Powers*.

here by a "word of wisdom" is more than simply a commonsensical aphorism or proverb. As a *charism* of the Spirit, it speaks to the recognition of God's activities in the world, activities that are rooted in Christ and the cross as the foundations of our wisdom (1 Cor. 1-3).[109] Such wisdom is the recognition of the nature of salvation that's rooted in the cross.[110] With this in mind, I appreciate the suggestion made by George Montague that this is likely a passing moment of inspiration, by which the community receives guidance in living the Christian life in light of the cross. It's practical in that it guides us in living out "the word of salvation which brings healing to the nations."[111]

If understood as words of discernment and guidance, likely brief in nature, these would be a welcome contribution to the life of the church. One who is inspired to give such words doesn't bear special authority. As with a prophetic word, these words must be tested by the community. Their truth will be found in their application to the life of the church. Do these words help us discern true spiritual realities that need to be addressed in our families, churches, communities? Do we see the practical implications of the cross – a call to service and suffering in the world?

These are words from God, revelations of the Spirit, which may pop up at the right time, perhaps from an unexpected corner. They may come as needed guidance at a crucial time in the life of the church. These aren't gifts that can be assessed or defined with any precision; they can just be tested and received when they come to our congregations. It would seem that we'll know if this is a true word of God.

TEACHING (DIDISKON)

Teachers serve an essential role in the life of the church, for they're the ones who pass on and interpret afresh the traditions

---

109 Fee, *God's Empowering Presence*, 166; Dunn, *Jesus*, 220-21.
110 Dunn, *Jesus and the Spirit*, 220-21.
111 Montague, *Holy Spirit*, 150.

Unfettered Spirit

of the Christian faith. Gifted teachers cause us to wrestle with difficult faith questions and help us discover practical implications and applications of that faith. The end result of this teaching is spiritual formation, and this formation is more crucial today than perhaps ever before. We live in an age of biblical and religious illiteracy. Some have suggested that the reigning paradigm in our congregations is Moralistic Therapeutic Deism. In other words, a majority of Americans believe in God and look to religion to make them feel good, and maybe even assist them in living well, but God really exists only in the background. For the church to become truly missional it will have to move beyond MTD to a much more robust understanding of God's presence and calling. The process of spiritual formation is designed to prepare the people of God to embrace their missional calling that is focused not just on the self, but on achieving the vision of God for the world.[112]

If spiritual formation is the key to preparing congregations for becoming missional communities, then surely Jesus offers us a model of what this Spirit-inspired process of formation would look like. He gathered a community of disciples and taught them through stories and parables that both enlightened and confounded. In the end, after the Resurrection and Pentecost this community of disciples was ready to carry the good news to the ends of the earth. Others, like Paul and Priscilla and Aquila would carry on this ministry of teaching, preparing new generations of disciples for apostolic/missional ministry. Teaching as a *charism* is revelatory in the sense that it unfolds the wisdom and knowledge of God in such a way that the people of God are prepared to join God's Spirit in bringing into existence the reign of God on earth James Dunn suggests that the teaching gift brings "new insight into an old word of God."[113] As interpreters of the text of Scripture, teachers take that word of God and make it fresh and applicable to the world at

---

112 Dwight J. Zscheile, "A Missional Theology of Spiritual Formation," in *Cultivating Sent Communities: Missional Spiritual Formation.* (Grand Rapds, MI: Wm. B. Eerdmans Publishing Co., 2012) , 2ff.
113 Dunn, *Jesus and the Spirit,* 237.

hand, so that the community is spiritually prepared to live out its mission in the world.

Gifted teachers can be found in Sunday school rooms, leading Bible studies, and teaching in seminary classrooms. At the congregational level, I have rarely experienced a teacher like Paul P. It has been many years since I participated in his church-school class, but I remember him to be a wonderfully gifted Bible teacher. He was by profession a university professor, but in this forum Paul didn't lecture. He simply led us to explore the text in a flexible yet structured environment, so that we could discover new insights and applications for our lives and for our world. While not every teacher will teach with the same finesse and power as this gifted teacher, an inspired and effective teacher will help us discover the fullness of the biblical text for our lives. Good teachers not only transmit information, they also help students discover for themselves ways of studying and applying the gospel to their own lives.

Evangelist (euaggelizō)

When we think of evangelists, the image of someone like Billy Graham immediately comes to mind. We say to ourselves – I can't do that – but that needn't be the primary model of evangelist. Evangelism is simply sharing the story of our faith in God as revealed in the person of Jesus with another person. It's a task given to every Christian, for we've all been commissioned to make disciples (Mt. 28:19-20). Evangelism is more than just words; it's a way of life that invites our neighbor to ask: "What is the source of your joy and your peace?" [114]

Many Christians are put off by the assumption that the point of evangelism is saving a person from spending eternity in hell if they don't convert. This idea makes little theological sense to persons who believe that God is just but also loving, but such a view

---

[114] On the question of evangelism a great place to start is Martha Grace Reese's series of books that begins with *Unbinding the Gospel: Real Life Evangelism*, (St. Louis: Chalice Press, 2007).

isn't required of us. The point of evangelism is offering a loving invitation to taste the relationship with God that we know in Jesus Christ. It is, Walter Brueggemann suggests, the retelling of the old story of faith in "ways that impact every aspect of our contemporary life, public and personal."[115]

The gift of evangelist is a more specialized gifting of God than what's expected of the general church. It describes a person whose focus is drawing others into relationship with God. Evangelists are often preachers, bringing an effective word of hope to a community. I'm mindful of the contribution made by Walter Scott to the founding of the movement of which I'm a member. Alexander Campbell was a great teacher, writer, and debater, but it was Scott who found a way of communicating the gospel message to the broader community. It's a gift, like that of apostle, that serves to empower those who hear the call to plant churches and cross ethnic and religious boundaries with the good news of Jesus. Although not excluding the possibility of mass evangelistic events, most likely this gift will be expressed in more personal ways that this. The focus is on building empowered missional communities that express in deed and in word the justice and the love of God for the world.

EXHORTATION/ENCOURAGEMENT (HO PARAKALON)

The name Barnabas means son of encouragement, and from the stories we find in Acts, he was definitely an encourager of others. Paul commended the runaway slave Onesimus for being an encouragement to him (Philemon).

Exhortation/encouragement, describes an ability to move people forward in life so that they remain strong in faith and service. The one who exhorts or encourages does so by the "mercies of God" (Rom. 12:1). Such a gifted person offers a word or message that inspires a community to new heights of worship and service. It's also possible that such a gift could take on a quieter form. Consider

---

115 Walter Brueggemann, *Biblical Perspectives on Evangelism: Living in a Three-Storied Universe,* (Nashville: Abingdon Press, 1993), 10-11.

John's description of the Spirit as the *Paraclete* (John 14). Therefore, just as the Spirit comes along side each of us, encouraging, empowering, and equipping us, the Spirit inspires and empowers some among us to carry on with a similar ministry. They might come alongside a discouraged, depressed, grieving person and lift them up. They could boost morale and challenge us when we begin to falter.

We find such people serving as counselors, as church elders, Stephen ministers, and members of pastoral care teams. They send cards to shut-ins, visit the sick, and stand beside others who lead. Every congregation has such persons, people who see it as their primary function to seek out those who need encouragement and draw them forward along the Christian journey.

Intercessory Prayer (enteuxis)

All prayer is Spirit-inspired and led. In fact, the Spirit is the carrier of our prayers to God (Eph. 6:18). When we can't pray as we would want, the Spirit pray on our behalf, interceding in ways that go beyond human words (Rom. 8:26-27). Thus, all prayer is charismatic activity, and as such it's a gift of the Spirit (although Paul never specifically calls prayer a *charism*).[116]

As a gifted form of ministry, we can envision the Spirit calling and empowering a narrower band of people to engage in intercessory prayer. With Abraham and Moses as models, these are people who take on a priestly role, stepping into the gap and speaking to God on behalf of another. Abraham intervened with God on behalf of Sodom and Moses on behalf of Israel, seeking to stay God's judgment. Jesus interceded for the disciples in the Garden (Jn. 17). Paul intercedes for the Colossian church, praying without ceasing that this church would be "filled with the knowledge of God's will in all spiritual wisdom and understanding." (Col. 1:9-12). The author of 1 Timothy tells a young pastor to intercede and make supplication for everyone in his purview including political leaders

---

116 Dunn, *Jesus and the Spirit*, 239-42.

Unfettered Spirit 123

(1 Tim. 2:1-2). Such an effort brings, this admonition suggests, a peaceable and quiet life.[117]

As a specific gift, intercessory prayer arises from a passion for prayer that goes beyond the norm. Such a person might devote extended amounts of time and energy lifting up those who are sick or grieve, those who exercise leadership, as well as the needs of the community and the world. In thinking about this gift my mind goes to Alice, who prayed daily for members of the congregation, for friends, community leaders. I remember her sharing how she had specifically prayed for me as the congregation's pastor when she felt like there were problems brewing in the congregation. Such people are a godsend to congregations.

As with some other gifts, this may be a gift for a season. Perhaps it's a gift that comes later in life when the active life is no longer possible, but there is time and energy available to devote to intercessory conversations with God.

Music

In the words of Paul: "I will sing praise with the spirit, but I will sing praise with the mind also" (1 Cor. 14:15). Singing, in Paul's understanding, is an activity of the Spirit, and by extension it's possible to consider musicianship, instrumental and vocal, as acts of the Spirit. The Psalms witness to the importance of song. "Sing a new song" the Psalmists say time and again. The 150th Psalm breaks out in joyous praise to God, inviting the orchestra of trumpet, lute, harp and Tambourines, strings, pipe and clanging symbol, to join in praise of God. Surely this is a *charism* of God!

I know of no better example of the inspired musician than my former music director, Harold. We weren't a large church and we didn't have great resources, just a few children and adults willing to lend an instrument and a voice. Nevertheless, he had the abil-

---

117 For a description of intercessory prayer, see Richard Foster, *Prayer: Finding the Heart's True Home,* (San Francisco: Harper Collins, 1992), 191-201.

ity, the gift, to lift our spirits into the presence of God. He knew, indeed he knows, how to let people break out in praise and make melody in their hearts before God. His ministry helps us understand that music in the Spirit is more than simply artistry, though that is involved. Spirited music lifts the souls of the congregation into the presence of God, baring their souls before their creator.

Music is often called the window of the soul, because it allows God's people to express what is on their hearts to God much more easily than with simple spoken prayer. David is said to have soothed the soul of Saul through his music (1 Sam. 16:16-18) and the Chronicler says that the Levitical singers and musicians brought praise to God (2 Chron. 5:12-13; 34:12). There's no biblically prescribed form of music. Neither organ nor guitar is holier than the other. What makes music holy is its ability to convey to the heart the gracious love of God lifting our spirit's into the presence of God. Sometimes such music will soothe the soul and others it will invigorate the spirit. Although many can sing and even play musical instruments, there are those whose gifts/abilities allow them to touch our souls in ways that move us toward the presence of God. As worshipers we're indebted to people like Isaac Watts, Charles Wesley, Brian Wren, Bach and Handel for the music that carries our spirits Godward. We're also indebted to the musicians and singers in our congregations who lead us into God's presence, musicians and singers who can step back and let the focus move from them to the divine audience, the one who is the giver of this precious gift of music.

Tongues (glossalalia)

Speaking in Tongues has been a distinctive mark of the Pentecostal and Charismatic movements since the beginning of these movements. Some Christians believe that this gift is the singular marker of the baptism in the Spirit. That is, if one is truly filled with the Holy Spirit they will give evidence of this presence with the gift of tongues. It does appear that in the book of Acts whenever an ethnic/religious barrier is crossed something akin to speaking in tongues occurs (Acts 2, 8, 10, 19). Thus, when Peter defended before the Jerusalem church his decision to baptize Cornelius and his household, he pointed to their common experience of speaking in tongues as confirmation that God had chosen to bring Gentiles into the church (Acts 11:16). There is, however, no pattern here that would suggest that this is *the* foundational and therefore essential sign of the Spirit's presence.

When we look at the various discussions of *glossalalia* in the New Testament, we don't find any definitive statement as to what it is. There's a significant gap between what we find in Acts and in 1 Corinthians 12-14. In Acts it appears that these are human languages or dialects known to the listener, but not the speaker. In 1 Corinthians we have ecstatic speech. Although this form of *glossalalia* doesn't appear to be unique to the Christian community, Paul wants to reclaim it for his community, especially since the church in Corinth valued it so highly. Paul's primary concern in this discussion is the possibility of schism. This gift was of little value if it served to divide the community and undermined the community's spiritual vibrancy.

What's unique about *glossalalia* is that unlike almost every other gift, it appears to benefit the recipient not the community. This may be why it has often been a popular gift – whether in Corinth or in many modern Christian circles. Although it might have such a blessing to the individual, Paul told the Corinthians that *glossalalia* would only become a blessing to the broader community only when interpreted. It's for this reason that Paul prefers prophecy over tongues – prophecy can be understood by all who hear it. Still, Paul can claim the gift for himself, but offers counsel on its proper and orderly use in the church. His counsel is this – if no one present is able to offer an interpretation (see below), then the one who feels led to offer a tongue should offer it to God and not to the community. In this sense, it may be seen as an expression of a personal, albeit nonrational, form of prayer.

Whether or not we have experienced for ourselves this gift of the Spirit, anecdotal evidence suggests that it can be a powerful ingredient in a person's spiritual life. I myself have experienced this gift, and while I've found it to be helpful in my own spiritual walk, I'm not convinced that it's essential means of communication with God through the Spirit. I would share Jürgen Moltmann's view of this gift:

It would seem to me that speaking with tongues is an inward possession by the Spirit which is so strong that it can no longer find expression in comprehensible language, and breaks out into sighing, shouting and incomprehensible speech – just as intense pain expresses itself in unrestrained weeping, or overwhelming joy in laughing, "jumping for Joy" and dancing.[118]

As for me, I have drawn on this gift at moments when I'm overwhelmed by a need or experience, and I've found it to be a source of strength. My sense is that this has been true for others. While not a necessary part of one's spiritual life, it can prove to be beneficial for some. But, if this gift is to have value it can't be seen as a spiritual prize according to the recipient some special status before God. The reason for the gifts is the up building of the body of Christ, and even if this has a more personal usage, it can't be the end but only a means to building up that body of Christ for the work of the ministry.

INTERPRETATION OF TONGUES

Paul made it clear that without an interpreter one should not publicly engage in speaking in tongues. If an interpreter (*hermēnia glōssōn*) isn't present, then this message incased in odd sounding syllables should be kept private. Without an interpretation a tongue is addressed to God not the community, because any message to the community requires clarity (1 Cor. 14:13-19). When one is present who has the interpretation, then it can be shared with the congregation, which must receive it with discernment.

---

118 Moltmann, *Source of Life*, 61.

Unfettered Spirit

If, as many presume, the form of tongues described by Paul is sub-rational ecstatic speech, then the interpretation that's offered isn't really a translation. Instead, as Anthony Thistleton suggests, it's "an intelligible description of the pre-conceptual mood or attitude which is expressed in tongues."[119] In other words, the tongue grabs your attention, while the interpretation offers the message that God seeks to make known to the community. The tongue may serve then to catch the ear, so that the "interpretation" can communicate the message of God with clarity of voice. When properly vetted by the community, then this word will stand as a gift from God.

Each community of faith must come to grips with these twin gift sets. History suggests caution should be in order. Perhaps the use of these gifts is best left to the small groups, as long as participants don't lose sight of the one who provides the gift. I would assume that public use of this gift would be disruptive, but it can also be disruptive if the small groups themselves begin to take on airs of spiritual importance. Therefore, any usage of this gift must keep the community's welfare in mind. Those who aren't so gifted should also keep in mind the biblical charge to refrain from stifling the movement of God's Spirit. The key is respecting the good of the community.

MARTYRDOM (MARTYS)

Jesus, Oscar Romero, Martin Luther King, Jr., and Dietrich Bonhoeffer seem to define for us martyrdom. Although not as well known to many readers, persons like Perpetua, an early Christian martyr who stood firm in her faith even as she was thrown into the gladiatorial arena, has a powerful story worth considering.[120] In the end, every death that removes a person of faith from our lives causes us to consider our own sense of mortality and life vocation. There are those who knowingly plan their own funerals in such a

---

119 A.C. Thistleton, "ἑρμηνευω" in Brown, *NIDNTT,* 1:582.
120 See Amy Oden, *In Her Words: Women's Writings in the History of Christian Thought,* (Nashville: Abingdon Press, 1991), 26-37.

way that a witness to God's grace and purpose is made known. That was definitely the case with Alice.

When we think of martyrs, however, we think of those whose lives are taken from them because of their witness to the coming reign of God in the world. Oscar Romero, for instance, was gunned down while celebrating the Eucharist in the cathedral in San Salvador. His death caused a nation to reconsider the social and economic divisions present in the land. When we think of such people we see in their lives and in their deaths examples of active nonviolent resistance to evil with a view to redeeming and transforming the human community.[121]

If a gift (*charism*) can be conceived of as an event in time rather than as a talent that's possessed, it's possible to view such an act as a sign of the Spirit's presence. Consider Stephen's willingness to boldly testify to his faith in Jesus in the face of an angry mob set on stoning him to death (Acts 6:8-7:59). Romero and Bonhoeffer offer examples of persons who die at least in part due to their decision to stand up for those on the margins – whether the poor (Romero) or Jews (Bonhoeffer). Probably neither man would consider themselves to be martyrs, and this is especially true of Bonhoeffer who was imprisoned because of his participation in efforts to assassinate Adolph Hitler (not an act of nonviolent resistance). But the very fact that their deaths continue to inspire us suggests that they were and are martyrs for the realm of God.

Although we usually think of martyrdom in terms of heroic deaths, this needn't be the only definition of martyr. The Greek word *martys* simply means witness. Thus, we can see this gift in action as Peter and John risk death in the name of a cause, but the event of martyrdom need not always end in death. This was bravely speak before the Sanhedrin (Acts 5:27-42) or in the efforts of medieval Catholic missionary Ramon Lull to share the gospel with the Muslims of North Africa. According to stories about his life, Lull went directly into the center of a North African community

---

121 On the practice of non-violent action of resistance to evil, see Walter Wink, *The Powers that Be,* (New York, Galilee Books, 1998), 114-27.

and preached the gospel. He gained converts and eventually faced execution, but what made him a martyr was not his death but his witness in the face of danger.

No one goes into life with the expectation of dying for their faith, but it's always a possibility when we face times when being true to our faith can lead to death. Martyrdom is a gift of Word in that it bears witness to God's grace, even if no word is ever spoken. We can take comfort in knowing that when these times arise, God will be with us.

Gifts of Word are a powerful testimony to the Spirit's presence in our lives, in our churches, and in our communities. In whatever form these gifts take, they speak to God's desire to bring all humanity back into relationship with God and with all of creation.

Thought Questions

1. Think of the ways in which you have heard words spoken in a church or religious context – when have you sensed that they were spirit-inspired?

2. There are three basic ways in which the word "prophet" can be understood. Discuss each and talk about how you have experienced these gifts in a church setting.

3. Evangelist is presented as a gift – consider the possible differences between a general call to share the good news (evangelism) and the work of an evangelist.

4. Music is mentioned here as a gift of word – discuss ways in which music and musicians might be understood to be Spirit-guided and inspired. Share your own experiences.

5. In what ways can you envision yourself as a martyr – that is, a person gifted in such a way that you can stand firm in your faith despite the possibility of death or imprisonment?

8

Gifts of Service

> Called as partners in Christ's service,
> called to ministries of grace,
> we respond with deep commitment,
> fresh new lines of faith to trace.
> May we learn the art of sharing,
> side by side and friend with friend,
> equal partners in our caring to fulfill God's chosen end.
>
> Jane Parker Huber[122]

Jane Parker Huber's hymn reminds us that at the heart of Christian life is a call to serve Christ in service to our neighbors She speaks of learning "the art of sharing, side by side and friend with friend, equal partners in our caring to fulfill God's chosen end." In discerning our gifts we discover how and where we should work with our sisters and brothers to "fulfill God's chosen end."

Diakonia, the Greek word for ministry and service – along with related words – reminds us that every gift and every ministry is devoted to the service of Christ and the world, whether it's a gift of word, leadership, power, or support. To be a leader, a prophet, a pastor, or a teacher, is to be a servant. Jesus defines his own ministry as one of service and he becomes a servant to his disciples by washing their feet (Jn. 13).

---

[122] Jane Parker Huber, "Called as Partners in Christ's Service," *Chalice Hymnal,* (St. Louis: Chalice Press, 1995), 453.

Still, there are other forms of giftedness that undergird and support the more visible ministries of the church. They're the behind the scenes efforts, without which nothing would get accomplished. These ministries are often overlooked by members or deemed less important to the church's missional calling. A person might offer this answer to the question: Do you have a ministry? No, I just take care of the babies in the nursery, or I just wash the dishes. Paul makes it clear that "the members of the body that seem to be weaker are indispensable, and those members of the body that we think less honorable we clothe with greater honor, and our less respectable members are treated with greater respect; whereas our more respectable members do not need this" (1 Cor. 12:22-24). Even those persons, whose ministries tend not to get noticed, deserve honor and respect, for they too help make a difference in the world. I've gathered together this set of gifts – service/ministry/assistance/helps, giving, compassion, celibacy, and craftsmanship – under the heading of gifts of service.

Ministry/Service/Helps (diakonia/antilēmpseis)

We've already noted that the word *diakonia* can be translated as ministry or service (Romans 12:7). A related term is *antilēmpseis*, which can be translated as assistance or helps. These two words often describe the provision of practical service. It could be service rendered to a person in need or in supportive capacities. As to the former, gifts of service and assistance, remind us of responsibility for the care of the indigent and the destitute, both inside the church (Acts 4:32-37) and outside the church. History is full of examples of people who have given of themselves to the poor and the needy. Mother Teresa and Albert Schweitzer serve as exemplars of service. They left behind the possibility of living comfortable lives to care for those who are in need of comfort, support, and healing. This is a gift that empowers people to give themselves fully to the work of homeless shelters or hospices. Not only are they able to fulfill these responsibilities, but they passionately give of themselves to feeding or bathing ones who are unable to do this for themselves. Because of these ministries, the church touches the least of Christ's brothers and sisters (Mt. 25:40).

There are also the gifts and callings of those who work behind the scenes to make the congregation a hospitable, welcoming, and inclusive place of worship and service. You may also find them trimming a hedge for an elderly person or driving a shut-in to the doctor. If something needs to get done, they make sure it happens. Though such people rarely make headlines, you know when they're absent. We might consider these to be humble, menial tasks that "anyone can do," and yet, unless they're attended to by diligent and competent hands, these tasks fall through the cracks. If someone is busy cleaning up dishes and making sure everything is in its place, we might suggest that this person is playing the role of Martha, who is busy in the kitchen while her sister Mary sits at the Master's feet. Although Jesus gently rebukes Martha for insisting that her sister join her in preparing the supper, without Martha's attention to the details of the meal, Jesus would not have been fed.

Bill exemplified the spirit of this ministry, always getting to church early to make sure everything was ready to go – the lights, the communion, and the windows. If there was a meal, he'd be in there washing the dishes and getting everything put away. With Martha and Bill in mind, could there not be a gift of the Spirit that encourages their sensitivity to the needs of the moment?[123]

GIVERS/GIVING (METADIDOMI)

Stewardship is a foundational practice of Christian life to which everyone is called. Stewardship supports the ministries of the church and extends its ministries of caring to the world. Paul calls on the members of the church to give cheerfully and not out of obligation (2 Cor. 9:7) in response to the bountiful gifts of God.

---

123 George Montague, *The Holy Spirit: Growth of a Biblical Tradition*, (New York: Paulist Press, 1976), 160-61.

Mindful of Jesus' request that the rich young man sell everything and give the proceeds to the poor (Lk 12:32), a directive that few of us feel compelled to embrace, we must consider that there is a range of giving that goes beyond the minimum, a kind of giving that comes not as a duty but as a passion. These are the kinds of people who often serve in the background, not calling attention to themselves or their gifts. Paul encourages them in their giving by calling on them to continue giving generously (Rom. 12:8).

One need not be wealthy to be a gifted giver, that is, a philanthropist of spiritual dimensions. Jesus contrasted the widow who gave her last few coins to the temple with the wealthy religious leaders who trumpeted their gifts, which paled in comparison with the sacrificial giving of the poor widow (Mk. 12:41; Lk 21:1-4). Whether you have amassed great wealth so as to endow ministries that will last years or you are a little girl who gives a whole fifty-seven cents to build a church, when the gift comes from the heart and leads to changed lives, then it's a sign of giftedness. The gifted giver gives generously without any concern for themselves or with attaching strings to the gift. The only requirement is that the gift be used in ways that express God's love for the world.

Compassion/Mercy (eleōn)

Compassion and mercy are the heart of Christian faith, and yet there are some who seemingly by nature are able to provide compassionate care for those who grieve, are sick or dying, or live on the margins of society (Rom. 12:8). Such a person might be drawn to one of the caring professions, such as medicine, social work, psychology, and hospital or hospice chaplaincy. They serve without regard for a recipient's gender, ethnicity, religious background, sexual orientation, or economic status. Mother Theresa's work with the lepers of India, and nineteenth century Belgian Catholic priest Father Damian's work with the lepers of Molokai, exemplify this kind of spirit. Albert Schweitzer's commitment to practicing medicine in Africa, even though he was a well regarded biblical scholar and musician in Europe.

In our churches, such a person might volunteer at the hospital, serve with hospice, join a pastoral care team visiting the homebound or the hospitalized, or host a grief group. This isn't a matter of office, but of opportunity to serve. Inherent in such a person is a cheerful and supportive disposition, along with a passion for healing of persons. By their very presence the person of compassion gives hope to the one who is hurting.

Celibacy

Since we live in an age where sexual fulfillment isn't just a right, it's almost a duty. Sex is used to sell everything from hamburgers to cars, so the thought that someone might voluntarily remain celibate – not just sexually chaste outside marriage, but committed to a life of devotion to God alone – seems odd, even unnatural. Yet Paul suggests that it might be best if all were gifted as he was, so that they might remain single and available for the tasks of the gospel without the distractions of family (1 Cor. 7:7-8, 32-35).

Paul's admonition to consider celibacy isn't easy to interpret. He may have had in mind the difficulties of raising a family in the midst of the uncertainties of the age, an age he believed would end cataclysmically. But, the passage also speaks to the freedom that the single person has to devote herself or himself to service. As a married father, I have had to keep in mind the needs of my wife and son, but if I were single I would be responsible only for myself.

Now celibacy is not a prerequisite for ministry, but it does offer freedom to serve. Therefore, celibacy isn't simply about chastity outside marriage, rather it's a *charism* that enables a person to forgo the intimate relationships of family for a life of service. However, neither marriage nor singleness should be considered the ideal, some marry and some don't. Among those who are single, some have been called to give of themselves more fully to the ministry of the realm of God by taking upon themselves the discipline of celibacy.[124]

CRAFTSMANSHIP

Bev's ability to create beautiful vestments and paraments for the church, Harry's knack of creating just what is needed by the church, from a cabinet lock to an advent wreath, or Lance's ability to take an idea and bring it to life in wood, give evidence of a gift of craftsmanship. If you have the ability to work with your hands and create something of value and beauty, that's truly a gift from God. Whether the medium is wood or fabric, steel or marble, clay or glass, works of art or works of utility, when they are created for the benefit of God's people and for the glory of God they are signs of the Spirit's presence. In the book of Exodus, Bezalel and Oholiab stand out as people filled with the "divine spirit, with ability, intelligence, and knowledge of every kind of craft" (Ex. 31:1-11). Although the work on the tabernacle involved human hands, it was also a work of the Spirit who inspired and empowered the workers. Bezalel and Oholiab have their modern descendants in the people in our churches, who filled with the Spirit of God, possess the abilities in every kind of craft and use these abilities to further the work of God's people.

Perhaps these same gifts used to create sacred spaces can also be used to build homes for the homeless, make clothes for those in need of clothes, or beautify spaces made ugly by neglect and pollutants. All this might be done to transform the world into the beauty that God sees in our midst.

---

124 John Koenig, *Charismata: God's Gifts for God's People*, (Philadelphia: Westminster Press, 1978), 102. Siegfried Schatzmann, *A Pauline Theology of Charismata*, (Peabody, MA: Hendrickson Publishers, Inc., 1987), 28-29. Concerning Paul's view of celibacy, there's much debate as to its intent and its application, thus one might be well-served in contemplating the questions raised by Jennifer Wright Knust in *Unprotected Texts: The Bible's Surprising Contradictions about Sex and Desire*, (San Francisco: Harper One, 2011), 81-83.

Hospitality (philoxenos)

Hospitality is more than knowing how to set out a proper table or cook a nice meal. Hospitality is the vocation of making the stranger feel welcome, of sharing love for the stranger. It's a willingness to welcome Jesus into our homes and our lives (Jn. 1:10-11). In Leviticus instruction is given for welcoming the alien: "The alien who resides with you shall be to you as the citizen among you; you shall love the alien as yourself, for you were aliens in the land of Egypt: I am your God" (Lev. 19:33-34). Paul reaffirmed this message and called for we who are God's children to "extend hospitality to the strangers" (Rom. 12:13).

Hospitality is at the heart of the Christian experience. The Lord's Table stands as a beacon of welcome (or at least it should). Jesus bids the stranger to come to the table to share in bread and cup, signs of his presence among us. Each of us is called to share in the ministry of hospitality, in welcoming the stranger to the table of our churches and our homes (Mt. 25:34-35). Hospitality is a pattern of inclusion of others, and so it's far more than simply throwing a party for one's closest friends and family.

In the life of the church, hospitality is more than hosting a coffee hour or potluck dinner. The gift of hospitality is directed at providing a place of welcome at the table for the stranger (Rom. 12:13). Throughout his letters Paul commends those such as Gaius (Rom. 16:23) and Stephanas, Fortunatus and Achaicus (1 Cor. 16:17) who had shown him hospitality. The same is true of Lydia, who after her conversion, invited Paul and his colleagues to stay at her home (Acts 16:14-15).

So, what is the *charism* of hospitality? Could it be a Spirit-guided and empowered ministry of leadership in the area of hospitality? We all know people in our churches that have the knack of making people feel at home, even if they are strangers. Ann and Bud made their home a haven for young people needing a family and a place to stay. I may have stayed that summer in the boat house, but I had a home, a bed and meals, and another family.[125]

To push this *charism* further, there is the broader question of how we welcome the stranger, the alien, and persons whose faith is different from our own. Consider the parable of the Good Samaritan, where the stranger becomes the exemplar of hospitality. Hospitality is, therefore, a ministry and calling that expresses the church's mission in a pluralistic world. Amos Yong writes that "believers in Jesus are sustained by the hospitable God not only because they have been born again by the Holy Spirit into a new community (the body of Christ), but also because the Spirit drives them into the world, even to the ends of the earth (Acts 1:8), to interact with and receive the hospitality, kindness, and gifts of strangers of all sorts, even Samaritans, public or governmental officials, and "barbarians" (from *barbaroi* in Acts 28:2)!"[126]

VOLUNTARY POVERTY

Involuntary poverty is a tragedy of human existence that the church is called to join in the task of alleviating its blight. No one welcomes the loss of a job, home, family, or farm. That such poverty is present in our world is a sign that the powers, the institutions of government and society are fallen and in need of redemption. Poverty is a sign that the reign of God isn't yet complete.

That being said, history and scripture suggests that for some, the renunciation of the material – a vow of poverty – like the vow of chastity (celibacy), frees you for service. It's also a reminder to the church at large that the pursuit of the material is not ultimate. The early church experimented with sharing the community of goods (Acts 2:44-45; 4:34-37) and a vow of poverty (sharing of one's goods with the body) has always been part of monastic movements. Though the practice of sharing community goods does not appear

---

125 Ana Maria Pineda, "Hospitality," *Practicing Our Faith*, Dorothy Bass, ed., (San Francisco: Jossey-Bass, 1997), 29-42.
126 Amos Yong, *Hospitality & the Other: Pentecost, Christina Practices, and the Neighbor.* (Maryknoll, NY: Orbis Books, 2008), 107.

to have been long lived in the early church, their experiment does suggest some in the church might have the calling or vocation of poverty so that they might walk in identification with the person who is without.

Barnabas is portrayed – in contrast to the infamous Ananias and Sapphira – as a person who voluntarily sold everything and shared it with the church (Acts 4:36-37). Barnabas goes on to serve as Paul's missionary companion, devoting his life to the service of God. Another exemplar, Francis of Assisi, the son of a wealthy merchant gave up everything in an imitation of his Lord, taking up the life of the beggar. The person who renounces material goods and chooses to live in community reminds us that the church is called to care for those who are hungry and needy. It reminds us as well that the way of discipleship is a way of simplicity. John Cassian wrote that "one does not become perfect just by stripping naked, by being poor and despising honors unless this love of which Paul speaks is there, a love which is found in the pure of heart."[127] Jesus' statements about wealth and property, especially his call for the rich man to sell everything and give the proceeds to the poor have always presented a problem for the church (Lk. 18:18-25; Mt. 19:16-22; Mk. 10:17-22). We have asked the question: Is this a requirement for everyone? As we struggle with these questions, we may affirm that some among us have heard the call to join in community and identify with those who are without material goods, so that they might better serve the needs of the neighbor.

THOUGHT QUESTIONS

1. Discuss the concept of service in our modern context – its nature and the way it's received in our culture.

---

[127] John Cassian, "Such trifling things!" in *The Westminster Collection of Christian Meditations,* Hannah Ward and Jennifer Wild, comp. (Louisville: Westminster/John Knox Press, 1998), 360.

2. Think of examples of service, are they honored and recognized? Why/why not?

3. Two of the gifts/callings speak of celibacy and poverty. How should we understand these gifts and their place in modern society? What are some ways in which they might be present in the church?

4. The arts and craftsmanship have long been honored; especially the work of those who are masters at these callings – think of examples of such gifted persons and discuss their contributions to the life of the church and the church's missional calling.

5. Hospitality stands at the center of the Christian experience. Discuss what this is and how it's present in the church. Remember that this is more than putting on parties and coffee hours.

9

Gifts You'd Like to Avoid, but Shouldn't!

> Intercession is spiritual defiance of what is, in the name of what God has promised. Intercession visualizes an alternative future to the one apparently fated by the momentum of current contradictory forces. It infuses the air of a time yet to be into the suffocating atmosphere of the present.
>
> Walter Wink[128]

When it comes to conversations about spiritual gifts, there are some gifts, at least gifts that are listed in the New Testament, that many Christians who are children of the Enlightenment would rather avoid discussing. Living as we do in a more scientifically sophisticated age (though the increased popularity of young earth creationism might belie that description), it's not surprising that many are skeptical of claims made about extraordinary healings and other demonstrations of what some would call "supernatural power." The whole idea of an interventionist God has become problematic for many (including me). We ask, or should ask, how can a loving God intervene on behalf of one person or community and not on behalf of another? So, what do we do with these descriptions of exorcisms, healings, and miracles?[129]

---

128 Walter Wink, *Engaging the Powers, Discernment and Resistance in a World of Domination*, (Minneapolis: Fortress Press, 1992), 298.
129 See Morton Kelsey, *Healing and Christianity: A Classic Study*, 3rd ed., (Minneapolis: Augsburg Press, 1995), 6-25 for a study of Christian

These more "exotic" gifts would seem to be best left to the side, and yet if we do this, do we not limit the way in which we understand God's engagement with us as the people of God? Perhaps these gifts remind us that what we see isn't always all that there is to reality. Maybe there are spiritual dimensions, like the ones that Walter Wink speaks of, that we should attend to. So, rather than ignore or jettison these gifts, let us ask the question, how can we engage these gifts in ways that transform the external realities to reflect the spiritual ones?

As we explore such "controversial" gifts as healing, exorcism, (or even tongues and interpretation of tongues, which we discussed under gifts of Word), we can do so in light of what Walter Wink calls an "integral world view." In this view, the spiritual and the material are interrelated as a reality. They represent the inner (spiritual) and outer (material) aspects of reality.[130] Following Wink's understanding of this interrelationship of spiritual and material, it's possible to view these gifts as the means by which we spiritually engage "the powers that be," so that they can be redeemed and transformed – even if that which is redeemed and transformed is the human body (healing).[131] We may not be able to adequately explain what's happening in the lives of those touched by the Spirit,

---

opposition to spiritual healing in the church. Bruce Epperly has written widely on the topic of healing from a Progressive Christian perspective, including his most recent book on the subject – *Healing Marks*, (Gonzalez, FL: Energion Publications, 2012).

130 Wink, *Engaging the Powers*, 5-6. Marcus Borg has attempted to write a primer on a Christian spirituality of a non-interventionist God, a spirituality that does allow for healing, even if not described in "miraculous" terms. For him the sacred is more metaphor than personal/material reality. Borg, *Heart of Christianity: Rediscovering a Life of Faith*, (Harper One, *2004*).

131 Wink, *The Powers that Be,* 31ff. Marcus Borg acknowledges that Jesus understood himself to be a Spirit person who exorcized the demonic and healed the sick and affirms the credibility of that claim. Marcus Borg, *Meeting Jesus Again for the First Time*, (San Francisco: Harper San Francisco, 1993), 36.

Unfettered Spirit 143

but we can see in this act of redemption and healing the hand of God.

Claims about witnessing dramatic acts of God have punctuated different eras of revival and renewal within church history. The most recent explosion of such claims began early in the twentieth century with the Pentecostal revival. Since the earliest stirrings of Pentecostalism, that movement and its more mainstream kin, the Charismatic movement, have spread widely across the world. In Asia and Latin America, Pentecostal and Charismatic Christians make up the largest share of Protestants. Additionally, since the beginning of the 1960s the Charismatic renewal has spread to the Mainline and Catholic churches, often serving as bridges of unity across denominational lines.[132]

In introducing myself earlier in this book, I admitted, even affirmed, my own Pentecostal background. Although my journey of faith has taken me out of that circle of religious experience, I don't discount the spirituality that is present in those communities, for I have experienced it. Indeed, as I noted earlier, we're all Charismatics – that is if we are people of the Spirit. Spiritual experiences and practices that include tongues speaking, prayer for healing, and exorcisms, may seem strange to many, and yet for many others these are vital experiences of faith. Therefore, if we're to consider the full range of spiritual giftedness, we shouldn't neglect exploring this set of gifts.

Exploration of this set of gifts must be done carefully, with all due attention given to discernment. Charlatans have long played havoc among those who are naive to the possibility of deceit among those who claim spiritual authority and power. Hollywood, however, has shown us in its portrayals of the Elmer Gantrys that such a possibility should be considered. Yet there is the other side of this,

---

132 Harvey Cox, *Fire from Heaven: The Rise of Pentecostalism and the Reshaping of Religion in the Twenty-first Century*, (Reading, MA: Addison-Wesley Publishing, Co, 1994), 71. A helpful book on the Holy Spirit written from a Pentecostal perspective is Amos Yong's *Who is the Holy Spirit? A Walk with the Apostles*, (Brewster, MA: Paraclete Press, 2011).

as in the Steve Martin movie, *Leap of Faith*. Even the charlatan evangelist Jonas Nightingale, a man who pretends to be a vessel of God's power, can be used by and transformed because of something – divine perhaps – that brings wholeness to a person's life. Therefore, even as we seek to find explanations for the healings of Jesus and Paul, we are forced to reckon with the unexplainable in our own age. An open mind and heart can lead to further enjoyment of God's presence in our lives.

Faith

Faith is "the assurance of things hoped for, the conviction of things not seen" (Heb. 11:1). It is trust placed in something or someone, who lies beyond your own self. In Christian theology, faith is the means by which we receive the blessings of God's reconciling love (Eph. 2:8). Faith isn't simply giving assent to the truth of factual statements or to creedal statements. It's not blind acceptance of things we cannot explain either. Faith can be seen as assent to the truth, but it's more than this; it's a sense of trust and fidelity. It can also be seen as *"visio"*, a way of seeing the world. Marcus Borg suggests that faith as *visio* is a way of "seeing reality as gracious." Although faith involves trust; it's more than trust, for it adds a way of seeing reality that transforms the world.[133]

If faith is the heart of Christian experience, what do we make of Paul's designation of faith (*pistis*) as a spiritual gift (1 Cor. 12:9)? After all, shouldn't we assume that everyone should have this gift (1 Cor. 13:13)? If faith is to be understood as a spiritual gift, should it have a more narrow meaning? Perhaps it's a burst of trust in God, a way of seeing the world that comes with a flash of enlightenment that moves a person to act in ways that are out of the ordinary. To speak metaphorically, it's a faith that moves mountains.

Elijah's encounter with the prophets of Baal at Mt. Carmel is illustrative of a faith that is willing to trust God when circumstances would suggest that one do otherwise. Faith is that sense of

---

133 Borg, *Heart of Christianity*, 34-37.

Unfettered Spirit 145

empowerment that enables one to continue moving forward even when the situation looks impossible.[134]

MIRACLES

David Hume's challenge to the miraculous has been a thorn in the side of supernaturalists for more than two centuries. He demanded empirical proof of any alleged supernatural intervention. He laughed off the traditional defense that such events were limited to an earlier age. If no one experienced them now, then how can we trust the ancient testimonies? Hume must be taken seriously, but his challenges aren't the only ones that face anyone seeking to advance the idea that we should embrace the miraculous. Most definitions of a miracle presuppose some form of supernatural intervention that changes the natural course of events. This could be the healing of a person or the redirection of a tornado's path. It assumes an interventionist God, but such an understanding has become increasingly problematic. There are obvious scientific questions to be dealt with, but more pressing are the moral questions. Any definition of miracle must explain why God could intervene in some events and not others.[135]

In the context of a theology of spiritual giftedness, discussions of miracles center on the question of divine agency, and how we as the people of God can be conduits of that agency. If we look to the biblical story, we find that miracles or works of power (*energēmata dunamis*) are definitely the provenance of God. The *Interpreter's Dictionary of the Bible* offers a very workable definition of the biblical understanding of a miracle: It's an event, whether natural or supernatural, in which one sees an act or revelation of God.[136]

---

134 For further reflections on this story see Arnold Bittlinger, *Gifts and Graces,* (Grand Rapids: Wm. B. Eerdmans, 1967), 33.
135 Philip Clayton and Steven Knapp, *The Predicament of Belief: Science, Philosophy, Faith.* (New York: Oxford University Press, 2011), 137-139.
136 S.V. McCasland, "Miracle," *The Interpreter's Dictionary of the Bible,* George Buttrick, ed., 4 vols. (Nashville: Abingdon Press, 1962), 3:392.

Whether you believe that God intervenes in the affairs of this world from outside or not, can you conceive of the possibility that there are events in time and space that reveal to us the presence and power of God? Can you envision points in time where the presence and work of God is revealed in tangible ways?

As scientifically sophisticated people we often find it difficult to incorporate "miracles" into our vocabulary, but perhaps Walter Wink is correct in speaking of a miracle as being "just a word we use for the things the Powers have deluded us into thinking that God is unable to do."[137] Miracles, in Wink's terms, are active engagements of prayer by God's people acting in resistance to the Powers that are themselves in need of redemption.

That Jesus acted to transform lives, whether those lives were challenged by physical or mental illness, or simply caught up in systems of oppression, the miraculous is God's act of liberation. Thus, in the biblical story a miracle is something such as a healing, an exorcism, the raising of someone from the dead.[138] However, we define the gift, it's something that we do not control or possess. Miracles happen as we allow God freedom to work in and through us to transform the world through love. They are, as Amos Yong suggests, "signs of the kingdom." These are events and actions that are works of the Spirit that anticipate the world to come, which is "freed from the bondage of suffering and decay." This new age isn't only future, it makes itself felt in the present age, so that this "charismatic activity of the Spirit points not to some future understood in linear terms as being ahead of us, but to the qualitative in-breaking of God's 'future' into 'present' human and (natural history."[139] Although this term can be, and often is, misused, it suggests the possibility that when empowered by the Spirit's presence we can

---

137 Wink, *Engaging the Powers*, 303. See also Amos Yong, *The Spirit of Creation: Modern Science and Divine Action in the Pentecostal-Charismatic Imagination*, (Grand Rapids: Wm. B. Eerdmans Publishing Co., 2011), 72-101.
138 Dunn, *Jesus and the Spirit*, 210.
139 Yong, *Spirit of Creation*, 93-94.

be vessels of divine action. To answer in the affirmative, one must look at these realities through the eyes of faith, even if critically informed.

HEALING/HEALERS

Healing is a sign of the reign of God present among us. Amos Yong, a Pentecostal theologian writes that healing not only leads to the restoring of human bodies, it serves as a sign that Jesus is "representative of the messianic promise to bring about the redemption, reconciliation, and release long associated with the year of the Lord's favor."[140] Jürgen Moltmann suggests that healing serves as "signs of the rebirth of life and herald the new creation of all things." They are tokens of "the resurrection world which drives out death."[141] Although such healings don't forestall death as a human experience, they remind us that in ultimate terms the curse of death has been defeated and wholeness is possible.

Every Sunday we gather in our churches and pray for the healing of our family, friends, neighbors. We pray in the belief that such prayers have an effect at the spiritual level, bringing wholeness to the recipients of our prayers. James told the sick to call for the elders to anoint with oil and pray that their bodies would be healed (James 5:14-15).

As we see from the Gospels, healing played an important role in Jesus' ministry. Jesus healed the sick, restored sight to the blind, made the lame walk. A total of forty-one separate instances of healing body or mind can be found in the four gospels. Morton Kelsey has written "that Jesus' ministry of healing is certainly in line with the constant emphasis in his teachings about compassion and caring about one's neighbor."[142]

---

140 Yong, *Who is the Holy Spirit?* 44.
141 Jürgen Moltmann, *The Source of Life,* (Minneapolis: Fortress Press, 1997), 64-65.
142 Morton Kelsey, *Healing and Christianity: A Classic Study,* (Minneapolis: Augsburg Press, 1995), 42-45. See also John P. Meier, *A Marginal Jew: Rethinking the Historical Jesus,* Volume Two: Mentor, Message, and

Gifts of healing (*charismata iamatōn*) are not an exclusive alternative or replacement to modern medicine. Instead, the work of the Spirit is a complement to the medical communities attempt to bring wholeness to the person. Medicine and the work of the Spirit need not be kept separate, even in our technologically sophisticated world. Today there's a growing understanding that prayer and faith play significant roles in recovery from surgery or illness. Not everyone we pray for is cured, but should this be our expectation? Perhaps healing is not always the same as cure. Paul himself spoke of his thorn in the flesh, an impairment that stayed with him throughout life. But, people of faith do seem to fare better than those without faith.[143]

And one needn't embrace an interventionist view of God to share in ministries of healing. There are a number of healing practices that are spiritually based such as Reiki and healing touch, and while controversial, they appear to provide support and healing for many. Some of these healing methods have their origins in eastern religions but seem compatible with the healing work of the Holy Spirit. It's important to note that these alternative forms of healing do not compete, but complement modern medicine. As Bruce Epperly notes, the gap between spirituality and modern medicine has begun to close in recent years. He writes:

> Scientists have discovered the wisdom of Jesus, who invited his followers to "consider the lilies" and trust that God would care for their deepest needs. Spiritual practices such as meditation, mindfulness training, and transformed attitudes toward time, work, and success have been integrated into medical treatment plans.[144]

Miracles, (New York: Doubleday, 1994), 678-727, for an in-depth discussion of the stories of healing in the gospels.

143 For an in-depth conversation about this question, see Amos Yong's book *The Bible, Disability, and the Church: A New Vision of the People of God*, (Grand Rapids: Wm. B. Eerdmans Publishing Co., 2011).

144 Epperly, *Healing Marks*, 12. In addition to Healing Marks, which explores the concept of healing in the context of the narrative of the

As we consider the question of the relationship between faith and health, perhaps a definition is in order. Jürgen Moltmann writes:

> Healing is the restoration of disrupted community and the communication of life. The "community" of our cells and organs is restored. The community of soul and body is restored. The social relationships which have been disrupted and which make a person ill have been restored.[145]

Healing is the process of making someone whole. That restoration to wholeness can be physical, emotional, or social. There is nothing in Scripture that would lead us to believe that everyone who comes to Christ will experience complete relief from physical or emotional suffering. There is, however, the promise of wholeness, even if that wholeness is not expressed in physical terms.[146] What is needed may not be physical relief, but a freedom from fear so that one can face life with boldness.

Consequently, we can say with confidence that God moves in the body of Christ using people of faith to pray for restoration to wholeness of their neighbors. Such a ministry is truly an act of love and compassion. I have never seen a dramatic act of healing, but I am open to the possibility that God might move through my hands and my voice to bring physical healing to another, and so in that hope I remain attentive to that calling. I have, on the other hand, anointed and prayed for a person shortly before their death. Might that not be an act of healing itself? As we become aware of this ministry, perhaps some among us will welcome the

---

Gospel of Mark, Bruce and Kate Epperly have written several books that touch on these topics and their books should be consulted. These include: *Reiki Healing Touch: And the Way of Jesus* (Northstone, 2005); and *God's Touch*, (WJK Press, 2005).

145 Moltmann, *Source of Life*, 66.
146 This point is made quite clearly by Amos Yong in his book *The Bible, Disability, and the Church: A New Vision of the People of God.*, (Grand Rapids, MI: Wm. B. Eerdmans Publishing Company, 2011).

opportunity to share in prayer for the hurting, so that they might experience God's saving and healing grace.[147]

Exorcism

Our conceptions of exorcism likely have been formed by films such as the 1970s horror flick *The Exorcist* or the kinds of wild experiences of "spiritual warfare" described in popular Christian books such as Frank Perretti's *This Present Darkness*. Such images fail to help us deal with the real presence of evil in the world.[148] As C.S. Lewis reminded readers in his *Screwtape Letters*.

> There are two equal and opposite errors into which our race can fall about the devils. One is to disbelieve in their existence. The other is to believe, and to feel an excessive and unhealthy interest in them. They themselves are equally pleased by both errors and hail a materialist or a magician with the same delight.[149]

We dismiss the reality of evil to our own detriment, for having bought into a materialistic world view we fail to see the spiritual dimensions of systemic evil. Harvey Cox writes that "in my opinion a century that has witnessed Auschwitz and Hiroshima and the Gulag is in no position to laugh off the ugly reality of diabolical forces that seem capable of sweeping people up in their energies."[150]

Walter Wink helpfully defines the "powers that be" as institutions and systems from governments to schools to churches that have the potential for good but that are fallen and in need of re-

---

147 Those interested in exploring the ministry of healing would benefit from working through Morton Kelsey's *Healing and Christianity*. Chapter 14 of his book offers a guide to implementing this important ministry in the church.
148 Wink, *Engaging the Powers*, 9. Cox, *Fire from Heaven*, 281-86.
149 C. S. Lewis, "The Screw Tape Letters," in *A C. S. Lewis Treasury: Three Classics in One Volume*, (New York: Harcourt Brace & Co., 1990), 213.
150 Cox, *Fire from on High*, 286. Walter Wink, *The Powers That Be*, (New York: Galilee Books, 1998), 124-27.

demption. Standing at the heart of this fallen reality is what Wink calls the domination system. It's a form of spirituality that embraces the "myth of redemptive violence." This myth suggests that violence can redeem us. Jesus, however, offers a different way, the way of nonviolence. Nonviolence isn't passive in the face of evil. It's quite active and creative, but it seeks to resist evil with good.[151]

Jesus stands as the alternative picture to this myth, offering a new way of engaging, and thereby reclaiming the powers and the people within their grasp. He is pictured in the gospels engaging in a ministry of exorcism (*exorcizō*) by which he casts out "evil spirits from possessed individuals."[152] In the New Testament, exorcism often occurs in connection with healing, representing a perceived connection between illness and possession by evil spirits. On several occasions Jesus healed a person by releasing them from the grasp of evil. In each case Jesus simply commanded the "spirits" to leave (e.g. Mk. 1:25; Lk 4:36). Like healing, exorcism is connected in Jesus' ministry to the breaking of God's reign. They are signs that evil cannot exist in the presence of God.[153]

If we're to embrace the concept of exorcism today, it's important that we not see this in disembodied or spatial terms (God is up, the devil is down below). Instead we must begin to see the spiritual dimension of world in which we live. Amos Yong suggests that "exorcisms do not merely cast out an immaterial, personal being, but they also cleanse and restore originally good creations according to the purposes of God." This can take place personally through the "healing of fractured self-identities;" or socially through the "reconciliation between people;" or politically through the enactment of a "shalom that includes justice." Although there are differences in perspective, Walter Wink writes that "in the biblical view the Powers are at one and the same time visible *and* invisible, earthly *and* heavenly, spiritual *and* institutional (Col. 1:15-20)." That is,

---

151 Wink, *Engaging the Powers,* 13ff.
152 John Koenig, *Rediscovering New Testament Prayer,* (San Francisco: Harper-Collins, 1992), 111.
153 Koenig, *Rediscovering New Testament Prayer,* 41-42.

"the Powers are simultaneously an outer, visible structure and an inner, spiritual reality." Whether that visible structure is a government, a corporation, or even a church or family, it has a spiritual dimension that's fallen and in need of redemption.[154]

The ministry of exorcism involves prayer, it may involve rituals that unmask and confront the evil that permeates a person's life or a structure's existence. It requires discernment and support, as one confronts and engages an evil spirituality that is not embodied in "demonic beings." The persons we engage aren't enemies to be destroyed, but fellow human beings caught up in systems and institutions that have been compromised. What they're in need of is liberation from these systems.

Perhaps the best way to understand exorcism in a modern context is to see it as an act of liberation from enslavement, whether that enslavement is to drugs, to addictive behavior, economic systems, or such ugliness as human trafficking. To engage in such ministry will take considerable discernment and strength. It's a ministry that requires a commitment to nonviolent resistance to evil. John Koenig suggests that at their best, those who engage in ministries of exorcism "work cautiously, praying with other believers to discern whether a demonic force is actually present and if so, whether a ritual to command to expel it is the appropriate mode of calling forth Jesus' power to heal."[155]

Concluding Thoughts

In offering descriptions and definitions of the abundant opportunities for spiritually-based ministry, I've only broken the surface. As we explore gifts such as the ones detailed in this chapter, as well as in earlier chapters, we must wrestle with our own understanding of divine agency. We must come to some understanding of how God is at work and how this relates to the laws of nature. For many

---

154 Yong, *Spirit of Creation* 222-223; Wink, *The Powers that Be*, 24.
155 Koenig, *Rediscovering New Testament Prayer*, 112-13. Also see Koenig's chapter on "Prayer as Peacemaking and Warfare" (146-59).

an overwhelmingly supernatualist understanding no longer works, but is what we see with our senses (as a Modernist world view would suggest) all that there is?

My hope and prayer is that the definitions presented here can assist those who seek to discover their own gifts, gain an understanding of what these gifts are and what they are intended for. These definitions and descriptions primarily focus on gifts found in 1 Corinthians 12, 14, Romans 12, and Ephesians 4. I've included other possibilities that seem to fit the patterns described in the more explicit statements. In the process of discovery, it's hoped that congregations can be empowered for service to God and to creation. In no way is this list definitive. There likely are other sets of gifts that when governed by love can be beneficial to the church. (1 Cor. 13). The value of these gifts diminishes if love does not motivate the user.

One should also expect that the exercise of spiritual gifts will strengthen the congregation and lead to spiritual maturity, but, if our embrace of our giftedness doesn't lead us to engage in ministry outside the congregational walls, then they will have failed in their purpose. Our calling into gifted service to God is to reach out to the principalities and powers, the domination systems that keep us from experiencing God's wholeness, and make ourselves available to God's work of redeeming this world. With this vision in mind, we as the church needn't fear opening of ourselves to the wide variety of gifts that lay at hand.

Spiritual gifts are designed to unify the body of Christ so that it might be a witness to the world of God's love and grace, a love and grace that will redeem and transform our world. No one person has every gift, nor is there one gift that everyone must have to be fully God's person. The key here is openness to the wondrous work of our God, who seeks to make us "ambassadors of reconciliation" (2 Cor. 5:20).

Thought Questions

1. How we understand these gifts will depend upon our world view – discuss how science influences the way in which we understand the ideas of power and miracles.

2. This section lifts up such gifts, healing, and exorcism. Discuss your understanding of these gifts and the ways in which these gifts, as well as the seemingly related gifts of tongues, may be present in the contemporary church.

3. How should we respond to claims that such gifts are present in the church? On what basis should we judge reports and experiences?

4. How should we make use of the admonition to make sure gifts are used for the purpose of building up the body of Christ?

PART 3

THE GIFTS, MINISTRY AND A SPIRIT-EMPOWERED CHURCH

10

BECOMING THE SPIRIT-EMPOWERED BODY OF CHRIST

> If the Church was a body composed of different members, it couldn't lack the noblest of all; it must have a heart, and a heart burning with love. And I realized that this love was the true motive force which enabled the other members of the Church to act; if it ceased to function the Apostles would forget to preach the gospel, the Martyrs would refuse to shed their blood. Love, in fact, is the vocation which includes all others; it's a universe of its own, comprising all time and space – it's eternal. Beside myself with joy, I cried out; "Jesus, my Love! I've found my vocation, and my vocation is love.
>
> Therese of Lisieux[156]

We've been exploring our callings as Christians, asking the question: Who am I as a child of God? We're asking questions about how the Spirit of God is at work in our lives, which leads to the question of our gifts. Although modern Christian experience, especially in the United States, tends to be individualistic in nature, our experiences with the Spirit of God eventuate in the creation of community. When the Spirit comes into the community as a refreshing burst of wind, the Spirit empowers and purifies each of

---

156 Therese of Lisieux, "The Way of Love," in *The Westminster Collection of Christian Meditations,* Hannah Ward and Jennifer Wild, comp., (Louisville: Westminster/John Knox Press, 1998), 238-39.

the members of the community so that together the members can build each other up in love.

The gifts that we've looked at are like puzzle pieces that fit together to create a whole and healthy community, the kind of community that strangers can wander into and discern that God is present in this place. This is the criterion that Paul puts before the Corinthian church – when strangers enter the community, will they have their lives opened to the Spirit and fall down and declare? God is in this place (1 Cor. 14:24-25)!

We live at a time when more and more people are abandoning institutions, including the church. They're setting out on their own as "spiritual but not religious." The church is more than an institution – it is an expression of the body of Christ. It's organic and growing. But, communities require structure to function. This structure is not the end, it's the means to the end – the revealing of God's vision for creation. To borrow from my own denominational motto, we are a "movement of wholeness in a fragmented world." These structures, which are informed by our giftedness, help us accomplish this task.[157]

In thinking about the way in which the church grows and adapts, it would be worth considering something every parent observes about their children. As a parent I can remember when my now fully grown son was so tiny and fragile that I could hold him with one hand. But as he grew and matured, that became increasingly impossible. In like manner, even as we can't remain babies

---

[157] C. Kirk Hadaway, *Behold, I Do a New Thing*, (Cleveland: Pilgrim Press, 2001), 35-47. In Hadaway's typologies of congregational life, the four types are the "club/clan", "company/corporation," "charismatic leader/follower," and the "incarnational community." This last model he defines as a "culture of transformation" (see figure 1, pg. 49). Reading *Christianity After Religion: The End of Church and the Birth of a New Spiritual Awakening*, (San Francisco: Harper One, 2012), can be a helpful antidote to institutionalism, but if a spiritual awakening is to have legs it will need some structure. Thus, for most of us will take both the spirituality and the religion.

forever, so churches must grow, mature, change and adapt, over time. Nothing organic stays the same, and the church as the body of Christ is a living organism.

Although there are other biblical images that can be used to describe the church – temple, household, bride, and vine – the metaphor of the body holds the most promise for understanding the relationship of gifts to the church. The church as we know it is the visible expression of Christ's living presence in the world. We are, as we're linked to one another by the Spirit, the manifestation of Jesus' body in the world. We are his hands and feet, eyes and ears. As the visible expression of God's love revealed in the person of Jesus Christ, the church's Spirit-endowed and empowered ministry will be marked by acts of compassion, healing, and liberation (1 Cor. 12:12-26).

THE CHURCH: THE BODY OF CHRIST

The body of Christ has many members, each is different in nature and in function, and yet this body is united in purpose. This body is knit together by the head, Jesus Christ, in whom all things hold together. Each member of this body is equipped and enabled to work together for the purpose of building the body in love (Eph. 4:15-16; Col. 1:18-20). Ultimately, in the mystical reality that is the church's existence in the world, Christ is both head and body.[158]

As a living body each member is dependent on the other:

> *If the foot would say, "Because I am not a hand, I do not belong to the body," that would not make it any less a part of the body. And if the ear would say, "Because I am not an eyes, where would the hearing be? If the whole body were hearing, where would the sense of smell be? . . . If all were a single member, where would the body be? (1 Cor. 12:15-19).*

Since our own gifts only represent a portion of the whole body, we must recognize that we're incomplete without the other

---

[158] William Robinson, *The Biblical Doctrine of the Church*, rev. ed., (St. Louis: Bethany Press, 1955), 70.

members. We need each other to fulfill our calling as the body of Christ. This idea is borne out in system's theory, which suggests that healthy communities are connected and interdependent. We all live in relationship to others – spouses, parents, children, siblings, co-workers, and neighbors. Healthy community is related to the way we relate and interact.[159] With this in mind a healthy congregation – as an expression of the body of Christ – must be more than simply a collection of autonomous individual Christians. As I say this, I recognize that much of our church life is designed to facilitate that autonomy we so desire.

Turning to a medical analogy, we know that heart attacks often result from blockages of the arteries. These blockages keep the blood from circulating, and the body suffers. In the same way, if the conduits through which the Spirit moves are blocked, the church suffers spiritual heart attacks. It divides, it fights, and it fails to fulfill its calling to bear witness to Jesus' love for the world. And what are these blockages? They include but aren't limited to race, ethnicity, gender, language, age, perceived disability, class distinctions, economic factors, and sexual orientation. These blockages can be removed if we're willing to let God have access to our lives through Christ. In other words, in the body of Christ there are no aliens or strangers. All are citizens and saints, members of the household of God (Eph. 2:15-20).

As we consider the ways in which spiritual gifts serve as expressions of Christ's living body, we must realize the temptation to seek spiritual experience and even spiritual ecstasy at the expense of common good. This happened at Corinth, where people sought after gifts such as tongues, believing that this experience of the Spirit put them on a higher spiritual plane. Paul attempted to counter this temptation by reminding the Corinthians that as members of the body of Christ their own spiritual health depended on the health of the body as a whole. In doing this, according to Hans Küng, Paul made it clear that "the church is never – as some

---

159 Peter L. Steinke, *Healthy Congregations: A System's Approach*, (New York: Alban Institute, 1996), 3.

in Corinth seem to have supposed – a gathering of charismatics enjoying their own private relationship with Christ independently of the community."[160] It may have been a gathering of charismatics, but Paul expected them to be living in relationship with Christ in community.

By thinking of the church as a body, Paul makes it clear that everyone in the church has value. There are no vestigial organs, no appendices, in this body. What may appear to us as insignificant or even inferior, God highly values. No part is unimportant and no part of the body stands above any other (1 Cor. 12:14-26). As we contemplate the image of the body of Christ, and our place in this body, we need to take into consideration that human bodies come in many sizes and even forms. In Paul's analogy of the body, when parts are missing, especially the parts we deem less significant, the whole body suffers. Such a body must compensate for missing members (1 Cor. 12:26). There is wisdom in this message, but as we hear it we need to remember that such a vision can have the effect of excluding or dismissing the contribution from the person who has disabilities – perhaps sight or hearing. So, in our vision of wholeness, let's remember that bodies experience wholeness in a variety of ways.[161]

By using an organic metaphor to describe the church, we can envision the church growing, changing, adapting, and evolving, just like the human body. It's not static – like a rock or a fortress. This metaphor also accents our interconnectedness as a church, through the head – Jesus Christ (Eph. 4:15-16). Whether or not our faith communities have the look of institution, it's clear that a detached individualistic faith doesn't match well with the faith envisioned by Jesus or Paul. It might be flat as some have suggested – the form is less the issue than the reality that a truly growing faith/relationship with God requires partners on the journey.

---

160 Hans Küng, *Church*, (New York: Image Books, 1976), 296.
161 Amos Yong, *The Bible, Church and Disability: A New Vision for the People of God*, (Grand Rapids: Wm. B. Eerdmans Publishing Co., 2011), 82-117.

This need for partners or community, whether small or large, is reflected in our call to be engaged in serving the broader community. It's good to remember that while Paul received a call to service on the Damascus Road, he was commissioned by the church in Antioch to engage in his mission work. He went on the first journey in the company of Barnabas and John Mark (Acts 13:1ff), and later he traveled with Silas, among others.[162]

It's good to remember that even Jesus lived in community. As he took up his itinerant ministry, he invested himself in a company of disciples to whom he imparted divine wisdom. It wasn't an easy life – Jesus told his potential followers that while "foxes have holes and birds of the air have nests; but the Son of Man has nowhere to lay his head" (Lk. 9:58-59; cf. Mt. 8:20). Jesus also reminds us that this community of the faithful transcends the human family: "let the dead bury their own dead" (Lk.9:60; Mt. 8:21). The true family of Jesus are those who do "the will of God" (Mk. 2:35). Community is the end of discipleship, but it's something the church has found it difficult to create.

In Paul's use of the metaphor of the body, he encompasses both the unity and the diversity of churchly existence, for the church is composed of many members while remaining one body. This church is healthy when all its parts are healthy and working together in harmony (1 Corinthians 12:12-26). Although the church as we often experience it may appear to be more institution than "body of Christ," the metaphor suggests that there is a deeper reality underlying the church's external existence. Because the organic tends to be harder to manage, we have a tendency to domesticate the church by focusing on institutional needs rather than on organic relationships. It will be a constant struggle, but it's not an impossible one. In seeking to hold this vision, we'll want to keep in mind the Reformation motto of "always reforming."

---

162 Howard Clark Kee, *Good News to the Ends of the Earth: The Theology of Acts,* (Philadelphia: Trinity Press International, 1990), 100-1.

THE CHURCH: SACRAMENTAL PRESENCE

Another way of envisioning the nature of the church is to turn to sacramental theology. The idea of sacrament, which is traditionally defined in terms of the visible/material serving as signs of invisible grace, allows us to peer beneath the surface of our ecclesial realities. In seeking to reenvision the church sacramentally, I'm not just suggesting that the church is the place where we receive sacraments, but that being in community we experience sacramental grace. If the church is by definition the living body of Christ in the world, then it's a visible sign of Christ's spiritual presence. As a sacramental sign, the church brings to an alienated and estranged world the reconciling and transforming work of the Spirit. It's as Leonardo Boff has written, "the sacrament, sign, and instrument of the now living and risen Christ, that is, the Holy Spirit."[163] Where the church as the body of Christ is present, working compassionately by caring for the homeless, the jobless, the oppressed, the imprisoned, then Christ is present and grace is made visible.

The church isn't the only sign of God's gracious presence in the world. To say this would limit God's ability to be present in ways that lie outside the walls of the church ("there is no salvation outside the church," for instance). The church is, however, a foundational sign, a "thin place" where we can encounter the creator.[164]

Thin places, are sacramental moments, "a mediator of the sacred, a means whereby the sacred becomes present to us." Thus, it's a means of God's grace to humanity, even to the creation itself. These sacramental thin places may come in many forms, ranging from geographical places such as Jerusalem or Rome or the mountains or the sea, to music or the arts. They are places "where the veil momentarily lifts, and we behold God, experience the one in

---

163 Leonardo Boff, *Church, Charism & Power: Liberation Theology and the Institutional Church,* (New York: Crossroad Publishing Co., 1986), 150.
164 Marcus Borg's *The Heart of Christianity,* (San Francisco: Harper San Francisco, 2003), 155ff.

whom we live, all around us and within us."[165] Because worship can be a thin place, the church as a visible entity offers the possibility of experiencing life-changing encounters with God. Unfortunately, in spite of our decision to make time and room for worship, we don't always recognize God's sacramental presence in our midst.

In the Protestant tradition two sacramental acts stand at the center of Christian experience, making visible to us God's gracious embrace of humanity, Baptism and the Eucharist. These means of grace or thin places help us gather our hearts into the presence of God so that we might taste a new relationship with the creator.

Baptism is a sign of God's covenant, a means by which we are initiated into the body of Christ (1 Cor. 12:13). It's a tangible way of identifying with Jesus' death, burial, and resurrection as we begin a new life as covenant children of God (Rom. 6:1-11). Baptism by immersion powerfully symbolizes the change of life that entering the covenant brings. In this watery grave we find ourselves "transformed after the likeness of Jesus Christ." Although baptism is not a mechanical conduit of the Spirit's presence, it is a symbolic marker of our status as "spirit-filled" persons. As bearers of the Spirit, we're thereby all ordained to ministries of the gospel.[166]

The Eucharist acts as a sign of the tangible nature of the real presence of Christ's body, a body into which we have been born through our baptisms. In Baptism and Eucharist, the disciples of Jesus are initiated into the new covenant. By participating in this meal we're joined to his destiny, as we share in the meal of remembrance. The first meal and its re-enactments hold the promise that the separation entailed in death will be transcended in God's new realm.[167] In these two sacraments we are swept into the covenantal

---

165 Borg, *Heart of Christianity,* 156.
166 James D. G. Dunn, *Baptism in the Holy Spirit,* (Philadelphia: Westminster Press, 1970), 227-29.
167 John Koenig, *The Feast of the World's Redemption: Eucharistic Origins and Christian Mission,* (Harrisburg, PA: Trinity Press International, 2000), 37-38.

Unfettered Spirit

relationship with our God. We become heirs of the promise that allows us to share in the goodness of God's reign

Although the sacraments have often been the cause of division (the reality of our differences often are magnified sacramentally), they're intended to be signs of unity. Paul wrote that "because there is one bread, we who are many are one body, for we all partake of the one bread" (1 Cor. 10:17). This stands as a reminder to the church that the barriers that keep us separated at the altar are signs that the body of Christ on earth is unhealthy. Health involves finding wholeness or unity at the table, so that in partaking of the one bread we become part of one body in Christ. As sacramental signs themselves, Baptism and the Eucharist remind us that the church as the body of Christ is the visible sign of Christ's gracious presence in the world.[168]

A Picture of Christian Community

If the church is the visible embodiment or sign of Christ's presence on earth – his hands and feet, what does this church look like in practice? As we consider this question, it should be clear that the church doesn't have just one form or expression in the world. It's been evolving and adapting over the centuries so that it can bring good news to each new age. There isn't even one specific form of church to be found in the New Testament, no blue print to be enacted, not even in the Book of Acts, which restorationist movements often looked to for such a blueprint. The differences between the churches in Antioch, Jerusalem, Ephesus, and Corinth offer us the freedom to create structures that fit the moment in time, while all remaining expressions of the one body of Christ on earth. Of course, it's easy to codify and solidify one particular image and make it the model for everyone and for every age.[169]

---

168 The image of the church as spiritual reality and even mystical reality can be found in William Robinson, *Peace in Heaven*, 11. See also Küng, *The Church*, 295.

169 For an interesting look at how the church adapts to its cultural situation and then solidifies, see Doug Pagitt's *Church in the Inventive Age*

When we look for patterns of church life in the New Testament what we see is both a call for unity and freedom to innovate. This same pattern gives us freedom to innovate even as we seek to find unity of purpose with other expressions of the body of Christ. Since there's no biblical blueprint that we must slavishly follow, then we can move forward, balancing the need to innovate with our heritage and theology.

As we think about the way the church exists today, it's appropriate to recognize that a long-established congregation composed primarily of older people will function differently from a new church plant made up largely of younger people. Having been a pastor of small, older congregations, I've found that much church growth advice appears to be useful on the surface, but in the end proves to be unrealistic and even counterproductive over the long term. Trying to impose a model of church life that works for a megachurch or a new church plant or a long established congregation can prove disastrous. It's not that we can't learn from each other, we just have to recognize the differences.[170]

If there isn't a blueprint with which we can use to create cookie cutter congregations, then perhaps the place to start is with the persons present in the community that is forming (or has formed long before). What's the age, gender, ethnicity of the group? What is the theological framework out of which they work? Then pushing further – what is their personality? Is it more introverted or extroverted? Central to the conversation will be the gift mix present in this emerging community. Do they have an inward or an outward focus? Answers to these questions can help provide a picture of what an actual community looks like. My sense is that as gifts are discovered and released, then the picture of the church will change.

(Minneapolis: Sparkhouse Press, 2010).
170 This point is well made in Kirk Hadaway's description of change strategies, especially for the club/clan type (smaller congregation), which is often tempted to moving toward a charismatic leader model or corporate/company model (programmatic). Hadaway, *Behold I Do a New Thing*, 55-60.

Unfettered Spirit

If it begins to see itself as Christ's body in the world then it will, if it hasn't already, embrace its calling to be misisonally present in the community. When this occurs, then it will be present not just in the form of one person (the pastor), but the body as a whole. As a pastor who is engaged in community organizing efforts, I found that we truly began to get engaged as a congregation when a few lay persons caught the vision and took leadership. Then it became the congregation's mission, not just mine.

Although we tend to lift up the megachurch as the exemplar of spiritual health, size isn't indicative of health. It's true that if a church is declining in size, then there may be health issues to deal with, unless the congregation is dealing with external factors (declining population base) that it can't control but inhibits growth. It's also good to remember that the vast majority of churches in America are small, with worship attendance under one hundred. This perceived smallness doesn't have to define the congregation's ability to make a difference in the lives of the people in the community.[171] This has always been true. Most early Christian churches met in homes (1 Cor. 16:19; Rom. 16:5), not large assembly halls.[172] Even today, many churches around the world meet for worship in homes rather than in dedicated sacred space. Jesus accepts this reality and acknowledges that size is not the determining factor in the effectiveness of communities of faith. For Jesus, "when two or three are gathered in my name, I am there among them" (Mt. 18:20).[173]

---

[171] On the prospects and values of the smaller church, see David R. Ray, *The Indispensable Guide for Smaller Churches,* (Cleveland: Pilgrim Press, 2003).

[172] Robert Banks, *Paul's Idea of Community,* Rev. Ed., (Peabody, MA: Hendrickson Publishers, 1994), 31-33.

[173] Ray, *Indispensable Guide,* 55. For a good description of the house church movement and how it can stimulate renewal in the church see Robert and Julia Banks, *The Church Comes Home: A New Base for Community and Mission,* (Sutherland, NSW and Claremont, CA: Albatross Books, 1986).

If size isn't the arbiter of success, then how do we gauge the church's effectiveness in mission? In answering this question, we need to recognize that while large churches can offer more programs and maybe even be more efficient, the biblical criterion for success isn't size or quantity of programs. Instead, the criterion is this: The stranger enters the community and declares "God is really among you" (1 Cor. 14:25). The true church of Jesus Christ is found whenever people encounter the Spirit of the Living God in such a way that their lives are transformed and they hear and respond to the call of God to embrace their gifts and join with God in the work of the kingdom of God.

As we envision what this church looks like, the picture that we're painting, we need to attend to the landscape or the backdrop to the congregation's existence. Is it rural, suburban, small town, urban? Although the church can serve and often does serve as a haven of rest in the midst of a wearying world, especially when times are difficult, so that going to church on Sunday morning can be a needed break from a world that seems out of control. Is this all that the church is called to be? Finding the balance between tending to the needs of the body and reaching out into the world is not always easy, but finding that balance is essential. A church that is always on the go, but never attends to its spirit, will quickly burn out. A congregation that simply attends to its own needs, likewise, will eventually fade away into irrelevance. As we look out into the neighborhood, what do we see and how should we be engaged?

If we embrace the call to be missional communities, we will see our neighborhood as a place to inhabit and add value. Without embracing theocratic visions, where we impose our values and ideas on our neighbors, it's incumbent on us to move into the world, to cross the borders and make a difference. One way to do this is to make use of the principles of community organizing. A church that sees itself as an agent of reconciliation and healing in the community is, in my mind, a healthy congregation. When congregations work together as part of a larger coalition, then smallness of size doesn't prohibit effective service and ministry or its ability to influence life in the broader community.[174]

Faith based organizing is rooted in the faith values of the congregation. As Christians our values are set by Jesus who made declarations like: "blessed are the peacemakers;" and "blessed are the merciful." (Mt. 5:1ff). This form of community organizing embraces power. Now power comes to us in a variety of ways, according to the principles of community organizing it includes recognizing the value of our own anger and grief at what is happening around us. From the perspective of a theology of spiritual gifts, we recognize that power comes first and foremost from the Spirit of God who is present in us and around us. It's this power that enables us to move from anger and grief to becoming peacemakers and bearers of mercy.

There are those who believe that the reign of God will come, but we will not see signs of it in this world. There is another possibility, which insists that the body of Christ is a visible sign of God's reign here and now. God's gifts of grace enable the body of Christ to faithfully live out the kingdom values in an as yet fully redeemed world. As God's gifts of grace begin to flow in the church we can join together in becoming agents of redemption and transformation of the principalities and powers of this world. One good example of this was that night in 1989 when the Berlin Wall came tumbling down. After the wall fell we learned that one of the central forces involved in this momentous occasion was the church, a church that had lived with persecution, but maintained its vision of freedom. As the people of God, empowered by the Spirit and claiming our gifts, we can participate in making similar signs of the kingdom visible in the world.

In everything we do, from our worship to our study of the Bible, in our evangelism and in our prayers, we see God moving in our midst, empowering us to embrace our calling to live faith-

---

[174] See Kendall Clark Baker, *When Faith Storms the Public Square* for an excellent discussion of community organizing and how it can enhance and define the missional nature of the congregation.

fully in the world. Congregations needn't compete or gloat at their success; rather they can rejoice that the gift-giving God is present in their midst.

When we ask the question as to what the church looks like, the answer needn't dwell on forms and structures, whether they're congregational, episcopal, or presbyterian. These structures are the means by which God's gifted people organize themselves so that they can effectively participate in ministries of healing and reconciliation. Like all human institutions, the structures and forms the church takes can be fallen and in need of redemption. But, having been redeemed, the church can be a powerful asset in God's work of reconciliation. Of course, this will involve change, but change needn't be feared (though we often receive it with fear). Letting go of long held beliefs and practices can be difficult. Sometimes we clutter our buildings with furniture that reminds us of earlier days, perhaps a time when our congregation was thriving and influential in the community. Remember that movement away from a geo-centered universe didn't come without great struggle. In spite of the difficulty we have dealing with change, and in the modern world change comes ever so rapidly, we should see this as an opportunity to help the world become a new creation itself.[175] What we need to remember is that a strong and healthy body is flexible. It will adapt as needed to address the needs of the moment, even as it remains true to its founding vision given to the church by Jesus.

One way for the church to attend to the changing times is to listen to voices present not only in the church, but outside the church as well. There's no better place to go than focusing on popular culture. What do we hear in the music, films, and television shows of the day? As much as I may enjoy the *Andy Griffith Show* or *Leave It to Beaver*, these shows don't represent the needs, concerns hopes and dreams of today. Tom Beaudoin wrote about the spiritual quest of Generation X more than a decade ago, and he

---

[175] An excellent starting point is Loren B. Mead, *Transforming Congregations for the Future*, (New York: Alban Institute, 1994), 1-23.

Unfettered Spirit

pointed out then that popular culture "is a major meaning-making system." What is true of Generation X is true of Millennials as well. Therefore, if these generations are on such intimate terms with popular culture it shouldn't appear strange that they'll "practice religion at least partly in and through this medium. We express our religious interests, dreams, fears, hopes, and desires through popular culture."[176]

One of the marks of the generation that Tom Beaudoin highlights, and one that the church must take seriously if it's to not only reach out to younger generations is that these generations are marked by a sense of irreverence. Beaudoin suggests that Gen Xers "tend to insert a large question mark after any religious idea, doctrine, or assumption that our elders have taken to be theologically certain or that they approach with reverence."[177] Since Beaudoin wrote his book in 1998, social media has become an increasingly important part of our cultural life, and the church will have to adapt to this medium of communication, even as it adapted to telephones, radio, and television. Although the irreverence of the present age may be off-putting to some, especially older generations, it seems to be here to stay. Jon Stewart and Stephen Colbert are the harbingers of the future, not Andy Griffith.

How does the church deal with generations of people who simply don't take things at face value and are willing to throw off traditional ways of believing and doing things?[178] Interestingly, it appears that evangelicals have been good at adapting to some parts of the culture (the performance aspects), while the more liberal/progressive congregations have offered a more open theological and social framework. The growing disillusionment with the institutions may stem in part from dissatisfaction with these two options. The good news, however, is that this apparent "irreverent"

---

176 Tom Beaudoin, *Virtual Faith: The Irreverent Spiritual Quest of Generation X,* (San Francisco: Jossey-Bass, 1998), xiv.
177 Beaudoin, *Virtual Faith,* 179.
178 Peter Rollins, *The Fidelity of Betrayal: Towards a Church Beyond Belief,* (Brewster, MA: Paraclete Press, 2008), 6.

spirit could be of service in tearing down walls that prevent us from moving into the community with the gospel of the kingdom.

By tuning its ear to the voices of popular culture, the church can ask the question: What do these songs, movies, and shows say to us about the world that lies beyond the doors of our churches? The issue is not whether one likes or enjoys a certain form of popular culture. In fact, one might be repelled by it, but that's not the point. What is important to take hold of here is the message coming through to the church about what makes the emerging generations tick.

By starting with the self-interests of those in our communities, we can discern the issues and concerns that are on the hearts of our neighbors. From there we can work together to find solutions, building power through relationships that are rooted in our faith values. In the midst of this relationship-building experience taking place outside the walls of the church, we'll begin to see healing of broken hearts, lives, and relationships begin to occur. Salvation will be experienced in all of its facets. As we do this work of relationship building we may also discern gifts that are present within the congregation and in the community. As gifts are discerned, then power is released.

Engaging in such community transforming ministry will require that we leave the comfort and safety of our buildings so that we can go where the needs are most present. This becomes ever more urgent, as fewer and fewer young adults, youth, and children will have experienced church life. When they enter our buildings, if they enter, it's likely that the music and biblical stories that mean so much to generations of Christians will be as if it were a foreign language. Our culture is no longer an expression of a culture of Christendom. It's not that these treasures have no value, but if they're to have value to a new generation then we'll have to do a lot of translating. But such is the calling of the Spirit-empowered and gifted church.

As we seek to translate the message of God's grace and mercy, we needn't abandon the rites and symbols and sacraments of our faith. Those symbols and acts of worship may be the keys to building bridges. The decision to remove religious symbolism that marked the Seeker Church movement has proven to be short-sighted. The point is not to abandon the symbols and sacraments, but rather to find new ways of embodying these sacraments and symbols so that they will prove welcoming to the stranger.[179]

The church that embraces its calling to be the Spirit-empowered and gifted body of Christ will release its members to explore and live out their giftedness. Such a church will always recognize the call to attend to the common good, not just of the congregation, but more importantly it will seek to live faithfully in and for the world that lies beyond the walls of the church building. As Hans Küng writes, "whoever has a share in the Spirit has a share in the gifts of the Spirit." Where ministry is limited to properly ordained church officials rather than being shared with the whole people of God then there is "grave reason to wonder whether the Spirit has not been sacrificed along with the spiritual gifts."[180] Such an entity, however, is not the church (body) of Jesus Christ that knows the enlivening presence of the Holy Spirit.

THOUGHT QUESTIONS

1. What images come to mind when you think about the church? Are the institutional images or organic ones?

2. Paul speaks of the church as the body of Christ? What does this image bring to mind? What is a body and how do we exist as part of this body?

---

179 See Phil Snider and Emily Bowen, *Toward a Hopeful Future: Why the Emergent Church is Good News for Mainline Congregations*, (Cleveland: Pilgrim Press, 2010).
180 Küng, *Church*, 246.

3. If the church is a body, and we're all parts of the body, how might we relate to each other?

4. When we think of spiritual gifts, how might they enable us to be part of this body?

11

LIVING AND WORKING TOGETHER AS CHURCH

> Living a life of purpose, then, doesn't require what the world considers special talent – just a readiness to respond when God calls, as Jeremiah did, or to follow the example of Jesus. If we examine our own hearts, minds, consciences, perhaps we'll recognize some simple things God has in mind for us to do, ways of reaching out to express God's love for the world around us. These will always be compatible with our talents and opportunities. And if we answer God's call, even though we feel inadequate, we will have the help and strength we need.
>
> Jimmy Carter[181]

We don't need special talents to serve God; we just need to be ready to act when God calls us. We each have what we need to fulfill God's call to service in the realm of God. No matter how old or how young, whether we're female or male, highly educated or poorly educated, rich or poor, we all stand before God as equals, and as equals we've been gifted for the ministries to which we're called. Sometimes the gifts are obvious, but many times they need to be uncovered and released. Often we'll make new discoveries over the course of time, but the point is – we have what we need. The question then is – where do I fit? Where is my place?

---

181 Jimmy Carter, *Sources of Strength: Meditations on Scripture for a Living Faith,* (New York: Times Books, 1997), 217.

NURTURING THE BODY OF CHRIST

If the church is the body of Christ, it is an organic entity rather than merely an institution. Bodies, of course, must be nurtured and fed if they are to survive. Remember how the angels came to minister to Jesus after his sojourn in the wilderness (Mark 1:12-13). This brief statement by the gospel writers remind us that the human body isn't self-sustaining, not even that of Jesus. The question then is – how should we nurture and feed this body? Or, borrowing from the principles of community organizing, we might ask the question – how does the church become and continue to be a community of power?

In gift-based ministry, it's assumed that every member of the body contributes to the welfare of that body. Each member is important to the body's ability to fulfill its purpose. The body is fed and nurtured as we share the gifts of the Spirit amongst each other. Using the principles of faith-based community organizing, we could say that while everyone in the community has leadership potential, that potential must be released and focused through training.

In gift-based understandings of congregational life and ministry, using Ephesians 4:11-12 as our guide, God provides pastors and teachers to equip the saints for the work of the ministry. These particular persons are gifted and called to lead and empower the members of the body to fulfill their own callings as part of that body. Pastors and teachers don't do the work of the ministry for the people of God. Instead, they equip them to fulfill their callings. To them is given the ministry of nurturing the body of Christ through preaching and teaching.

To get a sense of how this might work in practice, let's turn again to the principles of community organizing, where the community organizer is charged with recruiting, equipping, training, encouraging, and helping to empower the members of the coalition to achieve their purpose, which is to bring a moral vision into the public square. Using this imagery, pastors come to understand

Unfettered Spirit

themselves not merely as helping professionals, but as organizers, with the congregation being the entity being organized so that it can become powerful in its ministry and mission.[182]

Spiritually gifted ministry occurs both inside and outside the congregation walls, but before we move outward to the broader community, we must attend to what happens on the inside of the community. If the church is to move outward in ministry, to become missional, it will have to attend to such things as teaching, worship, and more. There will the need for teachers, for musicians, elders and deacons, trustees, worship leaders. Even those responsibilities that seem rather mundane often are central to the effectiveness of the church in its ministry to its neighbors. Unfortunately, in most churches there are more "jobs" to go around than willing bodies to fill them. We often turn to guilt or fear to get people to take the jobs, even when they don't feel called or equipped for this responsibility. In the end, the few fill the need and often burn out as a result. By embracing a gift-based model of church we hope to avoid this reality.

In envisioning what ministry is like in the church we'll need to avoid the equation of committee work with being church. That is a holdover from what Diana Butler Bass calls "religion." There are plenty of places where people can join a committee – from work to school to service clubs. I remember going to a meeting of a service club that was honoring a member of our church. I quickly saw the parallels between the service club and the church – it was all about being on this or that committee or task force. While I have nothing against service clubs, it's clear that younger generations are not apt to equate committee membership with ministry. They understand that jobs need to get done, but the job isn't their focus – it's the ministry that it engenders that's important. More specifically people want to do things that change lives, like building houses,

---

182 Kendall Clark Baker, *When Faith Storms the Public Square: Mixing Religion and Politics through Community Organizing to Enhance our Democracy,* (Cleveland: Circle Books, 2011), 184.

serving meals. They value study, prayer, and experiences that build community, but simply going to meetings won't suffice. This reality will force us as the church to decide what is important and essential and what no longer fits the congregation's mission.

Since we began the chapter with a quote from Jimmy Carter, the former president's own life could serve as a good example of what we've been discussing. Although President Carter held the highest office in the American government and continues to play important political roles that might seem to have few spiritual connections, we also know him for his church involvement. Carter has served for many years as a church school teacher, as evidenced by the book of lessons we began the chapter with. This is an important use of spiritual gifts. But, he appears to have other gifts as well that have allowed him to mediate disputes between rival countries or political groups. His gifts of leadership have led to the expansion of groups like Habitat for Humanity. I would venture to say that his spiritual gifts are equally at work in the Sunday School class and in the mediatorial work in a nation holding its first elections

When we gather to worship God, we have the opportunity to give thanks for God's gifts and graces that we are able to discover, develop, nurture, and ultimately express in and through the church. But, let us not forget that gifts transcend the boundaries of church life. Or better yet, we can begin to envision the life of the congregation, the covenant community, extending out to the furthest boundaries of creation. Thus, as we live out our lives in the world we become agents of reconciliation, often without even saying a word.

We each have a calling from God, a vocation for service. Some manifestations of this ministry take place within the walls of the church building, but other expressions of this ministry occur outside these walls. The ministries of worship leaders, church school teachers, providers of pastoral care to those in need spiritually, emotionally, or physically, provide a foundation for the ministries that take place outside those walls – whether they're undertaken ecumenically or with other faith traditions, these ministries express the mission God has given that congregation. If we're able to keep things in balance, then members of the congregation will be less likely to suffer from stress and burn out. This focus on gifts and calling doesn't make the work any easier, but it helps spread the load more equitably and it means that we will focus on areas we are more competent with. Then we will be free of that feeling that what we are doing is an impossible situation.

This effort starts with a rediscovery of calling. When we choose people to serve in leadership positions in the church, we have the responsibility of asking people to consider their particular calling. If we take on a responsibility, seeing it not as a job to be done but a ministry to be fulfilled, then when we are asked to serve as moderators, treasurers, committee chairs, church school teachers, or elders, we will see this work as a ministry. When we take on this perspective, we will abandon the principle of filling jobs with warm bodies and begin to ask who might be the best person to serve the kingdom of God through this ministry.[183]

FOUNDATIONS OF SERVICE IN INTIMATE COMMUNITY

I understand why many people find congregations stifling and oppressive. I've experienced this feeling myself on occasions. But as we've already seen, the body of Christ is best expressed in community. It's in community that we nurture and test our gifts. Congregations come in many sizes, from very small to very large. I've pastured smaller-sized congregations and I've been part of quite large congregations. Both kinds of churches have their strengths

---

183 See Brian Kelley Bauknight, *Body Building,* (Nashville: Abingdon Press, 1996), 44-45, for helpful instructions on the nominating process. Bauknight suggests a process that begins with connecting gifts with responsibilities. Candidates are sent a letter describing the candidate's discerned gifts and show why the person was chosen. The letter also includes a description of the responsibilities and time commitments. Nominees are asked to pray for a few days, after which a member of the committee calls on the person and seeks an answer. After this process takes place the congregation can affirm the person's call to this position.

and weaknesses. Whatever size of congregation we inhabit, it's important to find a sense of intimacy. In theory this is easier to accomplish in small congregations, where, as the famous line from *Cheers* puts it – "Everybody knows your name." It is more difficult to get lost in such a context, but larger congregations can provide opportunities to build intimate relationship through small groups. And even in small congregations, even the most intimate of congregations, not everyone really knows everyone else. I'm not even certain such a reality is possible in intentional Christian communities, though they are probably best equipped to build this kind of intimacy. As we consider this need for intimacy, we might keep in mind this observation from small church advocate David Ray: "So, if two is the minimum number for a church, is there a maximum beyond which a church becomes something else, when it starts being merely a religious institution or just a crowd?"[184]

Is there a point at which a church ceases to be a church? The question of course hinges on our definition of church, but the point is well taken. When does a community become so large that true intimacy is no longer possible? Does it come when we can no longer say "everybody knows your name?"

Once a church reaches a size beyond fifty or so, intimacy becomes more problematic. A congregation's ability to sustain intimacy diminishes as it grows, which means it must find other ways of building community. Small groups can provide an effective foundation for the renewal of church life. They can be the place in which gifts are discerned, nurtured, and set free. They become the locus of spiritual formation so that the community is prepared to be sent out into the world. This outward focus is important, so that these small groups don't end up becoming isolated cliques. There is a place for therapeutic groups in the church, but this isn't the place for that.

An effective model of a missional-type small group would be the base communities that formed in Latin America. These groups

---

[184] David R. Ray, *The Indispensable Guide for Smaller Churches*, (Cleveland: Pilgrim Press, 2003), 45.

Unfettered Spirit 181

helped empower the poor and the dispossessed to reclaim their human rights. They provide opportunities for education, community organizing, leadership development, as well as offering places of worship and Bible study. These more activist forms of community belie the American tendency to create cell groups along therapeutic lines (although physical, spiritual, and emotional healing is part of the Christian experience). They don't exist simply to serve a person's emotional needs or perceived need for spiritual experiences. Additionally, they serve as a place that challenges people to carry out ministry in the world in which they live.[185]

Cell group theory fits well with the organic nature of the body image. Growth comes as cells divide, replicating themselves within the body. In the church the groups divide as they grow (group theory suggests that when a group reaches approximately ten people, it's time to divide), and as the numbers of groups grow, organizational networks develop to facilitate communication and coordination of activities. Groups will take on the personality of the members who decide on matters of leadership, study, worship, and service. Growth occurs when permission is given by the congregation to the groups for them to discern God's direction. In time, as new groups are created, new opportunities for ministry emerge and new people are assimilated. The system remains healthy as long as the cells remain committed to maintaining the common good.

Cell groups allow for new ideas to emerge and valuable ways of bringing seekers into the community. They also provide important forums for empowering people for ministry, as they take ministry responsibilities within the small group. This is because, by their nature, small groups offer important opportunities for people to explore, discover, and make use of gifts of the Spirit in context that can be permissive and supportive. These groups offer the opportunity for interdependent (as opposed to dependent) relationships to develop and in the smallness of the community

---

[185] For a discussion of the base community see Alvaro Barreiro, *Basic Ecclesial Communities: The Evangelization of the Poor*, trans. by Barbara Campbell, (Maryknoll, NY: Orbis Books, 1982).

there is less pressure to perform. Therefore, people begin to work together with the interests of the other in mind, contributing their various gifts to the whole and ministry happens. Use of cell groups as the foundation for congregational ministry, therefore, moves the focus from governance to service.

MATCHING GIFTS TO MINISTRIES

Since we've been using the biblical analogy of the body to understand the church, it would be useful to see the organizational structure of the church as the skeleton that holds together the various parts of the body. This structure is firm enough and strong enough to support the body, but flexible enough to accomplish the tasks assigned to it. In connecting the gifts to the structures of the church, we need to ask how gifts are connected to responsibility within the body. So, we might want to ask about what gifts would be necessary to fulfill the ministry of elder. The answer to this question will, of course, depend on one's definition of this ministry (and not all traditions share the same definition).[186] But what about teachers or moderators or worship team members? What about those who provide care to those in need? What gifts are needed? Then, further on, how do these gifts fit with the structure as it now exists? Although I'm open to remodeling our structures, if necessary, I believe that a theology of giftedness can transform most ecclesial structures. Therefore, as we ask how gifts fit the structure, we'll also need to concern ourselves with the ways in which gifts reform structures.

To start with how gifts can inform the way people are brought into positions of leadership and service, perhaps it would help to look at a specific example. In the Disciples of Christ tradition, we have what some would call lay elders. These people, male and female, are called out from the congregation (elected) to serve several

---

186 In my Disciples tradition, Elders are lay leaders who provide spiritual leadership to the church, offer prayers at the table, and share in the pastoral care of the members of the church. In other traditions an elder is an ordained member of the clergy.

functions, both liturgical (at the Table) and pastoral. Since duties vary from congregation to congregation, a congregation will first need to give thought to what an elder is and does. Since in the Disciples tradition elders are seen as sharing with the pastor in the spiritual and pastoral leadership of the church, their gift mix could include gifts of teaching, pastor, encouragement/exhortation, intercessory prayer, leadership. The way in which an elder fills this ministry will depend in part on the nature of his or her gifts. Some elders may focus more on teaching and others on pastoral care. Their strength as spiritual leaders will be found in their sense of connectedness, their sense of interdependence. Those gifted for teaching will focus on teaching, while those gifted for ministries of encouragement and counseling will focus on that area of ministry. Together as a group, their shared commitment to the spiritual well being of the congregation will help them set the congregation free to discover and make use of their gifts in various ministries, all the while keeping the focus on the common good.

We can find the same sense of connectedness of gifts and ministries in every area of church life. Teams of pastoral callers might be formed from people gifts such as pastor, encourager, prayer, or mercy, for this ministry requires people who are empathetic, good listeners, and comfortable praying for people. Worship teams might include people gifted for ministries of teaching or music, but also craftsmanship, dance (could that be a gift?) or drama. Ultimately, it's the combination of people and their gifts that will create the texture of the ministry team. What may seem like a combination of disparate gifts can often serve to create a unique form of ministry that's needed in that particular congregation.

The principle that helps guide a congregation in its pursuit of living as an expression of the body of Christ is this: such congregations recognize that no one person has all the gifts necessary to fulfill God's calling to be a church, not even the pastor. We need each other's gifts, passions, visions, and personalities to fully express the church's existence as Christ's body. A congregation that pays attention to the relationship of gifts and the needs of the moment will be much more effective in creating proactive forms of ministry and facing new challenges. Knowing which gifts are needed for particular ministry tasks makes it easier to find people to take on those tasks.

We can begin this process with a few intuitive/reflective exercises. We start by listing the congregation's ministries in one column and noting the required gifts in a parallel column.

Exercise 1: Connecting gifts and ministries

Make a list of the possible ministries in the life of the church and their corresponding gifts:

Ministries	Gifts

The second step is to take note of the needs within the congregation. Although we might not want to acknowledge self-interest, self-interests must be taken into account. Remember Jesus calls on us to love our neighbors as we ourselves. Identifying needs within the community will allow for matching gifts with needs. To take the next step of missional engagement we must work toward creating communities of spiritual power.

Exercise 2: What are the needs in my congregation?

Having considered our self-interests as a community we're ready to look out into the world and discern the needs and concerns that lie out our doors. Again, taking note of the needs of neighbors we are enabled to match gifts with needs, so that ministry can take place efficiently and effectively. It's easy to limit the extent to which spiritual gifts define our lives. We can limit our use of gifts to the congregation, but surely there are needs in the community lying beyond the walls of our congregations that require our attention, and therefore ministry that is rooted in our spiritual gifts. If we're to be arks of blessing – bearers of the Spirit of God to the world – then we should expect God to be present and active wherever we're present in the world. Even when we're out in the world, seemingly by ourselves, we are in fact extensions of the body of Christ.

Exercise 3: What needs do I see in the world around me?

As we discern needs we can begin to plan strategically how to best fill these needs by unleashing the giftedness of the congregation. As we do this we may begin to see where we fit in the body of Christ. Am I a hand? An ear? A foot? The answers to these questions will lead to the realization that each of us is unique and therefore indispensable members of the body. After all, no one can fulfill your calling quite like you can.

Your personhood and personality will determine how and where you serve. That being true, it takes time to figure out the how and where. You have to get to know the other parts of the body and see where you fit. To shift metaphors for a moment, it's something like a jig-saw puzzle. You discern your place by seeing where your piece fits into the puzzle, and it's the Spirit who has the vantage point to bring these pieces into place. How these pieces fit defines the nature of a congregation, and because congregation is different, how we fit into the puzzle will change from place to place should we move to a new community.

Guided by the Spirit we're able to listen for the voices of the other members who draw us into place. Perhaps the voice calling out speaks of the need for tending the nursery during worship, and you discern that you have the requisite gifts and so you volunteer. The same is true of the church school, the pastoral care team, or property. Is this how we normally work as church? Probably not, but if we're attentive to the Spirit we can move in this direction.

Some of the ministry points will exist within the ecclesial community, as part of this community's spiritual self-care. Other ministry points occur outside the ecclesial community as the congregation expresses itself missionally. By drawing on one's spiritual gifts, persons are empowered to live and work and be a blessing to the wider community.

In discerning our points of service, we will ask questions like: Can I help provide meals to the homeless? Weatherize homes? Do the taxes for an older person? Tutor people learning a new language or tutor disadvantaged children so that they can make the next steps toward self-sufficiency? It could be assisting battered women find a place of shelter and safety, or serving as an advocate for women and children in society. It might involve advocacy for changing foreclosure or immigration laws. One might engage in building bridges across religious divides or work for civility in community dialog. The opportunities to minister in the public square are as infinite as the Spirit opens our hearts and minds to them.

Our ability to fully embrace our missional calling requires the sustaining presence of the Holy Spirit, who places us in strong support networks – that is – within congregations and communities. This work in the world is an extension of this body. It doesn't matter whether we go out as individuals or as groups, we do so as expressions of the body of Christ, so that we might "grow up in every way into him who is the head, into Christ, from whom the whole body, joined and knit together by every ligament with which it is equipped, as each part is working properly, promotes the body's growth in building itself up in love" (Ep. 4:15-16).

If we understand ourselves as being part of the body, knit together by the Spirit, then what are the needs addressed by my gifts, whether inside or outside the ecclesial community?

Exercise 4: Which needs might I address with my gifts?

Under normal circumstances we would want to engage in ministries that reflect our giftedness, but sometimes the needs of the moment require that we move beyond our comfort zone. When such times come, and they will come, the Spirit of God will make provision for this time and place. Giftedness is in part built into our personhood, but it's also something that the Spirit creates in the moment of time to fulfill a need of the moment. Sometimes, the needs of the moment ignite what appear to be latent gifts that have lain dormant until that moment. What might appear to be something outside our ordinary range of ministry becomes an act of faith in the provision of God. Realize, however, that the way you approach these new responsibilities will reflect to a great extent your mix of spiritual gifts as well as your personality.

Building a Ministry Team

I've been using the organic image of the body to describe the community, and this is a very biblical image and one that I have long embraced. But we could use a more modern image – that of the team. Being that I've been a sports aficionado, even if not gifted as an athlete, I appreciate the metaphor of the team. As with the body metaphor, this one also highlights interdependence.

Consider how a general manager and a manager fashion a baseball team. Such a team requires nine players (there are no designated hitters in this vision of the spiritual reality), and the gifts required by each player differs according to their responsibility. Center fielders, for instance, usually are rather speedy players because they have to cover more ground. Left fielders may not need as much speed, but hopefully they bring power. Shortstops need quickness, range, and leadership skills. Catchers needn't be fast, but they need quick hands and feet and great awareness of the game. When managers field their teams, they take into consideration the various skills, abilities, and personalities to set their lineup – both defensively and offensively. Not only that, but even if you're the best player in the league, if the rest of the team isn't commensurate in ability, the team won't succeed. The same is true of the church, and it is Jesus, the head of the church, who puts the team together.

If Jesus is the head of the church, the leadership of the church is the means by which Jesus builds the team. Although it's God who gives the gifts, and therefore, it's God who ultimately assigns us our ministries, it's the leadership structure of the congregation, including pastors, that set the lineups and in essence serve as player-coaches. Those who are called upon to discern who should be called to certain positions of leadership and service need to do so prayerfully, seeking God's guidance as they look at the various gifts and abilities possessed by the people before them and then work to place each person in the right ministry. They must do the church equivalent of scouting out the players and their gifts, and then after this can begin to develop and staff ministry teams.

Every team will have new players who need to discover and hone their gifts. This means giving people the opportunity to experience ministry in the church. I've known gifted preachers and musicians, but at some point someone gave that person a chance to stretch their wings and try to fly. Therefore, it behooves us to provide people opportunities to try out ministries in the church to see if they have particular gifts without having them make long-term commitments (similar to providing for some minor league experience). While playing in different positions, one might discover new gifts and new ministries. To prevent this process from becoming mechanical, church leaders will need to always keep the needs of the people in mind.

Most churches will have two kinds of people, volunteer ministers and paid staff. What is true of "volunteer" ministers is also true of paid staff. Churches that discover the need for additional paid staff should first look at the gifts present in the community, including the gifts of the pastor(s), and then decide which areas of church life need to be strengthened with new staff members. It does the church no good to hire staff persons with gifts and callings that duplicate those of the pastor – the exception being someone in an internship experience that involves a mentoring relationship. The goal is to expand the ministry of the church through team building.

As churches look at expanding paid staff, they might look first at persons within the congregation. Brian Bauknight suggests that "most if not all, staff can rise out of the membership of the congregation." There is wisdom in this approach, but there are also risks in hiring from within – if the need to dismiss an employee arises it can put a strain on the congregation. The pros and cons of such a decision need to be weighed, but recognizing and employing gifted members of the congregation is important.[187] The reason for employing staff is that it allows a person to give greater attention to the work of the body because they will be free from the need of employment outside the church.

We have already asked the question of the needs of the congregation and where individual Christians might serve, but as the church begins to build a team it will need to look more broadly at the total makeup of the church. Leadership will need to begin looking at the congregation and discern where gifts lie and how these gifts might be put to use in the meeting of the needs within the church.

Exercise 5: What are the strengths and needs of the congregation?

Building a ministry team, a process that involves paid and non-paid persons, ordained and non-ordained, also involves paying attention to the strengths and needs of the congregation. As people begin to discover their gifts, test them out, make use of them in real time experiences, they will grow in confidence. As this happens, the ministry team will grow in effectiveness.

For this process to be successful, church members must be in covenantal relationships with each other. The danger of focusing on giftedness is that it can easily lead us down the path of individualism, which can be very debilitating to the life of a church. "Covenantal relationships" Max DePree suggests, "rest on shared commitment to ideas, to issues, to values, to goals, and to manage-

---

187 Bauknight, *Body Building,* 68. Bauknight's book develops the question of staffing in some detail and should be consulted by churches seeking to expand their ministry staff.

ment processes." An advocate of participative management, DePree has called for the development of intimate relationships between management and workers. Being in covenant relationship, a mutual commitment to each other, allows for this sense of mutuality and intimacy to grow and develop. Covenantal relationships also allow for a hospitable response to the "unusual person and unusual ideas" and allow for the toleration of risk and the forgiveness of errors. This environment of forgiveness and trust is essential if the church is to release people to explore, discover, develop, and use their spiritual gifts.[188] It's not enough for people to volunteer; they must be committed to the common good, a good that depends on recognizing our interdependence (covenantal relationship).

WHO IS YOUR MENTOR?

Some things come easier to me than other things. I expect that's true of all of us. But even those things that come "naturally" need to be honed and developed. In an earlier church where I served as pastor there was a young child who amazed us with her ability to play the violin with competence and grace at the age of five. She was a natural, but even with such natural gifts, she required a teacher to guide her in her practice and preparation. This is true of any gift. Teachers need mentors. Master carpenters spend time as an apprentice. Although there comes a time when we're competent to go out on our own, the relationship between master and student never really ends. The relationship changes, but the master always is the master, even if I seem to surpass the mentor in ability and accomplishment. There is always something that I can learn from an outside observer.

Gift discovery and implementation is a life time process, requiring continual prayer and reflection on God's will for our lives. No one will ever get to the point of completion in this life. As people discover their gifts they will need to learn to use them, to

---

188 Max DePree, *Leadership is an Art,* (New York: Dell Publishing, 1989), 60-61.

practice with them, honing the skills that accompany these gifts. Giftedness doesn't mean that one can do any and everything without training or practice. A gifted cellist or pianist will go only so far on ability or giftedness. Hard work and continuous practice is required to master the instrument. One may be a gifted athlete but unless the raw talent is refined the athlete will be nothing more than potential. Many a potential superstar goes to the major leagues only to falter because they lack the discipline and desire to refine their natural abilities. The same is true of the gifted believer.

A gifted teacher or provider of pastoral care must work hard at developing the gifts God gives. The first step in effectively using these gifts is to experience a mentoring relationship. Remember Jesus invested three years of his life developing the gifts of the twelve; we can use something similar ourselves.

Mentoring begins as congregations realize that effective and long-lasting communities learn to pass on the wisdom of the ages. There's value in maturity and experience, for maturity involves learning. As a parent I had the responsibility of instilling in my son values and supporting him as he tried new things. As he grew older, he thought he could get along more and more without our help, but at the end of the day even in early adulthood he turns to mom and dad for help.

Mentors tell the story of the community. They give context to gifts and ministries. They help us realize our connectedness with one another. Mentors can be especially helpful to young people and to new believers, offering guidance in finding one's place in the community. Yes, the mature in faith play an important role in the life of the church, for they provide guidance in both word and deed. Honest mentors also let us know that it's okay to make mistakes.

If we read Ephesians 4, it's clear that a primary calling for those gifted as pastors and teachers is to equip the saints for ministry, and that includes mentoring persons (Eph. 4:12). But, this calling isn't limited to pastors and teachers – all of the mature in faith can take the opportunity to usher younger persons into full expressions of their giftedness in the ministries of the church.

Unfettered Spirit

As you find your place in the body, you may discover that you're a hand or a foot, a kidney or an eye. Whatever you are, even if society deems the gifts you bring to be "inferior," what you bring to the community is important, even essential. After all, where would the body be if everyone was an eye or a hand

THOUGHT QUESTIONS

1. Is it possible for one person to possess every gift? Why/why not?

2. What is the difference between a job and a ministry?

3. How might churches develop effective ministry teams?

4. What is a mentoring relationship? How might such a relationship help you in developing and using your gifts?

12

GET YOUR HANDS DIRTY:

ORGANIZING FOR MINISTRY OUTSIDE CHURCH WALLS

> The mission of the church . . . consists in proclaiming and teaching, but also in healing and liberating, in compassion for the poor and the downtrodden. The mission of the church, as the mission of Jesus, involves being sent into the world – to love, to serve, to preach, to teach, to heal, to save, to free.
>
> David J. Bosch[189]

From its birth at Pentecost until today, the church has been on a journey, carrying with it a Christ's message of grace, renewal, and hope (albeit, it hasn't always lived up to its calling). At its best this church has been an emissary of God's love, sharing in its words and its deeds a love that welcomes back the prodigal and cares for the stranger. It shows this love in its preaching and teaching, as well as through ministries of healing and liberation. As the body of Christ, the church has received from God the same calling as that of Jesus (Lk 4:16-21). Although the community is a place of preparation and support, the ministry of God most often takes place beyond the walls of our congregations. That is, the church doesn't simply

---

189 David J. Bosch, "Reflections on Biblical Models of Mission," in *Toward the 21st Century in Christian Mission,* James M. Phillips and Robert T. Coote, eds., (Grand Rapids: Wm. B. Eerdmans Publishing Co., 1993), 189-90.

exist for its own sake – it exists for the sake of the world that God loves so much (John 3:16).

The manner of the church's existence in the world has evolved and developed in a variety of ways and directions over the past two millennia. Sometimes it has adapted itself to better serve the community, and at other times it has retreated into the safety of its walls. The journey hasn't been a straight line. There have been hills and valleys, along with many a curve. If we use the metaphor of a river to describe this pathway, whenever that flow has dammed up, the Spirit has broken through, so that the work of God might continue on.

Over the course of time the church has faced persecution and hostile resistance, but in those areas where Christianity became the majority religion and Christendom held sway, the challenges often have come in the forms of complacency and triumphalism. Having come to believe that the culture was "Christian" many churches lost the spirit of mission. They might send missionaries to far off lands, but they didn't really see their own communities as places where the mission of God might take place. The church became the religious face of the culture.

Although many Christians hold on to the fading glory of Christendom, the day of a Christian hegemony in the West is over. Christianity no longer holds the same dominant position it once did. The world no longer waits with anticipation for the latest pronouncements by the religious establishment. With this change of cultural position, as we throw off the stain of complacency and triumphalism, comes an opportunity to become once again agents of transformation. As we do this, we reclaim our missional heritage, so that mission isn't just what some do over there, but it defines our identity as communities of faith.[190] We can become the leaven

---

[190] On the Mainline's possibilities for new life and ministry see Diana Butler Bass's book *Christianity for the Rest of Us: How the Neighborhood Church is Transforming the Faith*, (San Francisco: Harper One, 2007); and Carol Howard Merritt's *Reframing Hope: Vital Ministry in a New Generation*, (Herndon, VA: Alban Institute, 2010).

that prophetically challenges the status quo from within, allowing the kingdom of God to take root. Grafted into the Israel of God as heirs to the promise to Abraham, the church we might become is a sign of God's blessing in our world.

THE CHURCH AS AN AGENT OF TRANSFORMATION

If we try to look at the world through the eyes of God, we might look at things differently than we often do. What happens when we look at the world through the lens of love? How does this influence the way we see the world? Remember that when God looks at the world God doesn't just see human beings, God sees the entirety of creation and seeks to bring harmony or shalom to this creation of God's.

When God sees creation, God sees something that is good and worthy of redemption. Therefore, our ministry isn't bound up by ethnicity or geography, language or social class. But, having said this, it's important that we recognize and respect the differences inherent in the world's diverse cultures. Born in the Ancient Near East, the Christian faith became the dominant religion in Europe and over time Christianity became beholden to European culture, which proceeded to domesticate it. Indeed, sometimes it's difficult to distinguish between the Euro-American social-cultural elements and the distinctly Christian ones.

Christianity has been rightfully critiqued for embracing imperialist and colonialist ways. Too often Christian mission became a tool for pacification of a conquered people, and being a Christian became wrapped up in the adoption of the mores of western civilization. But things are changing. As Christianity has become an increasingly globalized faith, where the majority of Christians live in the Global South, these Euro-centric bonds are being broken and the colonialist vision of the faith is fading away.

Christianity is expanding most rapidly in Sub-Saharan Africa and Asia. Korea, a country that little more than a century ago received its first Protestant missionaries, is now more than thirty percent Christian. This new reality isn't only remaking the face of the church, the mission sending and receiving countries have become reversed. Europe is now receiving missionaries from countries where it once sent them. A call to mission isn't a call to civilize the natives, either there or here! Instead, mission involves living into a message that brings healing and grace to political, social, cultural, environmental, and economic arenas of life.

The story or our engagement with the world begins in the first chapter of the book of Acts where Jesus commissions his followers to embrace a mission that will touch the "ends of the earth."

But you will receive power when the Holy Spirit has come upon you; and you will be my witnesses in Jerusalem, in all Judea and Samaria, and to the ends of the earth (Acts 1:8).

The church, the temple of the Holy Spirit, is the bearer of the blessings of God's presence. The church as an institution is very human, but it carries a divine mandate. It's not a mandate to rule but to serve. With the coming of the promised Spirit of God, the church begins this mission in the world. It starts in Jerusalem, but with a bit of pushing and prodding and leading, the Spirit enables the church to move out into the world touching it with God's redeeming and transforming love.

In the beginning this community of Jesus' followers was a Jewish sect. It took time for this sense of identity to change, but we see hints of a broader vision in the gospels. We see an opening up of the gospel to the broader world in Jesus' encounters with the centurion, the Samaritan woman, and the Syro-Phoenician woman. In Jesus' ministry we see signs that the reign of God transcends religion, ethnicity, economic status, gender, and geography. In Christ, Paul tells us, "there is neither Jew nor Greek, slave or free, male and female." Instead we are all one in Christ (Gal. 3:28). Peter's dream at Joppa reminds us that what God declares clean is clean (Acts 10). All our walls of separation are falling down, which means that this mission has no boundaries. The message of the reign of God on earth as in heaven is an inclusive one, a message that builds bridges where chasms once existed.

Unfettered Spirit

This vision of church life seems to have been first experienced in the church of Antioch, where a community that was diverse in ethnicity and culture gathered in the name of Christ. It was this church that being attentive to the Spirit of God heard a missionary call. Composed of both Jews and Gentiles, it caught the vision of taking the gospel to Asia Minor and beyond (Acts 13:1-3). It also took seriously the call to care for the neighbor, gathering supplies to send to famine-stricken Jerusalem (Acts 11:27-29).

The mission that begins in Jerusalem and extends outward through Antioch will reach completion when all things are taken up into Christ (Phil. 2:9-11), giving impetus to a reclaiming of our missionary calling as Christendom fades into history. In order to reclaim this calling, we will need the same empowering presence of the Spirit that fueled the first wave of mission. The challenge is waking up to the realities of our day, recognizing that not only is attendance and membership on the decline but the depth of spiritual engagement in the West, in America as well as Europe, is shallow. But maybe this means we're ready for a new revival of the Spirit in our midst – another great awakening perhaps? Could it be that the awakening has been underway for some time and we're just catching on? And could this new awakening be one that reaches across religious lines, so that we can embrace a new vision of hospitality?[191]

If the church is full of Spirit endowed and gifted people, then it's capable of making a significant difference in the world. What it takes is a new vision of its place in the world. Instead of being a temple that never moves, it's a tabernacle that moves with the people bringing blessing or judgment (whichever is needed at the time) wherever it goes.

---

191 Diana Butler Bass, *Christianity After Religion: The End of Church and the Birth of a New Spiritual Awakening,* (San Francisco: Harper One, 2012), 239-245. Amos Yong, *Hospitality and the Other: Pentecost, Christian Practices, and the Neighbor,* (Maryknoll, NY: Orbis Books, 2008), 106-108.

Jesus says to the church: "You are the light of the world." If we're the light of the world, then it would be inappropriate to keep that light hidden under a bushel basket. If we're to be light-bearers who bring good news, then we'll need to bring this light into the places we live and work and play (Mt. 5:14-16). When the light begins to shine, then areas of need are discovered and work can commence.

The vision of God for the world comes to the church as it gives attention to the groans and cries of the world. It listens as the Holy Spirit interprets these groans and cries that are too deep for words (Rom. 8:18-27) to God and to the church. Our mission is rooted in these cries. It occurs not just in the church but wherever the church encounters the world (which isn't usually within the walls of the church). Remember that Jesus was criticized for dining with "sinners and tax collectors," but this very act of identification with those in need of healing reminds us of the places where ministry occurs. While technology, including social media, can extend the reach of the mission of God, it doesn't replace the human connection, and isn't the point of the incarnation. God touches us directly in Christ. So, if the Spirit of God is to be experienced, most likely it will be in the form of embodied persons.

As agents of healing in the world, we take the light we receive from the Spirit as a church and shine it in the world. Paul and Barnabas heard this call to take the light of God to the Gentiles, so that the word of salvation might be brought to the ends of the earth (Acts 13:47). Salvation means more than simply saving souls or making converts to the Christian faith. Without rejecting our evangelistic mandate (Mt. 28:19-20) it's important that we have a broader definition of salvation that involves the ideas of healing and wholeness.

The message that we've been entrusted with is a message of reconciliation. In bringing this message to a fragmented world, we recognize the alienation that's present not only in the world, but in our own lives. This ministry of reconciliation is more than one dimensional, even as our alienation is more than one dimensional.

Unfettered Spirit

It begins with the walls we've built to keep God out of our lives. That wall building exercise doesn't end there. We build walls between ourselves and our neighbors (isn't this the point of the second half of the Ten Commandments?), ourselves and the creation (our spoliation of the environment), and within our own beings.

One sign of this Spirit-empowered ministry of reconciliation is seen in the Pentecost reversal of the story of Babel. In the story of Babel, humanity seeks to storm heaven and take power, and God responds by confusing their languages and dispersing humanity across the world. Now, at Pentecost, with the gift of understanding (or gift of languages), the confusion is ended and a movement toward reconciliation begins. This work of breaking down walls and building bridges must remain at the heart of the church's mission. As we seek to move into this mission of God, our congregations need to be about permission giving, so that the people of God can utilize their gifts to bring this message of God's wholeness and healing to a fragmented world.[192]

If the church is to move outside its walls and bear witness to the gospel of Jesus in deeds and in words, then this will require that all hands be on deck. This isn't a ministry that involves just the pastor and a few committed lay persons. Clergy can play an important role in this work, but we all have roles to play if we're to be effective in this ministry.[193]

If our ministry is to occur outside the walls, it's important to remember that the call to service occurs within worship. Isaiah heard God's call as he was caught up in worship of the Living God. Even as he joined with the heavenly chorus in singing "Holy, holy, holy is the Lord of hosts; the whole earth is full of his glory," he heard God call out: "Whom shall I send and who will go for us?" With Isaiah, the church cries out: "Here am I; send me" (Is. 6:1-8). This is what Kirk Hadaway means when he says that the purpose of

---

[192] Kirk Hadaway, *Behold, I Do a New Thing,* (Cleveland: Pilgrim Press, 2001), 78-79.
[193] Loren Mead, *Five Challenges for the Once and Future Church,* (New York: The Alban Institute, 1996), 69.

worship is not to "alleviate, educate, and motivate," but is instead intended to "provoke, evoke, and transform."[194] In our worship, we hear the call and receive the empowering presence of God to complete the job.

As a missionary community, the church, seeks to be present where God is already at work. This call to mission, as we have seen, emerges in the context of worship that is vibrant and life giving. The style does not matter, it can be traditional or contemporary, but it will focus our attention beyond ourselves to the work that God is doing in the world.[195] This church is marked by flexibility and the ability to adapt to a changing landscape. When new people come in to the church they will be grafted in and made fully functioning members of the body. Like a branch grafted on to a vine, this new branch will become part of the whole. In the course of being grafted onto the vine, the stranger experiences healing and redemption.

Ministry Outside the Walls

When I began this project many years ago, I hadn't heard of the missional church. As far as I know, the missional movement didn't even exist at that point. Over the course of the past decade or so the descriptor – missional – has become pervasive. Although it originated in evangelical circles, the idea of being missional has taken hold within mainline Protestant circles. It resonates with people, like me who've realized that simply trying to "grow a church" for the sake of the church's survival won't work. Institutional religion as an end in itself is an idea whose time is gone. It no longer captures the hearts and minds of the emerging generations who are more inclined to the spiritual than the religious. The idea that you could build it and they would come is a premise that no longer

---

194 Hadaway, *Behold I Do a New Thing*, 98-102; Robert Cueni tells of what happens to a church that loses its focus in worship and becomes little more than a museum; R. Robert Cueni, *Dinosaur Heart Transplants: Renewing Mainline Congregations*, (Nashville: Abingdon Press, 2000), 125-31.
195 Mead, *Five Challenges*, 73.

holds true. It may have once been possible to put on a good show and attract a crowd, but the competition is too varied for this to work going forward. Religion based on institution and spectacle is giving way to a new model that is Spirit-empowered, Christ-centered, and mission oriented. No one was going to come to church for a concert or to join a committee. Ministry needed to touch lives and change realities.[196]

The missional model of the church understands the church to be an agent of transformation that is focused on touching lives rather than institutional survival. It's focused on moving across borders and being the presence of Christ in the broader world. Although I love Luther's grand hymn "A Mighty Fortress Is Our God," the church can no longer live as if it's a fortress, with walls designed to keep the world out. It's not a fortress where we wait out the world's siege until Christ comes to rescue us. But, if we're to move out into the world we don't do so as if we're "Christian soldiers marching as to war, with the cross of Jesus going on before." Such triumphalist images and attitudes undermine the gospel of Jesus. Although we may indeed storm the public square, the purpose for this action isn't domination but justice for those on the margins. Whatever our mission effort, we go forth in the healing presence of the Spirit. We go into the world to be leaven rather than be leavened.

As the body of Christ, its many members knit and sewn together by the Spirit, we bear witness to God's ministry of reconciliation (2 Cor. 5:20). This message is important because we live in a world full of people who know nothing but anger, grief, and skepticism. There is alienation, anger and fear, as well as feelings of powerlessness and despair. I believe that Christ is present in the midst of this reality, and that we can be bearers of good news as we embrace the work of Christ in the world, knowing that when

---

196 On the Missional Movement there are a number of helpful books, including those authored by Alan Roxburgh and Craig Van Gelder, but perhaps the best treatment I've found is that written by Gary Nelson, *Borderland Churches: A Congregation's Introduction to Missional Living*, (St. Louis: Chalice Press, 2008).

we move in the Spirit and let love have the freedom to work, then change begins to happen (Acts. 13:47).

You could say that each Christian is a mission station, for most Christians spend the majority of their time and energy in places outside the walls of the church. We might do this in the spirit of St. Columba, the Celtic monastic leader, who founded monasteries not as places of retreat from the world but as the staging ground for mission. With this in mind, how might our spiritual gifts enable us to be that mission station in the world that God loves?

This is really a question of vocation, of calling. Paul wrote about this to the Corinthian church: "Let each of you lead the life that the Lord has assigned, to which God called you" (1 Cor. 7:17). In speaking of vocation or calling, Paul doesn't speak to clergy; he speaks to every believer, telling them in essence to "bloom where you're planted." This is what Jürgen Moltmann means by the charismatic nature of the messianic community, which exists not only in solemn assemblies, but even more so as we are scattered into the world throughout the week.

The call to the fellowship of Christ and the gift of the Holy Spirit makes a charisma out of bondage and freedom, marriage and celibacy, manhood and womanhood, Jewish and Gentile existence. For the call puts the person's particular situation at the service of the new creation.[197]

If we're walking in the Spirit of God, this practice affects everything we do in life. These gifts that God provides allow us to serve God wherever we go – whether we're a teacher, a physician, a custodian or a nurse, a carpenter or even a politician. These gifts of the Spirit allow us to be agents of reconciliation. If we allow the Spirit room to move in our lives, then we can join with God in listening for the cries of the world and offer grace in response.

---

197 Moltmann, *The Church in the Power of the Spirit*, 296.

Churches Making a Difference

The church's mission is rooted in God's compassion and love for the entirety of creation. We participate in this mission of compassion and grace in a variety of ways. Indeed, the church is at its best when it sees itself as a servant to God's creation We see it present in the building of hospitals, schools, housing projects, provisions of nursing care, advocacy for the marginalized, environmental actions, even spiritually motivated political action. It takes up such callings with no expectation of reciprocity. Aid isn't given in exchange for conversion, but out of the love that flows from the heart of God. These are the good works that God promises to provide as the church shines the light of Christ into the world. Although words interpret and invite, the church's deeds demonstrate love in tangible ways.

Around the world, both at home and abroad, the church has reached out with compassion by establishing hospitals and medical clinics, homes for the elderly and for children without families. Albert Schweitzer may be best known for his biblical scholarship, but his lasting legacy was his ministry of medicine in Africa. In the area of education, the church has been a primary provider for the world's children and adults. Sunday schools, which today focus on religious education, originally provided instruction in reading and writing to the underprivileged. University education in the United States was originally church provided, and missionaries have made the establishment of colleges and universities a major priority.

Medical and educational ministries are usually supported financially by local congregations, but what about actual hands on ministries. There are opportunities that present themselves in every community for outreach. Habitat for Humanity, homeless shelters, counseling centers, and more, offer the possibility of getting our hands dirty. Many of these efforts require collaboration with other groups. Large churches may have the resources to tackle the problems of the community on their own, but smaller churches will need to join with other congregations, non-profits, parachurch organizations, and even governmental agencies.

I have come to believe that one of the most effective ways for the church to live out its missional calling is to engage in congregation-based community organizing. Groups like PICO National Network and Gamaliel work with congregations to build powerful coalitions. They provide leadership training and help coalitions develop strategies that will impact local communities. They advocate for justice, pushing governments and corporations to live up to their responsibilities for the common good. What is important to remember is that this kind of community organizing is value-based. Issues change, but values don't. Kendall Clark Baker has written an extremely helpful introduction to faith-based community organizing that lays out the rationale and methods of community organizing. In his discussion of values and issues, he points out how this works and notes the role clergy play in the process:

> Faith-based organizing is value driven. Values are embedded in stories. It's the clergy role, as steward of the values, to have a critical awareness of the stories of the consumerist world in which our people live, and to know by heart the stories of our people, and to set these stories in the larger context of the story of God which in truth expresses the only value that is "priceless."[198]

Groups such as these are working on voting rights, education reform, ending youth violence, and more. My own congregation has gotten engaged in founding just this kind of effort, and it bodes well for the church and the community.

When we step out into the community and begin to live as Christ-bearers, we never know how and when we'll be called upon to bring blessing and healing and hope to a part of the broader community. In a community where I formerly lived, the local

---

[198] Kendall Clark Baker, *When Faith Storms the Public Square: Mixing Religion and Politics through Community Organizing to Enhance our Democracy,* (Cleveland: Circle Books, 2011), 156.

hospital's spiritual care department engages the efforts of volunteer chaplain's aids who visit patients and offer prayer and other kinds of support. You can read to the blind, make recordings, tutor underprivileged children, teach English as a second language, or fix the cars for the elderly. There are endless numbers of opportunities to serve, all of which can be extensions of the congregation's ministry and make use of Spirit-endowed gifts.

Each of these efforts of outreach require gifted, passionate, and compassionate people to take up the struggle to make the world a safer, more civil, more compassionate place to live. Our journey of faith begins within our own hearts as we discern the walls that exist between us and God, between us and our neighbors, between us and the creation. That realization allows for openness to the Spirit of God that brings healing of the spirit. From that healing comes the opportunity to devote one's abilities (divinely given) to the service of the kingdom of God.

THOUGHT QUESTIONS

1. What role does the church play in the world? How might God use the church – as the body of Christ – to transform and redeem the world?
2.
3. What is the difference between an attractional and a missional church?

4. What kinds of ministries might one engage in that would have this kind of effect on the world?

5. How do we engage in this kind of ministry without becoming triumphalist or feel superior to others?

6. What gifts do you bring to this missional calling?

An Afterword

Reflections on Spiritual Gifts and the Ordained Ministry

I am an ordained minister. That's my confession. As a member of this clergy club (I'm an active member in an organization called the Academy of Parish Clergy), it would seem that I have a vested interest in sustaining my professional privileges, but I've long believed that ministry is a vocation shared by all God's children. I'm not sure how flat the church needs to be, but any vision of the church that exalts the clergy above the rest of the body does disservice to God's realm. In developing a theology of gift-based ministry, I'm less concerned about polity and more concerned with our willingness as clergy to allow the Spirit the freedom to empower the people of God for their ministry vocations. Although some churches are flatter than others, most faith communities have some form of leadership structure. The question for those of us in traditions that ordain persons to particular forms of ministry that go by the name "clergy" is how this form of ministry fits with a gift-based model of the church

Is it possible that as a paid ordained pastor, that I am something of an anachronism facing extinction? If we move toward a Spirit-led and Spirit empowered church form of church, does my "profession" have value to the church, to the world, to God? Or, should I find a new profession better suited for the coming age?

I've long believed that ministry isn't the sole domain of a select group of people whom we call ministers, pastors, or clergy. My years in the pastorate haven't changed my mind. But, I've also come to believe that pastors or ministers can have an important role to play in the life of a faith community. In part this is due to my experience in pastoral ministry. Although clergy can get in the way of the Spirit, as the Ephesian letter reminds us, there is a place for leadership and instruction and that God has provided those gifts to the church – both in terms of abilities and I would say offices.

Can a church get along without a pastor? History and experience suggest that the answer is yes. Churches need leaders, but ordained pastors, while helpful aren't a necessity. At least that is true for my own tradition, where neither the ministry of word nor sacrament is limited to clergy. Elders, who in the Disciples tradition are lay people, can preach, baptize, and celebrate the Lord's Supper. Still, even Disciples have rites of ordination that set some apart for specific ministries in the church. We give them certificates that they hang on their walls along with their diplomas. In a Disciples covenant of installation, a newly called pastor accepts this charge:

> *To lead in transmitting the Christian tradition*
>   *from one generation to another;*
> *to interpret the scriptures and proclaim the gospel of Christ;*
> *to administer the sacraments,*
>   *serving in the company of Christians*
>   *in continuity with the life and faith of the apostles;*
> *to serve God's people with pastoral care and to share in the*
>   *strengthening of the church in its life and mission;*
> *and to act as pioneers and leaders in the church's reconciling*
>   *work in the world.*[199]

This is a good description of what pastors do in their ministries, (though it does leave out all the administrative tasks that tend to dominate the typical week of ministry). But is there a reason why this kind of ministry should be limited to those we call and ordain as pastors or ministers? Most Christian traditions reserve certain

---

199 Colbert S. Cartwright and O. I. Cricket Harrison, eds., *Chalice Worship,* (St. Louis: Chalice Press, 1997), 198.

ministries to the clergy, which makes people like me necessary cogs in the machinery, but as I've been arguing since page one of this book, the gifts and calling for ministry fall on clergy and laity alike. And so, the question is: Am I necessary?

The Mormon Church does without clergy, though not without ordained leadership. Some Quaker groups rely on the Spirit, not the clergy. Might we not follow their example? In Islam the Imam's authority derives from his (at this point Imams are male) knowledge of the Qur'an not ordination. Might we look to this model? As a rabbi, Jesus was not recognized by any official board, and yet the people acclaimed him their teacher and master. They recognized in him a message of grace and truth that compelled them to follow him (this was truly a "charismatic" form of religious leadership – personal not institutional). What does Jesus' example say to us?

A Pastoral Identity Crisis?!

The question of whether ordination is essential or important in a gift-based ecclesiology, which I'm raising here, emerges at a time when a clergy identity crisis rages. It's clear that clergy have lost influence in society, but there are other factors that contribute to this growing identity crisis. There are two factors that seem at odds, but that contribute to the identity crisis. On one hand there's the fact that a majority of American churches are experiencing numerical decline making it more difficult to hire a seminary trained minister. On the other hand, there is the prospect of a clergy shortage due to retirement, the number of clergy leaving ministry due to stress and disillusionment, as well as a decline in the number of persons studying for ministry. Although there's a growing number of second career people entering seminary, the numbers of recent college graduates attending seminary has dropped precipitously. While prior experience in the world outside the church that second-career people bring to the ministry is of great value, the growing absence of younger clergy presents a loss of important voices in the church.

Those who remain in pastoral ministry will have discovered that this isn't a glamorous occupation. It may not even be all that respectable a vocation. It's not the kind of profession that parents hold out before their children as being worth pursuing. Business, medicine, law – these are a better future for our children, at least economically. Part of the reason for this is that very few pastors or religious leaders rank among society's most admired people. A Gallup poll from 2009 suggested that only 50% of Americans considered clergy to be honest, placing them behind police, nurses, pharmacists, police officers, and physicians.[200]

Although we would like to think there was a clergy golden age, clergy have always been viewed as different. Although there are exceptions, they've rarely been well paid or socially respectable. Frederick Buechner, who was himself a pastor, describes three popular and thus stereotypical views of pastors or ministers. The first stereotype suggests that pastors are "nice people" who try to make sure you know that they have their feet on the ground like everyone else. As such, they try not to offend anyone. A second view suggests that clergy "have their heads in the clouds" and don't get too involved in the real world. If you're a "normal" person, you will probably get embarrassed being around them, especially if you use "bad language." They are, however, supposed to have "a lovely sense of humor and get a kick out of it every time you ask if they can't do something about all this rainy weather we've been having." In this view pastors know their business is religion and leave other (more important?) matters to those who know better. Finally, there are those who see pastors being as "anachronistic as alchemists and chimney sweeps. Like Tiffany Glass or the Queen of England, their function is primarily decorative."[201] They do the marrying and the burying, but not much else.

---

200 http://www.gallup.com/poll/124628/clergy-bankers-new-lows-honesty-ethics-ratings.aspx
201 Frederick Buechner, *Wishful Thinking*, (San Francisco: Harper-Collins, 1992), 73. On the role of clergy in American history, see E. Brooks

Unfettered Spirit 213

Pastoral ministry doesn't have to live up to this stereotypical view of what it means to be a holy person, who is, as Donald Messer suggests, "a breed apart, oddly different from the rest of humanity, needing special care and treatment." Another stereotype that's equally untrue suggests that a minister is a "colorless, joyless, sexless creature."[202] Such stereotypes can make for lonely, separate lives. This needn't be our understanding of pastoral ministry. Although there are people who fit these stereotypes, most of us who have been ordained and serve in pastoral ministry don't see ourselves reflected in these stereotypes. But, with such bleak perceptions, it's no wonder that so few people would decide to join up for such an unrewarding career path

Pastors are human beings, who really aren't that different from others in the church. Their calling and responsibilities might be different, but just like everyone else they seek financial security, time with family, along with opportunities for relaxation and renewal. There may be differences between clergy and non-clergy, but there is little room for double-standards that suggest that clergy are to be holy and that laity experience that holiness vicariously.[203]

Still, in spite of everything we read, many still respond positively to the call to a dedicated form of ministry in the church. Some hear the call as young people and begin preparing to take up their calling early in life, as I did (although I did not take a pastorate until I was forty, thirteen years after my ordination). Others hear this call much later in life, and make incredible sacrifices to get their education.

Embracing a gift-based understanding of the church (ecclesiology) won't resolve all of the tensions inherent in the current system, but it raises the possibility of re-envisioning what ministry entails and what it means to be called to the specific form of ministry we

---

Holifield, *God's Ambassadors: A History of the Christian Clergy in America*, (Grand Rapids: Wm. B. Eerdmans Publishing Co., 2007).
202 Donald Messer, *Contemporary Images of Christian Ministry*, (Nashville: Abingdon Press, 1989), 13.
203 Messer, *Contemporary Images of Christian Ministry*, 13.

call ordained ministry. Clergy can begin to see themselves as part of a larger team of ministers called and empowered to live out the gospel of Jesus in the world. Clergy serve as mentors, teachers, leaders, but they don't do ministry on behalf of church members.

THE BIBLICAL CALL TO ORDAINED MINISTRY

Pushing the conversation further, we need to remember that there isn't a New Testament doctrine that envisions today's professional minister. The New Testament offers a variety of structures, some more formal than others, with Corinth and Ephesus offering contrasting examples. The Corinthians seem to have had a fairly informal structure, one guided by spiritually discerning elders (therefore it's not surprising that we find the bulk of teaching on spiritual gifts in a letter written to this church). The Ephesians letter, likely written a generation later, suggests a much more formalized structure that includes apostles, prophets, evangelists, pastors and teachers (Eph. 4:11). In a letter that may date even later than Ephesians, 1 Timothy envisions a church led by bishops (elders), presbyters, and deacons. In this discussion of presbyters (elders/pastors) and *episcope* (bishops/elders), the Pastorals flesh out a relationship between the church and its leaders that looks much different from the much earlier Corinthian church.

The responsibilities of what might be typical for a late first-century pastor are described in 1 Timothy, where an older experienced pastor writes to encourage a young colleague not let the people despise him for his youth (in the Pastorals at least it's pretty clear that pastors are male). Instead, Timothy's mentor tells him to set an example in his speech and conduct, and "give attention to the public reading of Scripture, to exhorting, to teaching." Finally, Timothy is told not to "neglect the gift that is in you, which was given to you through prophecy with the laying on of hands by the council of elders" (1 Tim. 4:12-14). This reference to a gift given by laying on of hands is the biblical foundation for an ordained ministry. Later in the letter, the author tells Timothy to rekindle this gift.

Unfettered Spirit

Vocational ministry, therefore, is in the words of this biblical writer a matter of giftedness, which must be rekindled on occasion.[204]

The way in which the church has conceived of pastoral ministry has evolved over time, taking on an increasingly priestly understanding, where the priest stood as mediator between the believer and God. Although this understanding was modified to some extent by the Protestant Reformation, the minister continues to have a mediatorial role, especially in terms of control over the sacraments. In Reformed theology, the pastor is minister of Word (preaching) and Sacrament (Eucharist/Baptism). A process developed by which persons – until recently this limited to males – were set apart for specialized forms of ministry through the laying on of hands. For some traditions, apostolic succession played a central role in this process. When a congregation, denomination, or perhaps a seminary has determined that a person is equipped and called to ordained ministry, hands are laid on them according to the pattern laid out in 1 Timothy, authorizing and empowering that person to carry out the duties of ordained ministry (1 Tim. 4:14).[205]

Although the way in which authority is conferred and understood, the assumption is that it's the Spirit of God who gifts, empowers, and commissions, while congregations, bishops, elders, affirm this calling. By recognizing a pastor's ordination, a congregation receives that person's leadership and guidance. Tradition and history help us understand how this authority should be exercised in the life of a congregation. Although our churches may use a variety of structural forms, it's important to recognize that the church isn't a democracy, ruled by majority vote. It's also not a clerical autocracy where elite groups of clergy hold sway. In a gift-based ecclesiology, there's the assumption the Spirit rules, and we are tasked with discerning where the Spirit is leading. This is true no matter what structure we happen to be a part of.

---

204 Messer, *Images of Christian Ministry*, 64.
205 Keith Watkins, *The Great Thanksgiving*, (St. Louis: Chalice Press, 1995), 210-11.

A Call to Representative Ministry

One way to make sense of ordained ministry while affirming the premise that all baptized Christians are priests of God is to see pastoral ministry defined as representative ministry. The pastor would embody for the congregation the call that all members share in. Therefore, whether standing at the pulpit or the Table, the ordained minister isn't just a representative of God to the people, but is also a representative of the people before God.[206]

By thinking of pastoral ministry as representative ministry, we start with the premise that every form of ministry is important. Therefore, no Christian is, by virtue of their office, holier than any other. There may be a difference in roles and even *charism*, but everyone is considered an important contributor to the health of the body of Christ. Those called to pastoral leadership don't do ministry for God's people, but equip and encourage the congregation in its ministries (Eph. 4:11-13). The goal of pastoral ministry is to help God's people reach maturity in Spirit, and that maturity leads to acts of service – the good works prepared for us by God.

Baptism becomes the place where the whole people of God receive their ordination to ministry. A further act of ordination designates certain people for specific forms of ministry. While God may issue the call, it's the church that affirms the call and through ordination this affirmation is witnessed to publically.[207]

The process of ordination allows the church to set standards and hold persons accountable to these standards. It's expected that those called to pastoral ministry will live lives of committed faith, devoting them to study and to prayer. There's the assumption too that since called to equip and lead, those called to pastoral ministry will seek the appropriate training so that they can effectively interpret and pass on the faith to those entrusted to their care (in Mainline Protestant Churches, there is an expectation that clergy will pursue the M.Div. degree) Most mainline Protestant traditions

---

[206] Messer, *Images of Christian Ministry*, 64.
[207] Watkins, *Great Thanksgiving*, 218.

Unfettered Spirit

require ministers to affirm a code of ethics. The Academy of Parish Clergy, which is a professional organization for clergy has a code of ethics that speaks to personal standards, institutional relationships, relationships with other colleagues, relationship to the community at large, financial standards, and relationship to the persons served by the clergyperson.[208]

While there should be no double standards, where lay people aren't expected to live up to the same standards as clergy, clergy are expected to model these standards for others. What persons who are ordained represent to the church is a way of being a minister in their daily life in ways that are commensurate to their gifts and calling. At the same time, those called into such ministries must recognize that they are not the whole expression of ministry in the church, or that everything of importance rests on their shoulders. As Bruce and Kate Epperly remind us, "while every preacher and worship leader is called to faithful excellence and healthy professional and personal boundaries in her or his ministry, she or he is not fully responsible for the spiritual growth of the congregation."[209]

A PASTORAL CALLING: EQUIPPING FOR MATURITY

What is the chief calling of the pastor? I believe we can find it in Ephesians 4:12 – pastors and teachers are called to help guide the people of God toward spiritual maturity. Those who are mature in faith will not be tossed about by "every wind of doctrine, by people's trickery." In an age of growing biblical illiteracy, with ever more groups claiming to represent God's message, the church needs

---

208 http://apclergy.org/clergy-helps/code-of-ethics.html. On the question of integrity in ministry see the chapter "Loss of Soul: A Crisis of Integrity, Passion and Wholeness" in his book *Clergy Table Talk Eavesdropping on Ministry Issues in the 21st Century,* Academy of Parish Clergy Conversations in Ministry, Robert D. Cornwall, ed., (Gonzalez, FL: Energion Publications, 2012), 9-12.

209 Bruce G. Epperly and Katherine Gould Epperly, *Tending to the Holy: The Practice of the Presence of God in Ministry,* (Herndon, VA: Alban Institute, 2009), 27.

to be equipped to be discerning listeners. Without undermining the valid ministries of all Christians, the church must not shrink back from calling, equipping, and ordaining qualified people to teach God's people so that they may grow into spiritual maturity and exhibit the grace and love of God in their lives.

The task of preparing people for service and helping them gain a competent understanding of the Christian faith faces significant hurdles. In an age when the medium has become the message and glitz is more important than substance, pastors and teachers attempt to call their people to service. They seek to help people to make responsible choices, especially ethical and moral choices, in a very complex world. Although pastors can't make the right choices for people, they can give them tools that will help them make good choices. As we grow in maturity we can tackle harder and more difficult situations; we can move from milk to meat.

Our theologies of ministry are rooted largely in our common practices. These practices in turn inform the ways in which we do ministry. If you believe that ministry is something shared by the body of Christ then you will place less emphasis on who does the work and more on what needs to be done. If you adopt a more priestly or liturgical model of ministry you will probably focus on who is entitled to perform certain rites and do certain kinds of work.

As ordained ministers go forth into the world, they must remember the hands laid on them, while also remembering that they are not "the" minister. As one among many ministers, pastors can have significant ministries, bringing the body of Christ to maturity through their teaching, nurturing, leadership, and pastoral care of fellow ministers. Remembering that it's God who has given us the gifts of ministry, we can receive our recognition and affirmation by the body. In the case of pastors that generally has been done through the laying on of hands. Then, in the course of time, we rekindle the gifts given us, whether as clergy or not, through prayer, worship, and study.

Ministry isn't about titles, though titles may accompany one's place of service. Indeed, it's wise not to get caught up in our titles, lest we become deceived by them. Frederick Buechner writes the following about the title "Reverend."

Reverend means *to be revered.* Ministers are not to be revered for who they are in themselves, but for who it is they represent."[210]

We, who are ordained, need to remember this. Those who serve alongside us might remember it as well.

---

210 Buechner, *Wishful Thinking*, 98.

BIBLIOGRAPHY

Ahmed, Akbar S. *Islam Today: A Short Introduction to the Muslim World.* New York: I.B. Tauris & Co., 2002

Ariel, David S. *What Do Jews Believe? The Spiritual Foundations of Judaism.* New York: Schocken Books, 1995.

Baker, Kendall Clark. *When Faith Invades the Public Square: Mixing Politics and Religion through Community Organizing to Enhance Our Democracy.* Cleveland, OH: Circle Books, 2011.

Banks, Robert. *Paul's Idea of Community.* Revised Edition. Peabody, MA: Hendrickson Publishers, 1994.

Banks, Robert and Julia Banks. *The Church Comes Home: A New Base for Community and Mission.* Sutherland, NSW and Claremont, CA: Albatross Books, 1986.

Barr, William R. and Rena M. Yocom. Editors. *The Church in the Movement of the Spirit.* Grand Rapids: Wm. B. Eerdmans Publishing Co., 1994.

Barreiro, Alvaro. *Basic Ecclesial Communities: The Evangelization of the Poor.* Translated by Barbara Campbell. Maryknoll, NY: Orbis Books, 1982.

Bass, Dorothy C. Editor. *Practicing Our Faith: A Way of Life for a Searching People.* San Francisco: Jossey-Bass, 2010.

Bauknight, Brian Kelley. *Body Building: Creating a Ministry Team through Spiritual Gifts.* Nashville: Abingdon Press, 1996.

Beaudoin, Tom. *Virtual Faith: The Irreverent Spiritual Quest of Generation X.* San Francisco: Jossey-Bass, 1998.

Bittlinger, Arnold. *Gifts and Graces* Grand Rapids: Wm. B. Eerdmans Publishing Co., 1967.

Boff, Leonardo. *Church, Charism & Power: Liberation Theology and the Institutional Church.* New York: Crossroad Publishing Co., 1986.

Bonhoeffer, Dietrich. *Discipleship*. Dietrich Bonhoeffer Works, Volume 4. Edited by Geoffrey B. Kelley and John Godsey. Translated by Barbara Green and Reinhard Krauss. Minneapolis: Fortress Press, 2001.

——————. *Letters and Papers from Prison*. Dietrich Bonhoeffer Works. Volume 8. Translated by Isabel Best, et. al. Minneapolis: Fortress Press, 2009.

——————. *Psalms: The Prayer Book of the Bible*. Minneapolis: Augsburg Press, 1970.

Borg, Marcus. *The Heart of Christianity: Rediscovering a Life of Faith*. San Francisco: Harper San Francisco, 2003.

Brown, Colin. Editor. *The New International Dictionary of New Testament Theology*. 3 volumes. Grand Rapids, MI: Zondervan, 1975.

Brown Taylor, Barbara. *Bread of Angels*. Cambridge, MA: Cowley Publications, 1997.

——————. *Preaching Life*. Cambridge, MA: Cowley Publications, 1993.

Brueggemann, Walter. *Biblical Perspectives on Evangelism: Living in a Three-Storied Universe*. Nashville: Abingdon Press, 1993.

——————. *Ichabod Toward Home: The Journey of God's Glory*. Grand Rapids: Wm. B. Eerdmans Publishing Co., 2002.

——————. *The Practice of Prophetic Imagination: Preaching an Emancipating Word*. Minneapolis: Fortress Press, 2012.

Buechner, Frederick. *Wishful Thinking: A Seeker's ABC*. Revised Edition. San Francisco: HarperSanFrancisco, 1992.

Butler Bass, Diana. *Christianity After Religion: The End of Church and the Birth of a New Spiritual Awakening*. San Francisco: Harper One, 2012.

——————. *The Church for the Rest of Us: How the Neighborhood Church is Transforming the Faith*. San Francisco: Harper One, 2006.

Cartwright, Colbert S. *Candles of Grace: Disciples Worship in Perspective*. St. Louis: Chalice Press, 1992.

Castelein, John. "The Doctrine of the Holy Spirit." In *Essentials of Christian Faith*. Edited by Steve Burris, 69-88. Joplin, MO: College Press, 1992.

Clayton, Philip and Tripp Fuller. *Transforming Christian Theology for Church and Society.* Minneapolis: Fortress Press, 2010.

Clayton, Philip and Steven Knapp. *The Predicament of Belief: Science, Philosophy, Faith.* New York: Oxford University Press, 2011.

Cornwall, Robert D. *Ephesians: A Participatory Study Guide.* Gonzalez, FL: Energion Publications, 2010.

_____. *Ultimate Allegiance: The Subversive Nature of the Lord's Prayer.* Gonzalez, FL: Energion Publications, 2010.

Cox, Harvey. *Fire from Heaven: The Rise of Pentecostalism and the Reshaping of Religion in the Twenty-first Century.* Reading, MA: Addison-Wesley Publishing, Co, 1994.

_____. *The Future of Faith.* San Francisco: Harper One, 2009.

Cranfield, C.E.B. *Romans,* International Critical Commentary, 2 Volumes. Edinburgh: T. & T. Clark, 1979.

Craddock, Fred B. *The Cherry Log Sermons.* Louisville: Westminster/John Knox Press, 2001.

Craddock, Fred B. et. al. *Preaching Through the Christian Year, B.* Valley Forge, PA: Trinity Press International, 1993.

Cueni, R. Robert. *Dinosaur Heart Transplants: Renewing Mainline Congregations.* Nashville: Abingdon Press, 2000.

Daniel, Lillian. *When "Spiritual by Not Religiouis" is Not Enough: Seeing God in Surprising Places Even the Church.* New York: Jericho Books, 2013.

DePree, Max. *Leadership is an Art.* New York: Dell Publishing, 1989.

Doran, Carol and Thomas H. Troeger, *Trouble at the Table: Gathering the Tribes for Worship.* Nashville: Abingdon Press, 1993.

Dunn, James D. G. *Baptism in the Holy Spirit.* Philadelphia: Westminster Press, 1970.

_____. *Jesus and the Spirit.* Philadelphia: Westminster Press, 1975.

_____. *The Christ and the Spirit: Pneumatology.* Volume 2. Grand Rapids: Wm. B. Eerdmans Publishing Co., 1998.

_____. "The First and Second Letters to Timothy and the Letter to Titus." *The New Interpreter's Bible.* Nashville: Abingdon Press, 2000. Volume 11.

Elnes, Eric. *Asphalt Jesus: Finding a New Christian Faith along the Highways of America.* San Francisco: Jossey Bass, 2007.

Epperly, Bruce G. *Healing Marks: Healing and Spirituality in Mark's Gospel.* Gonzalez, FL: Energion Publications, 2012.

_____. *Holy Adventure: 41 Days of Audacious Living.* Nashville: Upper Room Books, 2008.

Epperly, Bruce G. and Katherine Gould Epperly. *Tending to the Holy: The Practice of the Presence of God in Ministry.* Herndon, VA: Alban Institute, 2009.

Farley, Benjamin. *In Praise of Virtue: An Exploration of the Biblical Virtues in a Christian Context.* Grand Rapids: Wm. B. Eerdmans Publishing, Co., 1995.

Fee, Gordon D. *The First Epistle to the Corinthians.* The New International Commentary on the New Testament. Grand Rapids: Wm. B. Eerdmans Publishing Company, 1987.

_____. *God's Empowering Presence.* Peabody, MA: Hendrickson, 1994.

_____. *Paul, the Spirit, and the People of God.* Peabody, MA: Hendrickson, 1996.

Fosdick, Harry Emerson. *The Meaning of Prayer.* Nashville: Abingdon Press, 1980.

Foster, Richard J. *Celebration of Discipline.* San Francisco: Harper SanFrancisco, 1978.

Foster, Richard J. and James Bryan Smith. Editors. *Devotional Classics: Selected Readings for Individuals and Groups.* San Francisco: HarperSanFrancisco, 1993.

González Faus, José Ignacio. *Builders of Community: Rethinking Ecclesiastical Ministry.* Translated by Maria Isabel Reyna and Revised by Liam Kelly. Miama: Convivium Press, 2012.

Grenz, Stanley J. *Theology for the Community of God.* Nashville: Broadman and Holman, 1994.

Groff, Kent Ira. *Clergy Table Talk Eavesdropping on Ministry Issues in the 21st Century.* Academy of Parish Clergy Conversations in Ministry. Edited by Robert D. Cornwall. Gonzalez, FL: Energion Publications, 2012.

Hadaway, C. Kirk. *Behold, I Do a New Thing: Transforming Communities of Faith.* Cleveland: Pilgrim Press, 2001.

Halverson, Delia. *How Do Our Children Grow? Introducing Children to God, Jesus, the Bible, Prayer, Church.* St. Louis: Chalice Press, 1999.

Hanh, Thich Nhat. *Living Buddha, Living Christ.* New York: Riverhead Books, 1995.

Harbaugh, Gary. *God's Gifted People.* Minneapolis, MN: Augsburg Press, 1988.

Hauerwas, Stanley. *The Peaceable Kingdom: A Primer in Christian Ethics.* South Bend, IN: University of Notre Dame Press, 1983.

Hawkins, Thomas. *Claiming God's Promises: A Guide to Discovering Your Spiritual Gifts.* Nashville: Abingdon Press, 1992.

Holifield, E. Brooks. *God's Ambassadors: A History of the Christian Clergy in America.* Grand Rapids: Wm. B. Eerdmans Publishing Co., 2007.

Humbert, Royal. Editor. *Compend of Alexander Campbell's Theology.* St. Louis: Bethany Press, 1961.

Janzen, David. *The Intentional Christian Community Handbook: For Idealists, Hypocrites, and Wannabe Disciples of Jesus.* Brewster, MA: Paraclete Press, 2012.

Jones, Tony. *The Church is Flat.* Minneapolis: JoPa Productions, 2011.

Kee, Howard Clark. *Good News to the Ends of the Earth: The Theology of Acts.* Philadelphia: Trinity Press International, 1990.

Kelsey, Morton. *Healing and Christianity: A Classic Study.* Third Edition. Minneapolis: Augsburg Press, 1995.

Kenneson, Philip D. *Life on the Vine: Cultivating the Fruit of the Spirit in Christian Community.* Downers Grove, IL: InterVarsity Press, 1999.

Koenig, John. *Charismata: God's Gifts for God's People.* Philadelphia: Westminster Press, 1978.

_____. *Rediscovering New Testament Prayer: Boldness and Blessing in the Name of Jesus.* San Francisco: Harper-Collins, 1992.

_____. *The Feast of the World's Redemption: Eucharistic Origins and Christian Mission.* Harrisburg, PA: Trinity Press International, 2000.

Küng, Hans. *The Church.* New York: Image Books, 1976.

Lamott, Anne. *Traveling Mercies: Some Thoughts on Faith.* New York: Anchor Books, 2000.

Linn, Jan. *The Jesus Connection.* St. Louis: Chalice Press, 1997.

McLaren, Brian. *Why Did Jesus, Moses, the Buddha, and Mohammed Cross the Road? Christian Identity in a Multi-Faith World.* New York: Jericho Books, 2012.

Mead, Loren B. *Five Challenges for the Once and Future Church.* New York: The Alban Institute, 1996.

——————. *Transforming Congregations for the Future.* New York: Alban Institute, 1994.

Merritt, Carol Howard. *Reframing Hope: Vital Ministry in a New Generation.* Herndon, VA: Alban Institute, 2010.

Messer, Donald. *Contemporary Images of Christian Ministry.* Nashville: Abingdon Press, 1989.

Moltmann, Jürgen. *The Church in the Power of the Spirit: A Contribution to Messianic Ecclesiology.* Translated by Margaret Kohl. New York: Harper and Row, 1977.

——————. *Jesus Christ for Today's World.* Translated by Margaret Kohl. Philadelphia: Fortress Press, 1994.

——————. *The Source of Life: The Holy Spirit and the Theology of Life.* Translated by Margaret Kohl. Minneapolis: Fortress Press, 1997.

——————. *The Spirit of Life: A Universal Affirmation,* Translated by Margaret Kohl. Minneapolis: Fortress Press, 1991.

Montague, George T. *The Holy Spirit: Growth of a Biblical Tradition.* New York: Paulist Press, 1976.

Nelson, Gary V. *Borderland Churches: A Congregation's Introduction to Missional Living,* (St. Louis: Chalice Press, 2008).

Norris, Kathleen. *Amazing Grace: A Vocabulary of Faith.* New York: Riverhead Books, 1998.

Nouwen, Henri. *In the Name of Jesus: Reflections on Christian Leadership.* New York: Crossroad Publishing, Co., 1989.

Oden, Amy. *In Her Words: Women's Writings in the History of Christian Thought.* Nashville: Abingdon Press, 1991.

Oden, Thomas. *Pastoral Theology: Essentials of Ministry.* San Francisco: Harper & Row, Publishers, 1983.

Oord, Thomas Jay. *The Nature of Love: A Theology,* (St. Louis: Chalice Press, 2010

Pagitt, Doug. *The Church in the Inventive Age.* Minneapolis: Sparkhouse, 2011.

Patel, Eboo. *Sacred Ground: Pluralism, Prejudice, and the Promise of America.* Boston: Beacon Press, 2012.

Phillips, James M. and Robert T. Coote. Editors. *Toward the 21st Century in Christian Mission.* Grand Rapids: Wm. B. Eerdmans Publishing Co., 1993.

Putnam, Robert D. and David E. Campbell. American Grace: How Religion Divides and Unites Us. New York: Simon and Schuster, 2010.

Ray, David R. *The Indispensable Guide for Smaller Churches.* Cleveland: Pilgrim Press, 2003.

Reese, Martha Grace. *Unbinding the Gospel: Real Life Evangelism.* St. Louis: Chalice Press, 2007.

Richardson, Alan. Editor. *A Theological Wordbook of the Bible.* New York: Collier Books, 1950.

Riso, Don Richard and Russ Hudson. *Discovering Your Personality Type,* Revised Editon. Boston: Houghton Mifflin, 2003.

Robinson, William. *The Biblical Doctrine of the Church,* Revised Edition. St. Louis: Bethany Press, 1955.

Rollins, Peter. *The Fidelity of Betrayal: Towards a Church Beyond Belief.* Brewster, MA: Paraclete Press, 2008.

Roxburgh, Alan. *Missional Map-Making: Skills for leading in Times of Transition.* San Francisco: Jossey Bass, 2010.

Schatzmann, Siegfried. *A Pauline Theology of Charismata,* (Peabody, MA: Hendrickson Publishers, Inc., 1987

Smedes, Lewis. *Shame and Grace.* San Francisco: Harper San Francisco, 1993.

Snider, Phil and Emily Bowen. *Toward a Hopeful Future: Why the Emergent Church is Good News for Mainline Congregations,* (Cleveland: Pilgrim Press, 2010

Steinke, Peter L. *Healthy Congregations: A System's Approach,* New York: Alban Institute, 1996.

Stone, Bryan. *Faith and Film: Theological Themes at the Cinema.* St. Louis: Chalice Press, 2000.

Tillich, Paul. *Love, Power and Justice.* London: Oxford University Press, 1960.

Timoner, Rachel. *Breath of Life: God as Spirit in Judaism.* Brewster, MA: Paraclete Press, 2011.

Ward, Hannah and Jennifer Wild. Compilers. *The Westminster Collection of Christian Meditations.* Louisville: Westminster John Knox Press, 1998.

Watkins, Keith. Editor. *Baptism and Belonging: A Resource for Christian Worship.* St. Louis: Chalice Press, 1991.

_____. *The Great Thanksgiving,* (St. Louis: Chalice Press, 1995)

_____. Editor. *Thankful Praise: A Resource for Christian Worship.* St. Louis: CBP Press, 1987.

Weems, Jr., Lovett H. *Church Leadership: Vision, Team, Culture and Integrity.* Nashville: Abingdon Press, 1993.

Welker, Michael. *God the Spirit.* Translated by John F. Hoffmeyer. Minneapolis: Fortress Press, 1994.

Wink, Walter. *Engaging the Powers: Discernment and Resistance in a World of Domination.* Minneapolis: Fortress Press, 1992.

_____. *The Powers that Be: Theology for a New Millennium.* New York: Galilee Books, 1998.

_____. *Unmasking the Powers: The Invisible Forces that Determine Human Existence.* (Minneapolis: Fortress Press, 1986).

Yong, Amos. *Hospitality and the Other: Pentecost, Christian Practices and the Neighbor.* Maryknoll, NY: Orbis Books, 2008.

_____. *Spirit of Love: A Trinitarian Theology of Grace.* Waco, TX: Baylor University Press, 2012.

_____. *The Bible, Disability, and the Church: A New Vision of the People of God.* Grand Rapids: Wm. B. Eerdmans Publishing Co., 2011.

_____. *The Spirit of Creation: Modern Science and Divine Action in the Pentecostal-Charismatic Imagination.* Grand Rapids: Wm. B. Eerdmans Publishing Co., 2011.

_____. *Who is the Holy Spirit? A Walk with the Apostles.* Brewster, MA: Paraclete Press, 2011.

Zscheile, Dwight J. Editor. *Cultivating Sent Communities: Missional Spiritual Formation.* Grand Rapids: Wm. B. Eerdmans Publishing, Co. 2012.

ALSO FROM ENERGION PUBLICATIONS

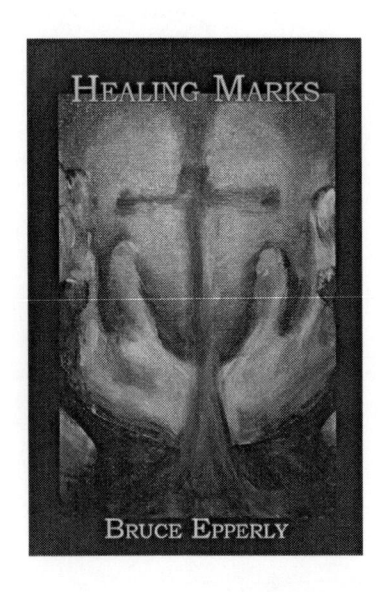

No theologian I know deals with the difficult questions of faith and illness with more clarity and insight than Bruce Epperly.

Patricia Adams Farmer
author of *The Metaphor Maker* and *Embracing a Beautiful God*

ALSO BY THE AUTHOR

Faith in the Public Square is a must-read for anyone and everyone concerned about the continuing role of religion in public life.

Ken Brooker Langston
Director
Disciples Justice Action Network

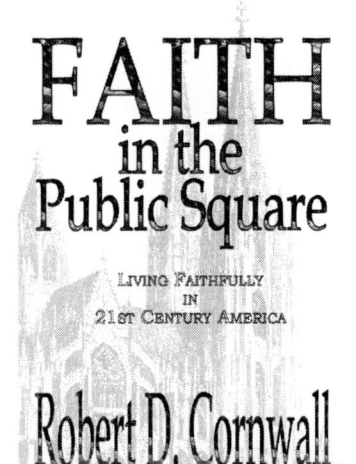

MORE FROM ENERGION PUBLICATIONS

Personal Study
Finding My Way in Christianity	Herold Weiss	$16.99
The Jesus Paradigm	David Alan Black	$17.99
When People Speak for God	Henry Neufeld	$17.99
The Sacred Journey	Chris Surber	$11.99

Christian Living
Faith in the Public Square	Robert D. Cornwall	$16.99
Grief: Finding the Candle of Light	Jody Neufeld	$8.99
Crossing the Street	Robert LaRochelle	$16.99

Bible Study
Learning and Living Scripture	Lentz/Neufeld	$12.99
From Inspiration to Understanding	Edward W. H. Vick	$24.99
Philippians: A Participatory Study Guide	Bruce Epperly	$9.99
Ephesians: A Participatory Study Guide	Robert D. Cornwall	$9.99

Theology
Creation in Scripture	Herold Weiss	$12.99
Creation: the Christian Doctrine	Edward W. H. Vick	$12.99
The Politics of Witness	Allan R. Bevere	$9.99
Ultimate Allegiance	Robert D. Cornwall	$9.99
Worshiping with Charles Darwin	Robert D. Cornwall	$9.99
The Church Under the Cross	William Powell Tuck	$11.99
The Journey to the Undiscovered Country	William Powell Tuck	$9.99
Eschatology: A Participatory Study Guide	Edward W. H. Vick	$9.99

Ministry
Clergy Table Talk	Kent Ira Groff	$9.99
Out of This World	Darren McClellan	$24.99
Wind and Whirlwind	David Moffett-Moore	$9.99
Healing Marks	Bruce Epperly	$14.99
Transforming Acts	Bruce Epperly	$14.99

Generous Quantity Discounts Available
Dealer Inquiries Welcome
Energion Publications – P.O. Box 841
Gonzalez, FL_ 32560
Website: http://energionpubs.com
Phone: (850) 525-3916